All Roads Lead To Cannonball

The tires screeched for kindness as the Lamborghini Murcielago's differentials exchanged hold for horizontal idleness. My kid hands faked certainty past their range of abilities and the bloodless essence of the unpracticed sales rep close to me neglected to radiate his ideal cool as we slid between a bicyclist and a street going farm hauler. I was smiling ear-to-ear as the V12 cry resonated off the Carolina trees. There is nothing similar to controlled power, besides obviously the impression of force just past full oversight - that is the point at which you exchange accuracy for general heading. Risky. That is the way it felt; hazardous and enchanting. In the most fundamental sense - I was alive.

Today's man isn't welcome to do bold things. Makers appear to venture out to England or Australia to see as a "genuine man" entertainer to play inverse a projected legend who is either a provocative geek or "sufficiently gay" to be acceptable and called "metrosexual." It appears as though being up on the most recent web images and unscripted TV drama dramatization establishes culture. We make light of the meaning of training and real explorative accomplishment behind web secrecy and online entertainment status. Where are the genuine heroes?

Men should be strong, risky, almost unapproachable.
They should be looking for chances to one or the other find or show boldness, sturdiness, and strength - both mental and physical. Maybe to win the esteem of womankind or just to display their strength over different men. There is a socialism of manliness happening where we need to have all betas instead of a periodic superb alpha.

Regardless of how much these carnal desires are subdued, they actually loom peaceful and determined underneath the surface only sitting tight for an open door to act.

But where are we to do that these days?

Cars. Wonderful, strong, savage, ludicrous, colorful vehicles. Challenges in vehicles. Beating records so incomprehensible that they were consigned to legend. Being shrewd and intense and working out and wicked. Taking off on a mission
with several different folks with enough testosterone and total surrender to

kiss the spouse, work, and perhaps independence from detainment goodbye.

You simply need to get up one morning and say, "Today I will begin arranging. It is something I just need to do." Then for the following decade it annoys at you, it pulls you toward it with an all the while threatening and invigorating attraction. It trickles behind the scenes like a latrine that won't quit running until that one day when it is all that matters.

It probably been around 8:00 PM. The vehicle felt taken care of and all frameworks were practical. I didn't know definitively where I was, the way quick I was going, or the way that long I had been driving. My vision was obscuring with extraordinary radiances around each light ahead and in my mirrors. My profundity discernment was no more. I was unable to understand what Dave and Dan were talking about. I advised them to observe the following service station. I had driven for what felt like hours straightforwardly into the Western Arizona sunset close to Kingman, wedging my head against the top of the vehicle to involve it as a stopgap sun visor since the real visor totally impeded my perspective out and about. My faculties were confused and battling to center. Whenever I got into the mountains headed towards the eastern California line, the winding streets felt totally strange to me.

Somehow, I came to the last corner store we would have to complete the outing. I peered down at the outing information showed on the Mercedes PC. I had driven for a little more than two and half hours at a typical speed of 95 miles each hour. It was our slowest leg of the outing up to this point. Our general normal was close to 100 mph and we were a little more than 500 miles from the Portofino, our objective. On one hand the Portofino felt inconceivably close, truth be told we didn't have to totally fill the fuel tanks to arrive. Then again, 500 miles was almost the distance that I used to commit a day to in a drive from Atlanta to Palm Beach, Florida seeing family on siestas and summer excursions. Considering the distance in that light stayed as disheartening and depleting as that leg of driving had felt.

It was nothing unexpected that no scenes from the Cannonball Run film were recorded here. Even Captain Chaos would have stumbled. It was by then when it hurt the most exceedingly awful and precisely that moment that everything appeared to be legit. Any blend of objectives, wants, and inspirations which could get me 24 hours into a drive, scarcely reasonable, and on target to do

something this groundbreaking must be genuinely special.

I love vehicles. I haven't generally adored vehicles. I don't cherish chipping away at vehicles, drawing vehicles, cleaning vehicles, or building vehicles. I love driving vehicles. It is the way that I make my living, the focal point through which I view the world, and my most loved sporting activity.

It kicked in exactly when I had the option to drive. Being a horribly arrogant youngster, I saw nothing out of sorts or discourteous in strolling into each colorful vehicle display area in the metro Atlanta region and asking the dedicated salesmen to test drive one of their fine automobiles.

Most individuals who are effective by any acknowledged measurement could be considered fanatical. My character has been described by a progression of fixations lumped together in succession - dinosaurs, ball, athletic shoes, reptiles, Ivy League schools, vehicles. It might have been running through each Mesozoic period dinosaur at age eight, playing in AAU ball competitions with Dwight Howard and Lebron James at thirteen, gathering Jordans at fifteen, going to the National Reptile Breeders' Expo at sixteen, attempting to get into an Ivy League school at seventeen, at age twenty attempting to drive 200 mph in my first Lamborghini without enough money in my ledger to make the following installment, experiencing passionate feelings for a young lady that was way out of my association around that equivalent time, selling supercars at 24, and barreling through Arizona intoxicated simply by depletion at 28. Life was for the most part an endless series of fixations on all the other things either becoming alright or falling by the wayside.

I began my first business when I was in center school. The thought initially came to me through my pet green iguana named George. Intriguing them with my strong fascination with hereditary qualities, I persuaded my oddly liberal guardians to put resources into an Albino Iguana rearing task. After a short time we had a storm cellar loaded up with 33 six foot long delicate monster reptiles. Given their craving, we were headed to turning into the biggest customer of collard greens in the territory of Georgia.

Mine was not a lemonade stand, pet sitting help, side of the road carwash or any of the platitude first pioneering projects you could expect of a youngster. I needed my work, even as a youthful youngster to imply a uniqueness to my personality and be something that would merit discussing. Anybody could have a pet

canine or feline. Very few individuals had a storm cellar that looked, smelled, and seemed like Jurassic Park.

Great White Reptiles was loads of tomfoolery. My dad and I fabricated elaborate enclosures together, took in the complexities of hatching, and took the reptiles to expos to sell. Unconventional is a good word to depict the segment of individuals who purchase reproducing quality reptiles as a mixed leisure activity and speculation. Envision concurrent excitement for calfskin clothing, body craftsmanship, and residing home style in a captivating emulsion. Add twenty foot reticulated pythons, eight foot Sumatran water screens, and young adult me to the blend and you have it.

I sold a rearing sets of iguanas that were heterozygous for albinism to two or three intriguing folks from Tampa. Their braids, self-modified denim wear, and general absence of cleanliness were very startling to Megan, whom I had as of late started dating. We figured out later how, not long after leaving the rest region where we had made the trade, they had delivered both thirty or more pound reptiles to meander about in the taxi of their truck. Fascinated by their hereditary transformation Noah's Ark, they forced their truck to leave gas in transit home and had to play paper-rock-scissors to see who got to walk five miles to fill a gas can.

Success was restricted. The iguanas appeared to be so sound and agreeable that maybe I persuaded them they would live for eternity. Whether or not it was shared comfort or some other herpetological moxie diminisher, prolific eggs were uncommon. My limited ability to focus before long made them look for my next fixation.

I was sixteen when I became stricken with vehicles. The certainty games to request test drives, magazine dashing, web recordings, and a blossoming influence into the neighborhood vehicle culture prompted the longing to turn out to be expertly fascinated in the vehicle business similarly as I had with iguanas. I thought I needed to be an auto writer, yet figured out it was anything but a lucrative industry. I would have had a ton of opportunities to drive dull vehicles for a couple of days yet just intriguing chances to drive an outlandish vehicle for five minutes, so it appeared to be beneficial to investigate other auto professions. It seemed obvious me assuming a task was broadly viewed as cool you'd presumably not be paid a lot to make it happen. I expected to change that.

My folks are astounding individuals. It has been said they didn't say "No" frequently enough to me however I think they are fantastic guardians. Both are architects, learned people, and dedicated Christians. They gave me each model and opportunity I might have requested to carry on with a balanced, typical life. I passed up that great opportunity or if nothing else regularly controlled it off base. Luckily they adored one another and cherished me through the numerous crazy detours.

Most guardians attempt to train their children to buckle down. Mine believed that me should work shrewd and know what I was referring to. Before long enough I was great at one and capable at faking the other. They raised me to be certain, put forth objectives, and go with choices well. I don't know they understood precisely the way that those attributes could show. The method involved with fostering a capacity to tackle issues in my own specific manner prompted some erosion with most power figures in my way and had a few remarkable ramifications through my life.

I turned into an energetic purchaser of vehicle culture. The standard of vehicle aficionado films was constructing rapidly at that point. Noteworthy greats like Bullitt, The Italian Job, Gumball Rally, Vanishing Point, and Cannonball Run were being joined by present day understandings and changes in Gone in Sixty Seconds, The Fast and the Furious establishment, another Batman set of three, and a revamp of The Italian Job. There were additionally some remarkable vehicle appearances in The Rock, Bad Boys, and The Transporter. From a diversion utilization viewpoint it was a highpoint of fascinating vehicle film appearances. This was flawlessly expanded by the beginning of novice made film tasks and web distribution of inadequately shot and gravely altered cuts. Teckademics and the Mischief establishment were reporting occasions like the Gumball 3000 and grassroots road hustling which added to the charm of significant distance cutthroat driving. The juggernaut of Top Gear was additionally building up some decent momentum in both the US and UK markets.

When I was a first year recruit in secondary school I was given a challenge to realize what genuine torment felt like. I was determined to have an extremely interesting knee problem called Bilateral Osteochondritis Dissecans Disease. It is a crumbling of the external chondyles of every one of my femurs. Basically, in the space where your femur boils down to meet your tibia in the knee joint it parts into two flaps. On the external projection, or chondyle, my bones began to disintegrate away. Now and again the piece of ligament that stayed set up attempted to keep up with strength, some of the time it didn't. Notwithstanding, it caused agonizing agony and would have had me in a wheelchair by age thirty while possibly not carefully tended to. It would take

me an hour to release my knees and stretch before a b-ball game to have the option to run because of the irritation. The main arrangement was a corpse bone and ligament tissue relocate from a dead, yet generally solid, giver near my age and level. I could not have imagined it then, but ten years later I would sell the guy who harvested the cadaver tissue in my knees a brand new Lamborghini Gallardo LP550-2 Spyder.

The knee medical procedures were a ton for a youngster to go through yet it offered me a chance to cover myself more profound into car way of life and fables. I had six medical procedures and took in a significant illustration about what I was fit for persevering. I love the tales of individuals going through training camp or their first visit through military assistance. What I went through dislike that by any means, except for one mental angle. Being pushed into something troublesome or excruciating absent much by way of comprehension of what you ought to expect will in general uncover a few intriguing things about what you are fit for surviving.

Sports had been a major piece of my life. The knee issues finished my AAU Basketball vocation and, from a clinical point of view, swimming was the main athletic pursuit that was a choice. I couldn't stand swimming. To me it is an exhausting, inconsequential movement except if you add sharks or gators to the mix.
Unfortunately, I was very great at it. My six and a half foot body and high limit lungs were significantly more helpful stroking through a pool than dunking a ball. I persevered through four years of varsity secondary school and club swimming.
The potential was there to swim in school however it sounded as tantalizing as one more round of knee medical procedure. I resigned joyfully to the hot tub.

I should concede day to day swimming was an extraordinary time for profound thought. There isn't anything more careless than rowing to and fro in a shallow pool checking out at a line on the lower part of it. You possess a great deal of energy for reflective thoughtfulness many laps. I recall exactly how forlorn life at that stage could feel and how I needed to accomplish something in my reality that sounds intriguing. Whenever the name Ed Bolian came up in discussions among my companions, I believed the following sentence should be, "Goodness definitely, the person who __________." That clear required to have been a mind blowing thing. The young adult desire to be unmistakable was in full force.

Obviously swimming was not safe from my endeavors to push limits. Somewhat out of the controlled aberrance of it, somewhat out of as yet attempting to win, and somewhat out of the strangely outsider impression of it - I
would persuade a couple of my colleagues to cover our bodies in petrol jam

before our swim meets. We would leave our shins and the undersides of our arms clear of it to keep up with foothold with the water. Somewhere else the water would dot off us like the hand waxed finish of a questionable British Sports Car whose non-running proprietorship esteem lay redemptively in end of the week cleaning sessions.

If you have never brought a plunge into a virus pool canvassed in Vaseline I enthusiastically suggest it. You will not have the option to wash regularly for a week and the ensuing skin breakouts are a con however the inclination must be like being shot out of a gun. It is multiple times more compelling than shaving your body.

It merits spending a second here to talk about something that emerged in my youthfulness - a flat out failure to regard any person or thing. I'm not quite certain where this began. I reproached educators into tears, disrupting guidelines if by some stroke of good luck for doing as such, and pushing against any line or breaking point available anywhere. It was an elitist demeanor that I didn't have any idea however it made me an entirely unlikeable individual for a couple of years while in secondary school. It might have originated from the rehashed aggravation of knee medical procedures, the overwhelming difficulties of scholarly future, or some blemish inside me I still couldn't seem to concede existed.

I find it undeniably challenging to keep a tranquil relationship with my bosses in a workplace. I don't acknowledge analysis well and my stomach reaction to a standard or inconvenience is dependably to consider how far it tends to be pushed. There is some dull traveler within me that just responds seriously to anything planning to limit me. I can say now this blemish is as yet a piece of me yet I have tracked down better ways of holding it under tight restraints. I never realized what reason my blemish served yet I generally trusted it could add to me accomplishing something intriguing down the road.

The way of young self revelation and soul looking through prompted the detailing of a day to day existence formula. I maintained that my life's objectives should be a combination 2 sections whimsy, 1 section inventiveness, 1 section aberrance, a sprinkle of importance with a gesture to authentic point of reference, embellished with some extraordinary style of exhibitionism, separated through some impediment I felt like most others wouldn't have the balls to go through. It would be served, obviously, in a glass of some kind of cutthroat triumph. Proof could demonstrate I was only a degree or two eliminated from either being a chronic executioner or certainty man. Or on the other hand a lion tamer.

School came simple yet inspiration didn't. I took a reiteration of Advanced Placement and significant level courses in secondary school wanting to acquire permission into an Ivy League school. After applying to most of them I found out coming from an unheard of public Georgia High School; even an experienced entrepreneur and swim team captain with a high SAT & GPA who had overcome a debilitating physical condition was not going to get much attention from the admittance teams. In the end I was owned up to Georgia Tech where I ultimately figured I would concentrate on open approach. That's what the reasoning was in the event that I didn't wind up doing business as my own boss in some limit, I would simply go work for the CIA.

I didn't give a great deal of consideration in school. I outrightly read vehicle magazines more often than not as opposed to paying attention to the talks. I did alright in the classes to pull off it however the greater part of my contemplations went continually to vehicles, organizations with vehicles, and driving vehicles. Each task I could twist towards vehicles and driving went straight there. The backs of every note pad page were loaded up with thoughts for vehicle clubs, driving encounters, and illicit street races.

One of the over the top plans was to get my grandma to parlay the assets from a land interest into the recently reported Bugatti Veyron around 2003. The world beating McLaren F1 had appreciated unequivocally and purchasing what was destined to be the new quickest vehicle on the planet appeared to be really smart. I set up a call with the CEO of Bugatti to examine my premium in the vehicle and my interests about its way to deal with market. My scarcely post-pubescent profound voice came in very convenient. They sent me a letter ensuring my portion of the vehicle and set up an arrangement for me to travel to Molsheim, France for seat and pedal fitting. Whenever my grandma chose hypercar theory was not for her I set up an arrangement with a German intriguing vehicle seller to sell my reliable spot for $100,000. The arrangement with their retail purchaser self-destructed yet it was an incredible illustration in the specialty of faking it until you make it.

Eleven years after the fact, as he tasted a cappuccino I had made him that he called "the best I have tasted in America," I imparted that story to the exceptionally Italian yet recently named President of Bugatti. He appeared to be entertained however it was presumably the espresso talking. My

Lamborghini sales rep barista abilities were
likely more noteworthy than the adolescence schemes.

The primary idea I needed to begin a colorful vehicle rental organization was in a discussion with my closest companion, Kevin Messer. We both cherished vehicles and we had caught wind of organizations in Miami and Los Angeles that would lease them. The thought was conceived. The principal armada we contemplated was a Diablo 6.0, Bentley Arnage, Ferrari 360, and Dodge Viper. Only one of these wound up making the finished product.

At that point, the car scene was evolving quick. In 2000, there were a couple of amazing execution vehicles sold in the US. The E39 BMW M5 had a normally suctioned 400 hp V8, the Porsche 996 Twin Turbo had 415 tremendous hp and would go 0-60 in 3.9 seconds, and the Ferrari 360 Modena was arising as the first genuinely usable supercar flaunting 400 hp. The Corvette Z06 was not too far off with 405 hp however the standard C5 Corvette was as yet a disappointing execution vehicle notwithstanding being incredible looking.

2003 and 2004 changed all of that - we got the Bentley Continental GT, Lamborghini Gallardo, Porsche Carrera GT, Ferrari Enzo, Mercedes McLaren SLR, Maserati returned to the US, Cadillac drew out the CTS-V, and Mercedes got into the genuine presentation vehicle game with 469 and 493 pull variations of a 5.4 liter supercharged V8 and a twin super V12 that they stuffed into a few models. You could get a medium sized E Class, a convertible SL, a standard S Class, or a 2+2 CL roadster with a constrained acceptance motor that would outflank pretty much anything more out and about, all while offering rubbing seats and downplayed looks. It was an abnormal suggestion to most well off possibilities yet a lightning quick Q-vehicle could without a doubt fit some niche.

I willingly volunteered to sort out which of these vehicles were the best. While still a youngster in secondary school, I would call up a vehicle sales center that had one of these vehicles available to be purchased, make sense of the idea of my business, being the reproducing of colorful and intriguing reptiles, and express my advantage in buying a vehicle. Obviously their assumption for a quick schedule for buy could have been inferred yet I never needed to deceive get to test drive the vehicles. I drove for all intents and purposes each model of Ferrari, Lamborghini, Porsche, Bentley, Audi, BMW, Mercedes, Maserati, and others and started to get a handle on what the choice of extravagance and colorful vehicles and individuals who encompassed them looked like.

I took in the intricate details of the present day sequential
manual gearboxes in a Cambiocorsa Maserati Spyder. I chose to check
whether it very well may be constrained into first stuff going decently fast
around a ninety degree turn. It could. The vehicle quickly kicked into a
powerslide with a direction soon to cross with an approaching Ford F350.
Some way or another, through no acquired ability of my own, I had the
option to right the vehicle and point it where we maintained that it should go.
The totally panicked sales rep communicated his extraordinary appreciation
for my advantage yet asked that I return to the showroom in a somewhat
more moderate way. As usual, I discovered some advantageous explanation
the vehicle simply wasn't so much for me at the time.

I had eBay cautions set up for whenever somebody would list a
fascinating vehicle available to be purchased with regards to the Atlanta
region. I would call them during extra energy at school and go test drive the
vehicles before swim practice, continuously offering some reason not to
perfect the buy that day. On one occasion a Ferrari 360 Spider sprung
available to be purchased as the individual vehicle of the proprietor of a
Toyota Dealership in my old neighborhood. They were all the while selling
at costs $100,000 over MSRP with everlasting stands by to get another one.
Our neighborhood Ferrari seller was never cordial to sightseers so I had not
had the option to convince them to allow me to drive one. I rang the Toyota
seller and took it for a twist. Many hours watching Top Gear, perusing
specialized details in vehicle magazines, and playing computer games
implied I was more knowledgeable on the vehicle than the sales rep. You can
envision his energy at the chance of selling the boss's
$300,000 supercar as a takeoff from the ordinary everyday practice of
Priuses sprinkled with a periodic Scion Xb. I showed him how the vehicle
functioned and we endlessly drove. We ran running on empty returning to
the showroom and needed to push/coast our direction in.

When it down-poured I would test drive lightweight back tire drive
sports vehicles like Honda S2000s, BMW M3s, and huge motor Mercedes to
level up my floating skills and to unnerve clueless sales reps. I never would
figure that 10 years or so later I would redirect similar recommendations
from inadequate leads as a sales rep of supercars.

The vehicles were extraordinary and the editorial composition of the day
was fantastic.
For all of the multi-vehicle shootout tests, quickest lap driving, drag times,
and different measurements - the point that you were unable to test the
capacities of these vehicles out on a genuine street was available in each and

every article.

"Why not?" my 17 year old self continued to inquire. "I'm happy that they can lap
the Nurburgring rapidly and it is incredible that they go from 0-60 so astonishingly, however which one might I at some point travel the 590 mile excursion to North Palm Beach the quickest in?" That was useful. That was fascinating. It very well may be any excursion so far as that is concerned. How would I partake in the drives that we do each and every day? I thought about a crosscountry race. What urban communities could intrigue? Detroit, New York, Chicago, Los Angeles, Miami, Seattle, Atlanta? It must be across the nation. That sounded right. New York to Los Angeles then. That is America basically with vehicles. What could be better?

Offering gearheads permission into a no limits crosscountry race seemed as though offering outing bins to bears. The cutthroat recommendation was basic yet the critical thinking methodologies would be fascinatingly assorted. It seemed like the best game of all time. I returned home and enlightened my dad regarding the thought. He said, "Goodness, you mean Cannonball? No doubt, that sounds like you. They did that thirty quite a while back. There are motion pictures about it."

Mind blown, directly to Best Buy I went to get all of the DVD's I could find on the strange Cannonball.

My examination drove me to Brock Yates, a supporter of Car and Driver Magazine and the organizer behind this fugitive brand of crosscountry hold nothing back road hustling. 35 or so years earlier he had been sitting some place thinking similar considerations I thought about while in my secondary school science class, and he concluded a criminal crosscountry race was a beneficial undertaking. He was the Godfather of the fantasy which had recently been touched off in my teen brain.

I found out about the soul of the thought, how Yates and his companions needed to show contempt for the foundation and dissent the inconvenience of a public speed limit. He had a thought for the formation of a Masters Level driving permit and accepted that thoroughly prepared drivers in fit vehicles ought to have the option to drive quicker than a regular person in a normal car.

I was shocked to figure out the number of authentic racecar drivers and groups had contended in the Cannonball. The vehicles were astounding, individuals were intriguing, the thought was perpetually convincing - I was snared. Individuals carrying on with common lives had secured the most impressive superior execution vehicles of the day, furnished them with state of the art gadgetry, and led a perseverance trial of both horse and administrator through the mysterious wilderness of the American expressway framework. I dove into analyzing the thought and thinking about what it would resemble with regards to present day vehicles on the present streets. Numerous restless evenings followed.

In my last semester of secondary school I took a class where I could characterize my own course prerequisites and content, highlighted an enormous scope research project regarding a matter of interest. We should characterize an educational program and an assessment scale for ourselves. There was to be some field research and a meeting with somebody who was compelling in the space of study.

I was proceeding with my propensity for test driving as frequently as I could and felt like I was turning out to be a remarkable beginner expert on the most recent harvest of sports vehicles. I decided to explore the calling of car news coverage for the task. The master in the field that I decided to meet with was Brock Yates.

CHAPTER 2

The Interview

The project supervisor at the vehicle sales center where I work from 2009-15 is named Bill Smith. Bill is one of my #1 individuals. He is essentially as American as a fruity dessert formed blue grass music guitar being utilized as a polished ash at Yankee arena on the fourth of July by Miss America wearing daisy dukes on the shoulders of Abraham Lincoln in an Elvis impersonator getup. He hates technology, loves the bumpy road of a past that has made him who he is, and is full of some of the best one liners and wisdom that you could ever find in a person. One of my number one things to hear him consistently say is, "The reason mightn't I at any point awaken and it be 1979 again?"

The 1970s in America was an insane time. The possibility of opportunity was in the air and the public mind was one of altogether testing limits, testing, and attempting to construct a character in an aggregate design. I was brought into the world in 1985 and it seems like I passed up a period exceptionally customized for my mentality by only a couple decades.

This was on the last part of a sublime time for the American vehicle culture and something that we will probably never see from now onward. NASCAR hustling had emerged from the 1930's North Carolina smuggling society and had advanced into display areas. This was the ideal racecar/street vehicle selling relationship that each vehicle producer actually cares about. "Win on Sunday, sell on Monday" implied that display areas of the 1960's were loaded up with vehicles that really looked like the ones that were shouting around the super speedways, just without all of the stickers.

The muscle vehicle period was a Great Awakening of vehicle culture in America. You could stroll into any display area in America and purchase a functional vehicle with the greatest motor they presented at a sensible cost. Nobody thought often about mileage, emanations, Al Gore, Ralph Nader, a dangerous atmospheric devation, carbon impressions, security, unfamiliar oil, or engine vehicle guidelines. Worries about oil reliance and embargos were as yet a couple of years away. What a wonderful time it was.

The mid 70's introduced a fuel emergency and a monstrous analysis of high

execution motoring. Regulations were passed that forced security, limited motor limit, ordered lower fuel utilization, and shackled down torque. It was the final knockout to the muscle vehicle. More regrettable than that, it additionally was the beginning of the 55 mile each hour public speed limit. This resembled observing a world brimming with drug addicts who had delighted in full legitimization and a limitless stock of whatever they might request and afterward switching off the fixture and watching everybody wriggle. Somebody ought to have played the ensnarement angle.

Brock Yates was a long-term staff writer for Car & Driver Magazine. He had an idea - what if we tried to see how fast we could drive from coast to coast? How would the world react if a group banded together to demonstrate just how preposterous a 55 mph national speed limit was? Eisenhower had built these roads to land military aircraft on. With cars that could go triple the legal speed, shouldn't we be allowed to use them? The idea was born and immediately gathered steam in the small underground world of cross country outlaw road racing, which at the time was his personal rolodex of racing contacts and connections.

The name Cannonball came from the legendary Erwin George "Cannon Ball" Baker who was known for doing hundreds of point to point motorcycle and car drives totalling more than half a million miles in his lifetime. His most popular trip was from New York City to Los Angeles in 1933 in a Graham-Paige Model 57 Blue Streak 8 of every 53 and half hours.

That record represented just about forty years.

The course was conceived - balls out NY 2 LA. The name advanced into The Cannonball Baker Sea to Shining Sea Memorial Trophy Dash. The incongruity dribbled from the intellectual editorial grandiosity of Yates who was both pleased with and unnerved by his new purposeful venture. He realized it was a thought that pulled at the heartstrings of any vehicle lover and filled in as an uncommon continuation of the incomparable American frontiersman soul. The "Go West" thought had plagued the United States mind for 200 years. Presently it had a new context.

Yates chronicled the historical backdrop of each running of the Cannonball in 1971, 1972, 1975, lastly in 1979 in his book - "Cannonball! The World's Greatest Outlaw Road Race," distributed in 2001. The tricks of the race were additionally intensified and portrayed in the 1980's movies by Hal Needham featuring Burt Reynolds, Dom Deluise, and the Rat Pack.

The best Cannonball story/stratagem must be the 1979 procedure of Yates and Needham. It was in the real race yet additionally later utilized in the 1981 film. They furnished a rescue vehicle and an implied conveyed along a lady to be a representative's significant other. Whenever they were pulled over for running lights on fire at 130 mph past a few medical clinics the police officers asked what they were doing. Some way or another without practice, the man in the back made sense of how the lady had a remarkable condition which must be treated by the staff of the UCLA clinical focus. She must be moved there by emergency vehicle in light of the fact that the compression of a plane lodge would have made her body emit into pimples. The police requested that they dial it back a little however allowed them to go on without capture or reference. Outright gold.

Of course when discussing Cannonball it is impossible to overlook the opening of each film featuring two gorgeous women piloting a Lamborghini Countach toying with the police and spraypainting X's over the shiny new double nickel speed limit signs. High Court Justice Potter Stewart said once that in spite of battling to utilize words to characterize erotic entertainment, "I know it when I see it." I accept this was the psychological picture he was attempting to describe.

The encapsulation of Cannonball cool additionally has a place with Yates' own support in 1971 when he requested Dan Gurney as a co-driver and had the option to arrange a credit of a Sunoco Blue Ferrari 365 GTB/4 Daytona for the outing. They did the drive in 35 hours 54 minutes, winning the debut serious occasion and making way for the years to come. Cart remarked to the disappointment of perusers wherever that "Absolutely never did we surpass 175 mph." The Yates/Gurney time would be dominated by a solitary moment in the 1975 winning run by Jack May and Rick Cline in a white Ferrari Dino 246 GTS. It is a horrendously lovely vehicle actually claimed and regularly shown by "Cannonball Jack" to this day.

The best time across the nation to emerge from the Cannonball runnings was held by Dave Heinz and Dave Yarbrough of 32 hours 51 mins. Heinz was a Jaguar Dealer and they drove a Jaguar XJS. The Cannonball cool component penetrated the showroom business for a really long time after the race.
Yarborough actually runs a Lexus store in Charleston. The XJS they utilized as of late reemerged available to be purchased, being purchased for reclamation by a person to come later in this story.

The Australian Jaguar Importer really equipped eleven XJS's with novel wheels, Cibie Driving Lights, a "Sovereign" trip PC, shut down chrome trim, and other intriguing adjustments. They were sold as "Cannonball Editions." This was not by any means the only "Cannonball" extraordinary release vehicle. In 1985 (the year I was conceived) Brock Yates joined forces with Bob Snodgrass and Brumos Audi in Florida to make a run of twelve redid Quattro 4000 game vehicles. They had a comparative set-up of changes in addition to euro spec lights, a bigger gas tank, and further developed suspension. Cannonball was turning into a social phenomenon.

When Yates was forced into halting the association of Cannonball both by the film makers and by his boss, there were plainly still individuals needing to keep getting it done. An occasion called the US Express was conceived and run in 1981, 1982, and 1983. The best break of this occasion was held by David Diem and Doug Turner of 32 hours 7 minutes. They drove a Ferrari 308 GTS, actually possessed right up 'til the present time by David.

Over the years, different limited scope copycat occasions kept on springing up, however the American hunger for such things was rapidly disappearing. Vehicles were less proficient, police watching was a lot more noteworthy, and the streets were turning out to be more packed with additional individuals possessing and driving vehicles. Never-ending suburbia was rapidly gobbling up the tremendous open areas of lacking locales of the nation and the populace was expanding quick. Remember there were half more individuals living in the United States in the year 2013 than there were in 1971 when the primary Cannonball was run.

In the epilog to his book, Yates said straightforwardly the way in which he didn't completely accept that that the records from that period could be tested today. The records had not progressed beginning around 1979 to him, not recognizing the side project style occasions. Even those had remained untouched since 1983. He refered to the undeniable reasons in general - more individuals, more police, more vehicles, better enemy of speeding innovation, crueler punishments for speeding, and something else altogether mentality which he thought would demonstrate considerably more threatening to the idea.

That was what I needed to converse with him probably as an eighteen year old secondary school understudy. I needed to comprehend what the way of life of an auto columnist resembled yet more critically I needed to be aware of Cannonball. Under a year earlier I had been longing for precisely the same thought he had spearheaded with practically no earlier information on its existence.

Why wouldn't someone be able to [I] make it happen? What might stop me? How much harder is it now? What might be engaged with an advanced attempt?

Yates was shockingly impending to a fair gotten his home youngster telephone number by feigning the secretary at the magazine. He actually cherished the possibility of Cannonball. It seemed like your granddad relating a night he enjoyed with Marilyn Monroe. It was an incredible apex, his proudest accomplishment, the tallest quill in his all around embellished cap. He had every one of the accounts new to him since composing the book only a couple of years earlier. They resembled his society stories from school. Those "you might have a hard time believing what we pulled off" type stories. He was the most sure sounding man I had heard talk. It was Tarantino wrapping creation on the last scene of Pulp Fiction. It was Michelangelo cleaning his brushes while the last strokes of the Sistine Chapel dried. It was Jordan pushing off of Byron Russell for the triumphant shot in game six of the '98 finals. These were the magnificence days projects that can transform your resume into a solitary detail, maybe a solitary word.

Everything was warm. He was incredibly kind. He hoped everything would work out for me in school and I let him know one day I planned to break the Cannonball records. Brock Yates dismissed pleasantly and marked saying, "Best of luck kid."

CHAPTER 3

Finding My Flaw

My young life dearest companion was named Kevin Messer. His father
was a long-term muscle vehicle fellow and Kevin was daring to the point of
carrying on a discussion with me about the things I was keen on. He was my
sidekick for the ill-conceived test driving, vehicle business dreaming, and
over and again stalling my first vehicle out in the mud. It was a 1995 Land
Rover Discovery with 150k miles. Suitably green, it was an amazing truck
with a driving rod thump that would make an old homestead farm vehicle
become flushed. We would escape and do doughnuts in his dad's 1960's
Corvettes and Camaros and dream about the days when we would have
extraordinary vehicles of our own. Before we understood how peculiar the
visual would be, we had a wagered to see who the principal individual is
have the option to purchase a Ferrari. The washout needed to back up the
driver for a day wearing a dress. Luckily I never made him settle up on that.
Two fellows moving around side by side in a Ferrari wearing appropriate
clothing is physically problematic enough.

We dreamt of the record. We talked about how we might do it, we
watched the movies over and over again, and we idolized the folklore of it
all. Neither of us had any idea what we would end up doing with our lives but
the conversations with him were actually where the exotic car rental concept
came from as well.

KevIn was not one to stay in line. He never did extraordinary in school,
got a ton of tickets, dated some unacceptable sorts of young ladies, and was
the sort of fellow your folks addressed you spending time with. I, then again,
was the sort of youngster your folks didn't understand was most likely some
unacceptable sort of individual to connect with until it was past the point of
no return. Kevin and I would download street racing clips on early file
sharing sites like Kazaa and Limewire of Ferraris doing burnouts and
Europeans getting arrested for bringing their cars to the US for driving events
and getting pulled over at preposterous speeds.

An occasion called the Gumball 3000 was established by a secretive man
named Maximillion Cooper in 1999. It proceeds with today as a yearly ~3,000
mile street rally for extraordinary vehicle lovers. It's anything but a race yet
whenever you get a
bundle of supercars and their proprietors' super-inner selves together, sticking
to as far as possible appear to fall just beneath modesty at the lower part of
their ordered progression of existential concerns.

It was broadly accepted that this was some continuation of Cannonball. Participants would claim to "win" stages or the event altogether but the organizers seemed to make it clear that it was not a race and that the only competition was to embody the Spirit of Gumball using decorated cars and generally adding to the endless party atmosphere. It was difficult to accommodate the legends of Cannonball with entitled global VIPs testing the restrictions of lack of sleep and blood liquor levels however it was the nearest thing that appeared to exist.

Similar occasions sprung up - the Bullrun, Player's Run, Cannonball Run Europe Events, and others. As a senior outing subsequent to completing secondary school I entered an occasion called the AKA Rally. It was similar thought, traveling commonly 3,000 miles the nation over from New York to Los Angeles, halting every night for a party. While I tried to do Gumball, the funds never made it conceivable. This occasion had a lower passage charge which implied there would be more changed Japanese vehicles and less Ferraris and Lamborghinis. I enrolled and drove an altered 2000 Audi S4 I had the option to secure because of the quantity of grants I had gotten surpassing the essential in-state spending plan at Georgia Tech. The vehicle was incredible - 350 overhauled hp with twin turbos for extraordinary force, updated suspension, decent six speed gearbox, all wheel drive, and entirely agreeable for sure. It was an extraordinary vehicle to gobble up the thruway on a long excursion. I purchased my first Valentine 1 Radar Detector, the Zach Morris cell variant of a Garmin GPS that weighed more than the PC I am composing this on now, and a Radio Shack CB Radio.

I had seen the recordings and heard the narratives from Gumball. It seemed to be an impact yet there was a reasonable boundary between the individuals who were regarding it as a tycoon's vacation and the people who were attempting to contend, either with one another or just with time as the opponent. I found the later tremendously compelling.
There were three names that stood apart of the members who appeared to approach the highlight point speed viewpoint in a serious way. They were Rob Kenworthy, Alex Roy, and Richard Rawlings.

Rob Kenworthy took an interest in a few Gumball occasions and different meetings. He was British and exploited not having US tickets sway his
driving honors back home. There were clasps of him winding through traffic in a changed Porsche 996 GT2 at almost 200 mph. It was fabulous yet he was appearing to simply drive quick for its adventure, not irritated by where he really finished.

Alex Roy was an alternate story. His goal was clear - he needed to complete first on each and every leg of the occasion, taking extraordinary measures to do as such. Where the other participants were clearly taking advantage of their selections from the cornucopia of exotic car offerings in the marketplace by driving Murcielagos, 360s, 911 Turbos, and even ultra-rare cars like Koenigseggs; he drove an understated Avus Blue E39 BMW M5. Truth be told, he furnished it as a global police vehicle every year with an alternate country's policing all over it.

Every time I would see a video or display of photographs web based archiving Gumball I rushed to pour through them. Very much like the vehicle measurement magazine racer that I was, I needed to be a specialist on this occasion I coming up short on means to participate in. I was flipping through some photographs from an European Gumball and saw an image of Alex Roy sitting at a work area. He was decked out in some unfamiliar country's police uniform with the stickers on the M5 set to coordinate. He was refreshing his route frameworks from a silver Apple PC comparably canvassed in vinyl decals. Topsy turvy in the edge was a telephone number in stickers outwardly of the PC. It must be his phone number. What else could you put on a PC when you travel out of the country? I put it into my telephone and saved it. I wouldn't involve it for a really long time yet I realized it would prove to be useful one day.

He additionally adopted an intriguing strategy to vehicle readiness. The vast majority of the vehicles were hitting strangely high rates without much in the method of police countermeasures. Alex did it another way. He had different radar identifiers, police scanners, lights, radios, route frameworks, and so on. It was plainly giving him a benefit in a race inside a convention that relatively few individuals minded about.

Richard Rawlings was a third blunt and in this manner productive member in the occasion. He drove an assortment of vehicles including an altered Chevrolet Avalanche and a Ferrari 550 Maranello claimed by his companion, Dennis Collins. Like Alex, he had radar indicators, fuel range broadening redesigns, and a CB radio recieving wire swinging off of the vehicle. He plainly needed to come in first and as often as possible did.

This was false Cannonball but rather it was the nearest thing to it I could find. I needed to be as close as possible to anything present day understanding existed. As I was setting up my vehicle for the AKA Rally in 2004, I bought my set-up of hardware to imitate their readiness. A few agents from the MTV True Life creation group reached me and let me know they needed to follow three distinct groups in their cooperation in this event.

They inquired as to whether they could film me, some history about me moving on from secondary school, and us driving. It was loads of tomfoolery and the episode broadcasted as "MTV True Life: I'm Rallying to LA" in October of 2004.

The excursion was an impact. My co-driver was an old buddy from secondary school and AAU ball colleague - Lee Burrell. He figured out how to drive a stick to go along with me on the excursion. He was the ideal co-driver. I realized him alright to appreciate his conversation yet the relationship was relaxed an adequate number of that we may as yet fly off the handle with one another and be straightforward. Like the Gumball, this was not a race but rather an assembly. That being said, there were four groups that regarded it as a rivalry. Lee and I were continually attempting to get to each objective first, just like a two young lady group out of New Jersey and a person named Tom Greulich from St Louis. Another extraordinary contender and co-member was Nick Reid. He drove a Subaru WRX STi quite well and was the existence of each party.

The young ladies were a fascinating pair. Alicia was a sea life scholar from the Smithsonian and Kelly was shrouded in Tattoos and the proprietor of the pristine BMW E46 M3 that they drove capably. They enjoyed the benefit of really having been to the majority of the urban communities where we were going instead of Lee and I who had voyaged very little.

Tom drove a Honda S2000. His decision of vehicle for the meeting didn't make any difference since Tom's folks had a Jaguar XJ220 which was one of the most crazy hypercars to at any point exist by 2004. I guess that didn't make any difference either on the grounds that they never drove it and I have come to embrace the place that in the event that you don't have the testicular courage to really drive an extraordinary vehicle you own, you should not try to buy it in any case, especially assuming the vehicle is of questionable speculation potential like a XJ220 had been since its delivery ten or so years prior.

Tom and I fostered a lovely companionship through the outing. He drove quick yet mindfully. He had a good time yet put resources into making friendships
en route. We stayed in contact for a long time after the drive, talking vehicles and life. Incredible guy.

In the resulting exposure of the meeting and the MTV show I met a person named Chris Staschiak. He had done Gumball multiple times with Roy and Rawlings, and was a genuine vehicle fellow. He drove a 1973

Corvette, dressed as a L88 with bass boat sparkle green paint. He sought to one day own a Ferrari or a Porsche 911 Turbo. Chris and I would talk consistently however really didn't meet face to face for a very long time. Chris was the main individual other than Kevin who I realized that had at any point thought often about the Cannonball Record. He cherished discussing its technique, the most ideal vehicle to get everything done, and how we could do it one day. You would never truly tell how genuine he was tied in with proceeding with the thought though.

Around that equivalent time there was another re-arrival of a 1976 short film by Claude Lelouch called C'était un rendez-vous. It included an unknown driver, as a matter of fact Lelouch himself, passing through the city of Paris dangerously fast mid one morning. The legend was that Lelouche's own Ferrari 275 was the horse for this film however it was truth be told a Mercedes Benz 450SEL 6.9
- the first German super car with the resonating Italian V12 named over in altering. During the drive you see the vehicle go by the famous tourist spots of Paris like the Arc de Triomphe and Champs-Élysées. It had the awesome total surrender to pull at the gearhead heartstrings in every last one of us. Pigeons being dispersed, no faltering in the running of red lights, smoky sideways slides around turns, the agenda finished with just a Dukes of Hazzard span hop left out.

The film closes as the vehicle pulls up to a neglect and a lovely lady approaches meet the driver, willfully unaware of the dramatization of the drive carrying him to her. This would clearly be the specific way in which I would meet my own significant other sometime in the future. Who could oppose such a proposal?

The film, and all the more strikingly its new push to advertise where I learned about it, exhibited the new range of crosscountry driving occasions and highlight point speed records were front of psyche in American vehicle culture. Even the production strategy - taking something that would be sexy to do in a Ferrari but actually using a more functional and capable German super sedan, mirrored the intellectual's approach to a modern Cannonball.

After we got back from the meeting I secured my first position in the vehicle business. I was a nonexclusive representative of a hustling school at Road Atlanta called the Panoz Racing School and Audi Driving Experience. They hustled authorizing and general driving abilities preparing at the track. I gleaned some useful knowledge, lived it up, and was not welcomed to apply there to work the following summer.
Apparently they were not keen on perceiving how high the Audi A4's could

hop, how well their pit trucks could do doughnuts in the unpaved regions around the storerooms, for sure an astonishing rough terrain rally circuit could be made interfacing a couple of parts of the assistance streets through the infield of the track.

The New York to Los Angeles Rally and the resulting vehicle business work did a considerable amount to control my quick interest in breaking the record. Now, nobody had made a new endeavor as far as anyone is concerned. The 1979 Cannonball and the 1983 US Express records actually stood and the entire thought had not gotten a ton of press. The craving was as yet alive however there was no psychological picture of what a cutting edge endeavor would look or feel like. I realized it was definitely past my financial plan and I knew to the point of realizing I was unequipped for completely understanding the dangers and long haul liabilities of being related with the record at that point.

In the fall of 2004 I entered Georgia Tech as a first year recruit, studying Mechanical Engineering. I loathed essentially everything about Georgia Tech other than Intramural Sports. It was testing, my colleagues were hard to connect with, and it obscured any vision I had of what way my life planned to take. I was familiar with applying a fair exertion and getting passing marks. The assumption became to invested some extreme energy to get fair grades. I scraped by however observed my own self-esteem in Intramural Slam Dunk Contest Championships and short film rivalries instead of a Dean's rundown streak.

Growing up I was never one to avoid a valuable chance to have a go at something that others feared. Every year my flat mates and I would enter a brief film challenge with something that we called Lecture Crashers. It was a montage of tricks and interruptions we would complete in the huge auditoriums and study halls of Georgia Tech. In a school of withdrawn self observers laser zeroed in on their 9-5 fates, this was an over the-knee skirt in Amish town.

I viewed the school as loaded with the sort of individuals I realized I would have rather not been like. I don't claim to believe that a great many people approach life, rules, goals,
and fixations the way that I do, nor will I battle that my methodology is better. I additionally know my perspective is commonly entirely gone against to the heading of bliss and happiness. At the time there was an ardent incongruence between where my reality was pushing me and where I was expecting to control. I expected to track down better approaches to intrude on that inertial draw of the institution.

I got pretty discouraged. I was unable to rest. I didn't eat well. I remained in respectable shape yet was sincerely tangled. The proportion of folks to young ladies at Georgia Tech was 4 to 1 which didn't help. I sincerely had never had a lot of progress in that area. I never found it hard to track down a date for prom or a homecoming dance in High School however the possibility of a significant sweetheart relationship was still very foreign.

Georgia Tech is an extremely different spot. You could normally count seven or eight dialects being spoken in the understudy place or library. I became capable at outwardly knowing between Chinese, Japanese, Korean, Vietnamese, Thai, and Malaysian individuals. One way I appreciated alleviating pressure was playing what I called Godzilla ball. Almost immediately the end of the week mornings the Asian understudies who never stayed in bed would be up playing in the amusement place. Yao Ming was an oddity and by and large it was a genuinely low expertise game where you had basically no contact. I recall one game to 11 where I had 1 help and 10 focuses with 7 sure things. Bunches of tomfoolery and a confidence support I wanted frantically at the time.

Around evening time I would leave my destined to be denounced dormitory, leave to the closest disabled spot. My Audi S4 was stopped there, actually using the long term lapse from the secondary school knee medical procedures. I would go out at a few AM and drive laps around I-285 which is the ring street around the edge of Atlanta. It is around 62 miles and I would by and large drive it in around 45 minutes, a typical very nearly thirty miles each hour over the limit.

I went quick yet it wasn't necessary to focus on that. I generally anticipated attempting to do it quickly yet never found time for it. I was exorcizing evil presences, not practicing myself or the vehicle. It was splendid. Just me, the drivers, and the streetlamps gushing by. Nothing was achieved, nothing was learned, I just got back home prepared to rest for two hours and to get through the dejection of one more few days.

The significant choice of a mechanical designing way was because of the business program having an awful standing and the supposition it was a preferable course to auto reporting over the current other options. I immediately concluded that was a dumb thought. They don't pay you enough and the classes were more earnestly than appeared to be needed. I had already resolved myself into the idea that my profession was unlikely to be closely tied to my major and that the main service this institution was going to provide me was a name on a resume line rather than vast subject matter knowledge.

I searched for choices and tracked down the moderately new Public Policy Department. I was generally drawn to the major by one of the teachers who was an ex overseer of the CIA. Now that seemed like tomfoolery. In the thoughtfulness of my downturn I had come to see a few things about myself. One was the means by which I coming up short on enthusiastic awareness a great many people appeared to have. The mindfulness was excessively new to get a handle on it. I needed to discover some objective or vocation where it could act as a benefit. Working for the CIA appeared to actually take a look at a great deal of boxes. I questioned they would give me a permit to kill however it seemed like fun at any rate, especially with no quick innovative other options. I changed my major to Public Policy.

The second explanation that I picked Public Policy was the planning. The major was little to such an extent that there was compelling reason need to offer products of similar classes every semester. This implied they were generally all on Tuesdays and Thursdays. I could keep a full time plan with 18-21 hours nevertheless have weekends lasting four days. I went to class from 8-6 two days every week and afterward lounged around without a lot to do. It was awesome. Luckily the classes were not extremely hard. Most assuming it was papers and presentations.

It was in those introductions that I mastered something different about myself - I love talking. I love it considerably more when I don't have a clue. I love it significantly more when I don't have a clue and a lot is on the line. I wanted an adrenal high and this was the principle line of it. Talking into an ocean of critical eyes selling a feign and fabricate a rationale in view of a few handholds of verifiable data was an euphoric rush. Whenever I could pull that off it stimulated each nerve that I really wanted caressed.

It was an intriguing time with regards to political and mental exploration. The openness to PCs fit for running progressed relapse models on especially ridiculous thoughts was introducing an age of Freakonomics styled business analysts and specialists. Certain individuals were taking a gander at the world such that I connected with. It appeared to be a fascinating, though practically futile field of study. I adored eliminating feeling and run of the mill supposition from a thought and making quick work of what it could really take to tackle the problems.

The overall educational plan and significant prerequisites were new in the Georgia Tech School of Public Policy. The course load strolled you through the political theory process presenting another component every semester and requesting that you compose a paper involving that point as a vantage point. What no other person appeared to get was you could utilize a similar paper again and again. Additionally, nobody in the classes knew what was happening at all.

In my introduction class I composed a paper on the other hand energized vehicles. This was, typically, a subject I coming up short on sure excitement for and by and large contradicted all that I had confidence in or held dear about the world. I had barely any insight into them however I recently began talking. The quicker I talked, the more individuals tuned in and the less inquiries they posed. I began with a few things I knew without a doubt and afterward incorporated from insane suppositions into a genuine show. I went on through every semester analyzing similar subject according to the points of view of overall influence, regulative cycle, partisanship, layered government, administration, execution, and aimlessly constrained my direction into the array of friend and instructor audits.

By my senior proposal I had incorporated the paper into a recipe that really evaluated, in dollars, the gradual expense of each human vehicle mile driven on American culture. It caught off-guard the scholarly staff since it was a multi week task worked more than four years, half truth be told and the other close to 100% totally manufactured with such an extreme arrogance behind it they really accepted I hadn't made up the entirety of the factual work. My professor asked if I would present it to a larger audience or explore publication of the work but I knew well enough to stop while I was ahead and in front of an audience that did not know enough to call me out on its shortcomings. Never sell past a yes.

Between the late night parkway runs, excursions to the hot tub, and reusing papers, I was looking. Trust me, I get that this has sounded a piece self-lauding and keeping in mind that looking back I am pleased with a portion of my autonomous reasoning, this is all approaching from a person who observed life exceptionally detaching through

immaturity. Maybe it was organizing me for something fascinating, maybe it was shaping me into the spouse my better half would require, maybe it was simply ensuring a striving Italian vehicle sales center wouldn't leave business one day. I had no clue about where my life was going and the way that I planned to arrive. I had no lack of goal and thoughts ran transiently through my head with pop star closet change speed however I was unable to build up some forward movement. I got into the propensity for building an archive every year I basically named "The Plan."

The Plan was a territory of Ed's association. It talked about my mental state, social victories and disappointments, business thoughts, life vision, companionships, and objectives. I assumed if I at any point got captured or achieved something incredible there would be an engaging thing about them. They additionally filled in as my own Last Will and Testament to circulate the iguanas and my car.

A common topic of the mental piece of these works was really psychopathy. I didn't get it at that point yet clinically I have been informed that I am an insane person, which is basically characterized as lacking appropriate sympathy, dread, and aversion to specific dangers and other expressive gestures. Like most mental circumstances, everybody falls some place along a range of psychopathy. Contingent upon test organization, I fall somewhere close to 65% and 95% of the way toward the furthest edge of the range from the individual who might be my future spouse, Mother Theresa, and Elmo. All I knew was that I didn't feel the manner in which I accepted individuals regularly did about day to day circumstances. It doesn't make me a terrible individual, it simply makes it significantly more straightforward for me to go with awful or perilous choices. I additionally truly enjoyed Dexter.

I battled with a grip of this as an understudy. It was a sincerely inconceivable obstacle as a creating young person. I experienced childhood in an incredible family with wonderful, balanced guardians. They tried sincerely and ingrained a few extraordinary thoughts - the best of which was Christianity and an enduring confidence in God. Salvation is set apart by a day to day existence change, abandoning an existence of transgression and perceiving that effortlessness saves us and accommodates us to God. This was a piece intense for me since I never knew a daily existence where I didn't feel like I was a Christian. I was conceived the day after our minister's girl. Each of the books I recall from my nursery were Bible stories. It was not overbearingly pounded in yet it was in every case part of my life I readily acknowledged and I fostered a reasonable solace towards everything. Right up 'til the present time, I view confidence in God as perhaps the least difficult idea for me to stay unfaltering to.

The psychopathy showed itself in what felt like not being apprehensive. I never felt humiliated and I diverted affronts without trustworthiness on the grounds that my valuation scales for me and the remainder of the world felt so fundamentally skewed. It was great that I was a Christian since it seemed I could make a generally excellent criminal.

The issue I looked as a youngster was that I just couldn't stand everybody. I was unable to stand my educators or any individual of power. I was pretentious, pompous, and didn't actually like the sensations of others. It made me into a genuine jerk and set me back a great deal of fellowships as I explored a glass instance of feelings. I clearly recollect the battle of accommodating the Christian thought that we need to adore individuals to cherish God genuinely. Feeling like I would never figure out how to adore or even like individuals, I had no clue about how this made sense.

The distinction between my earnest sentiments and what I realized I was called to do both as a Christian and as a citizen was troublesome. The main thing? It is the way that you respond and treat individuals? Is it the way in which you feel within? At first they were exceptionally close. I was unable to endure or enjoy the shallow absurdity I saw from the regular person and I let him in on that. Over the long run, however, I had the option to isolate my throaty proclivity from how I could act. It implored a few moral inquiries with respect to genuineness however that is a conversation for one more day. Luckily I discovered an equilibrium that permitted me to acquire a few companions, a few partners, and keep away from certain foes that I deserved.

I realized God was genuine, I knew how He had helped me through hardships, recuperated me actually and inwardly, and favored me in manners I really wanted not a great reason for past effortlessness. I accepted the Bible and I accepted I expected to think often more about the suppositions and prosperity of others yet I just proved unable. Who else has full confidence and comprehension of the power and presence of God however felt the way that I did? Satan. The Devil. What number of thirteen year old children need to get their folks to work them out of the possibility that they are a manifest type of Satan? Well I did. Luckily they did a decent job.

CHAPTER 4

$1 Million In Debt At 20

Another incessant component of The Plan every year was a status report on my advancement in beginning my purposeful venture business - a fascinating vehicle rental organization. In 2006, the late spring after my sophomore year at Tech, I at last gained some headway toward the thought. My field-tested strategy as a fifteen year old five years earlier really emerged into something genuine. This was the pinnacle of the US loaning economy and furthermore the environment that accelerated the slump. You could get a home loan without pay and you could get a vehicle credit basically by requesting it.

I was twenty and I purchased my first Lamborghini. I offered my Audi S4 to use as an up front installment and began the business without enough cash extra to make the primary installment on it. It was a Giallo Midas (pearl yellow in lay-carperson) 2004 Lamborghini Gallardo. I constructed a site that was simply past the vibe of an all around created Angelfire page however it began to work. I got calls, got the vehicle leased a lot, made the business seem to be something past a shoelace project run out of an apartment, and really educated a lot.

What I realized most was that I was so ill-equipped to run a genuine organization with genuine dangers. There was a great deal of breath holding through the bets of a startup climate trusting the chances never worked out as they ought to have. Obviously my bookkeeping technique was a case of receipts similar as Vince Vaughan's "managers" from Dodgeball, my promoting was me posting on message loads up and heading to vehicle shows, and my agreements had a greater number of openings than a butterfly net yet I was in business.

It was the discussion of grounds. "The person on that awful MTV show has a Lamborghini and some way or another rents it out." I received an irregular message through this new site called The Facebook that us undergrads used to sort out who had a similar class plan. Georgia Tech was quite possibly the earliest school to get it actually had the "Imprint Zuckerberg creation" slogan at the lower part of each page. The message was from an extraordinary vehicle aficionado first year recruits who needed to know how a youngster my age had a Lamborghini. His name was Dan

Huang. The discussion was brief. Dan was one of those paranoid notion monstrosities persuaded you expected to monitor your web character by utilizing mysterious profile pictures so I had no clue about what he looked like.

The rental organization developed consistently. I purchased a Ferrari 360 Modena a couple of months after the fact and a 360 Spider (convertible) right when the organization turned a year old. Gumballer Chris Staschiak really flew down to Palm Beach with me to get it and drive it back to Atlanta. It was another of those incredible life travels. 600 superb miles in a Rosso Corsa, six-speed gated manual, mid-engined V8 Ferrari with a Tubi fumes. That vehicle was so clearly it would shake the whole structure when I would begin it inside my distribution center unit. Ferrari planned the exhaust systems on those vehicles to crumble inside over the long haul so when the vehicle had 50k miles it screamed like an appropriate Formula 1 car.

The organization was becoming laid out, acquiring some reputation inside the Atlanta region vehicle scene, and my client base was progressively loyal.
Most of my business in year two was from rehash clients. I observed an

exchange with a recurrent leaseholder was right multiple times as important to me than tracking down another client. They didn't have an expectation to absorb information in the vehicle, they started to consider the vehicle theirs, and they habitually told their companions they possessed them. These elements made them lease more to keep on keeping the act up and they treated the vehicles better. It benefitted me to limit their rentals and proposition bring motivators back. That's what I did and my rental volume expanded in a genuinely necessary fashion.

Literally that very week I integrated Supercar Rentals I went on my first date with Megan. She was the young lady I would wind up wedding 37 months and after twelve days. I grew up with Megan. We went to rudimentary, center, and secondary school together. She is a year more established than I am so while we was aware of one another, we never hung out in school.
Her mom and my mom moved on from secondary school together and our grandmas were in a secondary school graduating class of twelve together. Luckily, they did the backtracking to affirm that we were not related before we remembered to do it.

I realized she had an incredible standing and that she was well out of my association yet like each and every part of my life - I was optimistic. I recollect a discussion I had with Kevin Messer four or five years before I asked
Megan out of our first date. I genuinely can't recall how she arose during natural discourse yet I communicated some interest. His reaction was, "Just drop it. She has a Master-Lock between those legs." His relationship objectives and mine were totally different at that point. The discussion didn't go on however I recall strikingly believing that was definitively the sort of thing I would believe that somebody should say about anything young lady would ultimately turn into my wife.

Megan was the ideal young lady both to date and to wed. Normally I had viewed most young ladies as possibly either. She had been in an adequate number of awful connections to see the value in somebody who was not a total simpleton but rather she did so early enough to stay away from difficult issues or long haul enthusiastic scarring. She had invested some energy being single and was exceptionally free, had a profession way as a main priority to turn into a primary teacher, and she thought often enough about her family to cherish them and furthermore gain from their missteps. She was prepared to be wooed.

Dating resembled unexpectedly giving introductions in school. Begin with two or three things you know and afterward continue to talk. I cherished it. I cherished the profound, drawing in discussions where you study yourself than the other individual. We observed our assets and inadequacies were adequately inverse that we filled in every others' holes in a shockingly fortunate way.

Megan is an extraordinary Christian young lady. She assisted me with understanding how to experience the thoughts that I thought often about and made me a considerably more touchy individual to what it really took to keep up with sound associations with individuals. The adoration God/love individuals polarity was beginning to appear to be legit, even in my hindered psychopathic passionate development curve.

She had a bigger number of companions than anybody ever. We never went anyplace that Megan didn't see something like three or four individuals that she knew. I needed to level up my abilities of utilizing unclear pronouns to pretend commonality since I was unable to monitor which ones I had met previously. An expertise has made an interpretation of well into the vehicle business. I'm really horrendous with names. There were heaps of, "Hello man," "How are you pal?" and "Extraordinary to see you! How are things?"

I might want to imagine that through our relationship I have made Megan a 10% better, more compelling individual. Not that such an assistance would be fair since she has worked on all parts of me, dependability prohibited, by 1000%. I was batting out of my association yet I was proceeding to partake in consistently of
it.

Megan isn't extraordinary at math yet she knew to the point of understanding the rental
business was nuts. I had nearly a million dollars in debt by the time I was twenty-two and while I had good answers for all of it she was purely in the relationship through faith in me rather than in the visible outcomes of what I was doing. It would have been electrifying to eavesdrop standing by listening to her make sense of for her loved ones how everything would have been okay despite the fact that more often than not everything felt kept intact by the most slender of reused tape.

Running the colorful vehicle rental organization without anyone else certainly reduced and occupied me from my school work. It was a detail of need previously barely surviving. I actually gained ground through the educational plan and was on target to graduate on schedule. Notwithstanding these victories I was continually tested by the way that I was unable to gain ground towards status to endeavor a New York to Los Angeles drive and one day do so quicker than anybody at any point had. Regardless of how invigorating the closer view of my life got, the foundation presence of the Cannonball prodded constantly me.

The most effective way to portray the psychological occupation the New York to Los Angeles record held in my awareness is this. You have a latrine that is continuously running. It is far enough away from your bed that you can in any case rest. The hole is little sufficient that it doesn't affect the water bill. You have never fixed a latrine or even removed the cover from one however you accept you can make it happen. You accept you should simply invest some energy, liberated from all the other things that with such ease takes need, and check it out. When you do, it could go on an outing to the home improvement shop yet you will observe the flapper you really want to supplant and you will pop it right in there.

Before you find time for that, however, you utilize the restroom multiple times, go on a couple of excursions, have a few visitors over who can't help thinking about why you don't deal with the spot, you do some math on how much the tarrying could have set you back. You issue to a few unsympathetic companions about how irritating it is and they couldn't care less. Your folks drop by and they think you are not adequately convenient to realize which end of a nail to begin hitting. You even keep away from that washroom through and through for a brief period before you at last separate and shut the world off to the point of fixing your toilet.

CHAPTER 5

Two Lightning Bolts In The Darkness

Even as it stayed not too far off I was unable to place why it was so convincing to me. The objective of breaking the record for driving from New York to Los Angeles is anything but a typical one. It conveys bunches of hazard and little award. In light of my discussion with Yates and the set of experiences that I could explore it was not satisfactory assuming it was even conceivable. I kept on letting myself know it very well may be done yet was my wavering because of an absence of means to achieve it or the worry it was really inconceivable? I had not by and large permitted my important choices to be constrained by dread, passionate gamble, or constraints so I decided to accept I just was not prepared. The fantasizing continued.

The vehicles were quicker, streets were better, and the course was presently more limited however there were 50% more individuals in the nation and the quantity of vehicles utilizing those streets had expanded by a comparative size. There was no open contest so confirmation and legitimacy ultimately depended on the driver. There was a genuine opportunity I would get captured. There was most likely a genuine opportunity I would pass on. It would surely be incredibly costly. I realized I was probably not going to break it on the main attempt which would make it much more costly. The method involved with endeavoring it could annihilate a vehicle or it could end up requiring significantly more support than I could expect to add to the cost. It was an awfully hard thing I would presumably pour a ton of time and cash into and wind up getting nothing from. It was sounding a ton like golf. I disdain golf.

The "Why?" question is one of the hardest and generally pleasant to wrestle with. The tingle came from the social references in general and to the characteristic delight of getting out on an open street in a quick vehicle. It was an engaging test to the vehicle devotee, contender, and issue solver in me. I felt the abilities and gifts I had loaned themselves to beating the obstructions to outcome in a genuinely special blend with the end goal that being me, notwithstanding the characteristics in general, could really be an advantage.

It additionally appeared as though something that could interest the client base that I would take special care of consistently in the intriguing vehicle business. If similarly as a publicity stunt, most likely it would be salubrious to my different endeavors here and there. Obviously that support sounded a piece like purchasing season passes to a baseball season since you want a new hat.

Its truth is both shallow and profound simultaneously. Like Everest, a brief mile, or a chicken across the street - you do this is on the grounds that it is out there. But was that enough? It is an idea that can permeate everything about you and potentially help to define who you are. I hold back nothing my relationship with God to be the primary thing individuals see when they are around me yet as we live in this world and seek after various things, this was one of those individual mountains and a resume thing that genuinely made a difference to me. Could any other individual mind? I had no clue and I didn't know how much the public allure made a difference to me yet I needed to find out.

There was no real way to know how the world could respond. I had no genuine thought if claiming Supercar Rentals would be the last work I would require. What might a business say assuming they Googled me and observed I was famous for overstepping regulations? Could they even find out? It appeared to be possible that the entire accomplishment could really go unrecognized. The media environment was substantially less great for demonstrations of public rebellion than it was during the 1970s. Would I even have the option to get insurance?

I worked at the hustling school a couple of years sooner with an incredible person. He attempted to show me how to clean a vehicle appropriately. That was a disappointment and the water spots and solidified dust on my Murcielago can in any case verify it. His name was Tony. Tony's better half had kind of fallen into a gospel singing profession yet his most noteworthy expertise, past itemizing twelve racecars a day, was in storytelling.

In the mid 90's he was the guardian of a well off man's vehicle assortment. He had a decent assortment of vehicles however he was preparing to take conveyance of his pristine Corvette ZR-1. It was an American vehicle that, without precedent for north of 10 years, an Italian vehicle fellow could adore. He advised Tony to get his Countach and that they would see which was quicker coming back. Tony got on the parkway headed back right close to his manager in the new Corvette however it was no counterpart for the powerful bull. Tony pulled away rapidly in the Lamborghini and put some genuine distance between them.

Tony peaked a slope at around 180 mph and saw a cop coming in the other heading. Realizing what might occur straightaway, he felt free to head over to the roadside. It took the cop a couple of moments to move beyond Tony coming
from the other way, get turned around through the middle, and pull to a stop behind Tony. The trade resembled this:

"Do you have at least some idea how quick you were going?" The

official asked Tony. "I have a very decent idea."

"I was astonished that you stopped."

"No doubt, didn't want to run today," Tony guarded, trusting that he could have tracked down the great graces of the cop and get off with a warning.

"Well you can't surpass the radio."

"Sir I was doing around 3 miles per minute, I likely had a shot."

"Is this your car?"

"Do you have any idea about what? It isn't. It has a place with my chief." Sarcasm in a period of hazard and misfortune. No big surprise I adored this guy.

"Well what is his take of you driving it like that?"

"You can ask him in a one moment." Like the lovely accuracy it could be, Tony's manager blew directly past them in the Corvette at simply that exact excellent moment.

His supervisor came and rescued Tony of prison. He paid a $5,000 fine to try not to relinquish his permit however it didn't significantly benefit him for sure in light of the fact that Tony couldn't get protection for the following couple of years. Would this kind of criminal standing bring an end or possibly an impermanent break to my own driving career?

In May of 2007 I found a great deal of those solutions. Toward the beginning of the yearly Bullrun crosscountry rally, somebody bet Richard Rawlings $50,000 that he was unable to break the Cannonball record. Like Brock Yates, Richard didn't recognize the US Express records so he saw the 32:51 Heinz/Yarborough time from the 1979 Cannonball as the current imprint to beat. He was at that point ready to do a more than relaxed crosscountry drive in a Nero Daytona 1999 Ferrari 550 Maranello with its proprietor, Dennis Collins. It was furnished with radar identifiers, a dated Scorpion radar jammer, CB, traffic signal transformer, scanner, power device, and the overall agenda of aggressive excursion items.

Rawlings acknowledged the demand and redirected to Manhattan to begin at the Red Ball parking structure. He moved into the Portofino in Redondo Beach 31 hours 59 minutes after the fact, beating the 32:07 US Express record also. He burned through no time in announcing the triumph, having proactively been in discussions for a TV bargain. He and Dennis completed a few meetings and the story got some incredible web exposure. It was by and large certain and persevered on message loads up for a long while. There were inquiries concerning legitimacy yet they appeared to pass. There were inquiries concerning ensuing indictment however nothing at any point appeared to materialize.

For me, sitting in my apartment perusing the web, this was a Mars Rover landing. This was the primary present day broadcasted endeavor at the record. It was in an extraordinary vehicle by somebody who was known to be of the capacity to drive quick. It got a sensible measure of positive consideration and appeared to need adverse result for the most part. This was splendid. It appeared to be slow, however, a two hour endlessness away from the thirty hour time I had been thinking about my own benchmark. Was Brock Yates right about such a period being impossible?

There was one unusually candid web voice contrary to Rawlings' record. The naysaying, authenticity testing, and disparaging came from his noteworthy Gumball rival Alex Roy. He was incredulous of the absence of verification, the little edge of triumph over the 32:07 US Express record time, and the overall disposition that Richard had about the entire thing. Alex contended that the computation and accuracy he felt would be important to achieve such a Herculean auto task was not shown here. Alex sort of appeared unexpectedly on this and his legitimate position was fairly bizarre. He was sure quick to comment though. The supposition of the crowd was that the new record would challenge the striking nature of the US Express narrative that Alex Roy had put resources into and was chipping away at close by Cory Welles.

Roy's resentment seemed OK only a couple of brief months after the fact in October of 2007. He delivered his new book, "The Driver." He uncovered how on Columbus Day few days of 2006 he and co-driver Dave Maher had driven his 2000 BMW M5 from the New York Classic Car Club to the Santa Monica Pier in 31 hours 4 minutes. Cory Welles rode in the rearward sitting arrangement and caught video. Alex had held up a year to finish his book and to permit the legal time limit to terminate on a portion of the speeding regulations. He had outperformed the Rawlings/Collins time and done it before their drive really took place.

Right up 'til today, neither accepts the other truly made it happen. Essentially that each cases to me. Neither have distributed any wholistically definitive evidence they did it however the documentation that was freely accessible and the apparent media reality checking made it a lot harder to uncertainty anything about the Roy/Maher claim.

Alex professes to have a cornucopia of video, photographs, cost receipts, gas receipts, witness accounts, and so forth. Richard professes to have a few video and a telephone log with his better half. I disdain the possibility that anybody would lie about this kind of thing and I find it sincerely pointless to address by the same token. Both had been over and over asserted on the web and pretty much nothing remained to be acquired by guaranteeing a "record" that was more slow than either.

The game had obviously changed. I was never again pussyfooting towards this record in obscurity. There were two considerable contenders who had a special interest. One could all the more effectively excuse Rawlings' prosperity as favorable luck in view of its suddenness however

Roy had made this his life's main goal. He was logical, determined, and ready. Was I capable of that level of preparation? Would I ever be able to afford it? Could I chase a goal as intently if I truly doubted I had what it took to compete on that level? I wanted to find out but I didn't know how. I likewise had the dark opening of the rental business consuming any abundance cash I had for the sake of armada expansion.

Kevin, Chris, and I had incessant discussions about it. Megan realize that it lingered in my mind and that one day I would likely get it done however she never appeared to give the discussions much trustworthiness. We set off to characterize the vital factors in the equation.

The Car - We really wanted something exceptionally quick. It ought to could convey three individuals, bunches of gas, have a suspension to deal with the weight and execution, and get sensible mileage. It additionally should have been agreeable. It should have been able yet additionally subtle and ready to fly under the supposed and strict radar. In the event that it became newsworthy it would be great to utilize something intriguing. Clearly a M5 was out.

The Route - I expected to observe a harmony between the briefest course and the quickest course founded on an expressway inclination. I would likewise require the gear important to keep up with the course. It was more than by and large New York to Los Angeles. Alex had driven from the New York Classic Car Club to the

Santa Monica Pier. Richard stuck to the most well-known Cannonball end focuses - the Red Ball Parking Garage and the Portofino Inn. I adored this beginning with Yates and the later was a simple choice. The subject of deterrents likewise introduced - traffic, climate, mishaps, development. Evasion of these potential preventions would likewise be critical.

The Prep - We would require a ton of hostile to cop contraptions to keep away from identification. I had a portion of these from the 04 AKA Rally yet this excursion was on an unheard of level. Alex's M5 seemed to be a space station inside. The establishment would should be perfect and intentional. Ergonomics and admittance to the fundamental information were top priorities.

The Team - This didn't appear to be something that I could completely design and execute myself. I really wanted a genuine accomplice who could share the driving, the enthusiastic burden, and its funds. While Kevin and Chris both adored the conversation it stayed sketchy regarding if they would turn out to go along or contribute monetarily to the endeavor.

The Obstacles - Construction, climate, traffic, mishaps, and each and every other street risk should have been managed. Any deficiency here could without much of a stretch render the optimistic times unthinkable. These difficulties would demand a gigantic time interest in planning.

The Verification - I wanted indisputable confirmation. This would be simple from the GPS beacons I utilized for the rental organization yet I would require overt repetitiveness. Alex's campaign against the legitimacy of the Rawlings/Collins time raised the requirement for definitive evidence. Without an authority administering body or coordinated occasion, giving layered evidence was a challenge.

The Reveal - The delivery should have been controlled. More press would be better and it expected to understand right. It seemed like a story which could with such ease get crucifyingly negative. I expected to ensure we painted it in a light that was honoring this convincing part of vehicle history as opposed to in the equivalent fighting the-framework soul that had initially generated the arrangement of the event.

The psychological test of forming a system to break the record was a gigantically intriguing. We had perceived how Richard and Alex made it happen, a significant asset incomprehensible only a couple of brief a long time earlier. We had a couple of thoughts of our own to toss in as well.

While I was an understudy at Georgia Tech, I was informed there was somebody I expected to meet. Forrest Sibley was an electrical designing major enthusiastically for police countermeasures. Everything about Forrest fit the capriciousness of this undertaking. He cherished distance cycling, had a sweet blonde braid, wore Hawaiian shirts and spandex simultaneously, and enjoyed an awesome chuckle. An offbeat social ungainliness exists inside us all in this domain yet his was its very own brand. He fit in great.

His purposeful venture was not breaking a New York to Los Angeles driving record yet it was exceptionally free to it. He needed to fabricate a completely compelling regular citizen radar jammer. He called it the Bacon Blocker and by then it was essentially only a very much framed hypothesis in his own head. In my restricted comprehension of hardware it seemed like it could really work.

He claimed a few laser weapons for testing and had essentially every current enemy of police contraption introduced in his fight scarred Acura RSX. He had some other seriously interesting ideas that applied to my pursuit such as anti- laser paint, strategic police scanner programming, and a MiRT which is an LED traffic light changer as used in ambulances around the country. He offered some extraordinary [expensive] increases to my inevitable shopping list.

Obviously, life was not done getting in the way.

Megan and I got occupied with 2007. She was in her first year of instructing and I was approaching graduation. We intended to get married after I got out of Tech, at which point she hoped to move closer to the Atlanta area but at the time she was still teaching near the University of Georgia, from which she had recently graduated. I would every now and again go up to peruse to her group, take on the appearance of Johnny Appleseed, or get a companion's pet Alligator and go play Crocodile Hunter (because of some exceptionally compelling emergency the board with respect to the Discovery Channel, none of the children realized he was dead).

Engagement was the most hopeless a great time. You have the burdens in general and tensions of being forever together without the advantages - operatively for our situation were the comfort of living respectively and the fulfillment of sex. We had both chosen to remain sexually abstinent until marriage and while it certainly strengthened our relationship both then and now, it was a profound challenge at the time.

In 2008 a couple of things ended up bringing the Cannonball objective nearer to

reality. One of my old buddies and clients crashed my Ferrari 612. He was really involving the vehicle for a crosscountry vehicle rally and the mishap occurred in Texas. In Georgia and most different states after a protection supplier pays to fix your vehicle, they are as yet expected to remunerate you for the reduced worth of the vehicle. I was the beneficiary of the greatest lessened esteem settlement ever in the territory of Georgia at almost $50,000. It was an incredible money implantation into Supercar Rentals, permitted me to take care of Megan's wedding band, and left a smidgen for something discretionary.

Megan's folks were most certainly not excited about the possibility of her wedding a business person with a heap of obligation collateralized on devaluing resources and a money unfortunate business that was scarcely steady on a month to month basis.
Despite the strain - she held undaunted and continued to put stock in me. And still, at the end of the day however, life was not without its incidental jabs by Megan to investigate something new and safer.

Graduating from school was one of those intriguing vibes that totally satisfied my hopes of it. The difficult exercise between Megan, business, and school had been so extraordinary it seemed like at long last observing an exit from an extreme club. The ears were all the while ringing and it required investment for the anxious aversion to die down however the cool, dull air simply washes over your body and purifies the nervousness from each fiber of your electrifying being. It felt precisely as great as I had ever imagined it would.

I moved out of the six room/six washroom/double kitchen house I had resided in with my flat mates and intramural colleagues for the beyond two years. I tracked down a calm distribution center a piece north of the city, beforehand a rescue vehicle station. It had all of the suitable fire concealment dividers to legitimately store vehicles inside. It was off in an unexpected direction enough to protect the vehicles. My plan of action principally involved conveying the vehicles to clients so it was essentially an incredible spot to store the vehicles and as it ended up - me.

The distribution center was worked out with a lot of workplaces. It was just a utility sink changed over into a shower away from the ideal single guy cushion. I managed this issue utilizing my mountain man level of carpentry capability. Obviously, therefore I figured out the distribution center just had a five gallon water warmer so I could scrub down at around a 30% stream for 45-60 seconds all at once. Megan didn't visit often.

I made one of the workplaces into a room, one more into a kitchen (room with a microwave, hot plate and an ice chest), and one more into a wardrobe. That left an exquisite space for an office, client seating region, and afterward an open space to store the vehicles. It was flawlessness. You have never rested until you did as such in the main room of a stockroom where the hotness is completely practical that is forty feet from any room with an outside window.

Ferris Bueler encouraged all of us to buy a Ferrari 250 GT LWB California assuming we had the means. Extraordinary exhortation. On the off chance that you happen to not possess the ability to bear the cost of customary lodging, I firmly suggested stockroom living. It was all that I believed it should be. I lived there for a long time between graduating school and getting hitched. I consistently inquire as to whether we can move back. It is vacant.

It had generally appeared to me that such an intriguing car accomplishment could act as an incredible showcasing ploy or exposure stunt for a maker. It unquestionably existed on the edge of social worthiness yet I needed to rely upon the possibility that awful exposure can't exist. An organization like Mercedes or BMW was probable too enormous to even consider facing this sort of challenge yet a portion of the periphery fascinating or extravagance brands seemed like great contender for a proposal.

After the Bentley/Rolls Royce split, BMW purchased Rolls in 1998. The standing of Bentleys as vehicles that you drive and Rolls Royces being the vehicles that you ought to be driven in was beginning to obscure. Volkswagen brought Bentley into a significantly more standard market position with the presentation of the Continental GT. It was basically the same as Audi's effect on Lamborghini with their part in the origination of the Gallardo. Rolls Royce was a piece more slow to the corporate development strategy.

They deliberately got rid of the Silver Seraph and made the new Phantom for 2004 much to the joy of each hip-jump craftsman of all time. In 2008 they drew out the two entryway Phantom Drophead and afterward in 2009 they planned to deliver a proper rooftop rendition. Rolls Royce charged the vehicle as the most ideal way to travel significant distances. They said it was a genuine option in contrast to personal luxury plane travel. This was an intriguing case. Most likely they required somebody to test that.

I sent a letter in 2008 toward the North American promoting delegates of Rolls Royce with a proposition. Send me one of your vehicles and I will utilize it to break the Cannonball New York to Los Angeles record. Without a doubt there could be no greater demonstration of the distance capacity of the vehicle than the most

incredible highlight point record ever.

I got no reaction. Great - presently I had another person to demonstrate myself

to.

The rental organization was drifting alongside an intermittent weave yet I was periodically able to add something new to the fleet. Obviously, such augmentations typically diminished crosscountry vehicle purchasing assets. On one occasion I got a call from the nearby Ferrari seller's administration division. Given the questionable dependability of Italian vehicles and the burdens of rental driving I was an incredible customer of their products. It was the month's end and they expected to finish off a $9,000 ticket on an Argento Nurburgring (silver) 360 Modena. It had around 21,000 miles and despite the fact that they previously had it destroyed the client had said he was unable to bear to pay to complete the job.

It worked out that he had been given the vehicle as a gift when he endorsed to a hip bounce mark. He had never determined the vehicle much and it had sat in his folks' carport until one day they chose to check whether it would in any case run. Attempting to kick off the vehicle, they put the links on in reverse and seared the whole electrical framework. The vehicle required motor PCs alongside brake cushions/rotors/calipers (because of the liquid cementing), a major help, and a few minor beauty care products. It was surely not the type of vehicle they needed for their trade-in vehicle stock so they went flipping through their rolodex searching for somebody that would put a hard number on a non-driving Ferrari with a clothing rundown of requirements. Luckily, they had the perfect non-knowing client with a hunger for a miscreant vehicle - me!

Mark, their administration consultant, called me and inquired as to whether I needed it. "Sure," I said accepting it would be modest yet at the same time having no clue about how I could pay for it. They simply needed their administration charge paid and they had the proprietor's consent to impart his contact information to me assuming I was intrigued. I got the proprietor's telephone number and gave him a call.

The vehicle was worth about $75k at that point assuming it were awesome. It was anything but an especially fascinating illustration of a 360 and the proprietor was out of choices. There were likewise no contending bidders in light of the fact that the showroom was not excited about being left with a neglected help bill. After they observed me they halted looking.

I offered him $30,000 for it. He was a canny mediator so he finished up making me pay $31,000. I settled up the bill at Ferrari and wound up possessing the vehicle for $40k. Indeed, I ought to say Megan possessed the vehicle for $40k. While the pay bringing in and cash holding tides have moved since we got hitched, Megan came into our relationship with about $50k in a speculation account from living reasonably, getting loads of grants, and buckling down in the summers. I don't think the stormy day reserve was expected to be either an endowment or the resources to be a money buyer of a Ferrari as a 23 year old teacher yet she was presently exactly that.

We gotten it, leased multiple times, drove it a piece, and sold it for $60k. That was a major assistance in inducing her faith in the incredible things that can emerge out of possessing outlandish vehicles. It was a speedy, simple, attractive profit.

Life was moving quick. At the point when I had headed out to Georgia

Tech and begun the rental business and afterward met Megan, Kevin Messer and I were not close to as close as we had been growing up. He was associated with a muscle vehicle rebuilding and financier business and getting along admirably. We talked more than once per year and our ways met at times. The discussions generally elaborate a status report uncovering my absence of progress toward the record.

Early in 2009 I got a call from my dad. Kevin had been out drinking one evening and acknowledged a ride home from a companion who had likewise had a couple too much. Returning, a cop saw them and endeavored to pull them over. The driver chose to attempt to sidestep the cop and in doing so ran off of the street and into a field. Kevin was speared by a fence post and killed right away as a traveler. The driver was fine.

The passing of my young life dearest companion hit me truly hard. He was the individual that had been there at the beginning of the possibility of Cannonball and I had generally expected that regardless of how far off things had become it would ultimately be something that we completed together. It generally seemed like the chances had been if both of us were ever to pass on in a vehicle, the other would back up the driver. It reignited the fire in me to seek after the Cannonball much more forcefully. With some cash left from the 612 decreased esteem repayment and a portion of the returns from the ex-rapper 360 deal, the time had come to go vehicle shopping.

I found a white 2003 Mercedes Benz S55 AMG on Craigslist for $25k. It had 90,000 miles, a ton of corrective requirements, a minor mishap on CARFAX, and was the least expensive one in the world...ever. In my conversations with Chris
and Kevin of what vehicle would be best for breaking the record, the AMG Mercedes vehicles held ascending to the first spot on the list. It turned out Carmax had offered him $16,000 for the vehicle. We chose $16,001. It was utter perfection.

I drove it for around 90 days until somebody made an illicit left move toward my path, hitting me head on when I was en route to a couples' wedding shower. I recall the mishap clearly. I saw his dynamic cycle and the inevitable direction toward my front right guard. There was a reasonable inclination I was going to figure out what it seemed like to be hit by an airbag.
Fortunately, they didn't send however the remainder of the wellbeing frameworks did. The seat repositioned, the belt tensioners terminated, radio went off, and the dangers turned on. It destroyed that silver Honda Accord yet luckily the two of us were fine.

It was a marginal complete misfortune however I asked for help at my nearby body shop, another neighborhood business where I had regular customer honors. I told the proprietor I would prefer not to see the vehicle once more. They ended up adding up to the vehicle and that gave me a reestablished greeting to go vehicle shopping, my most loved pastime.

The best individual to at any point offer a vehicle to you is another person's protection supplier. With the ink of my particular scarcely dry on the title, they got me a check from the insurance agency for $27,500 for a fast 72% benefit. I utilized that to purchase a lot more pleasant dark 2003 S55. The fantasy remained alive.

The week prior to our wedding, in June of 2009, I leased two of my vehicles to a recurrent client. He was beforehand an Atlanta Police Officer. He leased the Bordeaux Pontiveccio Ferrari 612 Scaglietti and the Giallo Midas Lamborghini Gallardo. That Wednesday night I was at my unhitched male party hustling go-karts and I got a call from an obscure number. The lady on the opposite stopping point made them premium things to say.

"My significant other is the person that purchased your Ferrari today and gave you our BMW and the $15,000 in real money as an initial investment. He committed an error and we need to fix the exchange." I am Jack's startling stomach punch.

There were such countless things amiss with that assertion. I could see the following couple of long stretches of what was at that point the most active seven day stretch of my life beginning to disintegrate into mayhem. The rental client had concluded that he was going to sell

the vehicle, which I came to find out was called Auto Theft by Conversion. He took a BMW 750 and some money as an up front installment and consented to allow the purchaser to pay after some time. Obviously my client was presently neglecting to answer his cell phone.

The GPS beacon on the Gallardo said it was in midtown Atlanta. I observed it in a body shop with the front crushed off of it. That allowed me a half murmur of help. I got it towed to my favored body shop and documented a case with the tenant's insurance agency. Luckily his cooperation was not needed. The Ferrari was another story.

Without a method for getting the BMW and their cash back the "purchaser's" self declared legal advisor spouse was not ready to give my Ferrari back. Clearly I let them know I was detailing the vehicle taken yet their reaction was to conceal it instead of give it back. Obviously the type of individual who purchases a Ferrari with practically no desk work or documentation is on a somewhat unique degree of the real world. They pursued numerous sketchy choices in different aspects of their lives as well.

I at last reached out to the rental client on Friday. He didn't have the person's name, address, telephone number, or something besides the way that he went by Lucky. He had no great explanation for selling the vehicle yet appeared to have persuaded himself I may be blissful about it. There was an overall insanity about him not completely conflicting with the remainder of my client base at the time.

When you know who stole your car, the police don't try very hard to find it. Since the theft officially occurred in one county and the car was in another county, the normal BOLO/All Points Bulletin reclamation strategy did not happen. I would get reports of the car showing up in restaurant valets, mall parking lots, etc. but it kept moving. Beyond the whack a mole location effort, my satellite tracking device was malfunctioning within the typically unreliable electronic system of the Ferrari so that was no help. Fortunately, GPS/Cellular technology, particularly in capacitance, has been quickly improving since then.

I was on the telephone with companions who were out searching for the vehicle, police, my legal counselor, the rental client, valets in and out of town, and every other person I could imagine all through the evening of our practice supper and the day of our wedding. We were unable to gain any headway. Typically this was not a

incredible method for intriguing my new spouse and her loved ones. Luckily, we had the option to get a couple of wedding photographs without a Blackberry standing out of my ear.

It is significant here that extraordinary vehicle rental protection is one of the hardest to observe items in the protection commercial center and it is ridiculously challenging to keep. In addition to the fact that there is an unmistakable getting that assuming you at any point record a case against the strategy you can not restore, yet additionally on the off chance that they figure out you encountered a misfortune that you wind up paying cash based they actually may drop you. Revealing the vehicle taken through the organization insurance contract would have gotten me paid yet shut me of down only a couple of months later.

We passed on the following morning on our special first night to Jade Mountain Resort in St Lucia. The vehicle was all the while missing and progress was at an impasse. I left it in my legal advisor's hands and let him know that I would be back in seven days. It is hard to articulate in composed structure the degree of uneasiness I needed to smother to partake in my vacation with my new spouse however I figured out how to. We lived it up and in spite of the chances my circulatory strain remained where it expected to be.

When I got back there was still no advancement. I was at long last ready to reach out to Lucky. He consented to return the vehicle for $5,000. I had been in correspondence with the cops running the case so I enlightened them regarding the solicitation. Their response was to ask Lucky if he could take a check. Then they said to stop installment on the check after I gave it to him and got the vehicle back. I advised them that bobbing a check for that measure of cash is a crime however they told me not to stress over it. Policing work.

Lucky was glad to take a check. We met at the questionable midtown parking area where he had reserved the vehicle. The battery was totally dead so I called a tow truck to return it to my stockroom. He was agreeable and accommodating. He even drawn out a Maserati that he had bought all the more truly that was some seafoam green metallic tone repaint. The paint has tumbling off in square foot pieces so I gave him a body shop recommendation.

I am not one for firearm proprietorship and individual security. I don't esteem my life enough to put away huge amount of cash, time, and energy into collecting an individual weapons store. I did marry into a one family militia though. I had called my father by marriage of multi week and requested that he follow me to the gathering in the event things went a piece pear formed. I later figured out that this was not the best
foot forward in my prospering union with his girl. Disdain needs to begin some place I suppose.

Everything was genuinely predictable. After we headed out in different directions I got a call from my bank. "There is a person here attempting to cash a check dubiously," the exceptionally affable delegate of the bank asked calmly.

"Goodness better believe it, that is a coercion installment for the arrival
of taken property.
Please don't respect that solicitation and obliterate the check. There ought to be a stop installment in your framework too." She was glad to oblige. Fortunate was not. He appeared at my stockroom a couple of hours after the fact, conveyed a few void intimidations, and we headed out in different directions. I never heard from him or the client that had leased the vehicle

once more. I did get his insurance to pay the $30k to fix the Gallardo though. On to the following one.

CHAPTER 6

Lawyers, Politicians, And Used Car Salesmen

I met Alex Roy without precedent for mid 2008. He was in Atlanta for a BMW occasion coordinated by a shared companion. We shared a brief discussion I am certain was effortlessly excused. He was visiting the area to participate in the establishing of another standard. It was one of his stops around the nation advancing his as of late delivered book.

The shared companion was named Mitch DeFrancis and he was arranging an endeavor to break the record for the longest escort of vehicles from a solitary make - for this situation BMW. I had really helped Mitch find and money a very much like 2000 E39 undercarriage BMW M5 to the one Alex Roy used to set his cross-country record only two years earlier. Alex was in participation to act as a lead pace vehicle for the occasion. He was friendly even after Mitch and I had transferred my advantage in breaking his record one day.

Later that year Alex and I talked at more prominent length. I dove into my telephone directory, observed the number put away from the Gumball photograph display, and made a phone call to him where I advised him that one day I planned to make my own endeavor. Right now I had an alternate request.

One of my regular rental clients adored my Rosso Corsa Ferrari 360 Spider. He would lease it once consistently, by and large frequently enough to hold up the appearance to his companions that he claimed it. One of his vehicle fellow companions was contending with him that the fixation that he had for the 360 was silly a direct result of the new deal execution choice of the 505 hp Chevrolet Corvette C6 Z06. It was the affectionate liking of each vehicle magazine at that point and it was winning most comparisons.

The client called me and said he needed to lease my vehicle and his companion needed to lease a Z06. They needed to "race crosscountry." He had been to my stockroom and seen the S55 that I expected to use for the record myself and he really needed to make it a three way race with me in play also, put everything on the line charges. I let him know I was not exactly prepared to make my own endeavor yet however I would investigate what it would take to put something to that effect together.

Obviously this sort of rental utilization was not something I was eager to hear yet I was genuinely not in a monetary situation to indiscreetly turn down any enormous business recommendations. I chose to sort out the amount it would take for a booking like this to check out and give them a proposition. I likewise let them know that I was [loosely] companions with the person that presently held the record for doing one or the other I would reach him to chip away at the best groundwork for the vehicles. Obviously this was a self serving suggestion since I completely expected the cosmic rental rate I would propose to make their premium in this thought die down rather quickly.

THe statement came to about $25k per vehicle to which they nimbly and fortunately bowed away. The conversation with Alex was great though. He was as against this as a race as I was nevertheless he was still incredibly accommodating. Each discussion I had with Alex before my own endeavor was absolutely approaching, well disposed, and positive with the always present interest not to hurt myself or any other person. He, similar to every other person who had at any point been related with the Cannonball pursuit, was extremely glad for the wellbeing record of the compatibility of the idea.

The main known injury in 45 years is a messed up arm from an all young lady group during the 70s that ran off the street in an undramatic one vehicle episode. I don't think safety belts were in play. I accept here the indecent nylon driving suits worn by the Countach film young ladies came from, pink in the genuine model. In the event that my head fit inside and I could contact a solitary pedal at a time, I don't figure I could oppose the appeal of a Countach.

Alex and I discussed vehicle prep and countermeasures. I had perused his book and knew by and large the way in which he had gotten it done. We talked about which frameworks functioned admirably, which ones didn't, and what further enhancements may be conceivable. The primary point we examined was really check. He was extremely reproachful of the absence of confirmation presented by Richard Rawlings and was pleased to have full video of the whole drive. Nobody has at any point had the interest or tolerance to watch everything except in the event that a tree falls in the forest and there is nobody around to hear it I guess a logger can in any case guarantee the kill.

In this rental race situation I would have to administer who won. I informed him regarding the satellite GPS beacons I kept in the vehicles and inquired as to whether he would dislike that. He concurred it would be the most indisputable and handily shared type of verification accessible. It had not been accessible on a

customer level when he attempted it or he said he would have utilized it.

As the rental race suggestion burnt out, the steam of business for Supercar Rentals was beginning to peaceful also. From when I began the organization in 2006 to that point in 2008, the US Economy had encountered a flood and afterward a gigantic decay. Devaluation in extravagance resources was at an unequaled high, showrooms were shutting, new vehicle deals were down, funding was troublesome, and as different organizations battled it turned out to be less and less socially adequate to be seen cruising all over in an unbelievably shaded costly automobile.

That decline had really helped the rental business. I was selling my utilization item as a proprietorship elective. Leasing a vehicle for $1,500 each day was much less expensive than the genuine expense of claiming one. People were paying me to rent my cars because it was a more intelligent decision than paying a quarter of a million dollars to own one. These were better individuals than the typical intrigue somebody for-the-night swarm so I partook in that random situation. It did well until it didn't anymore.

Early in 2009 costs had reached as far down as possible. Even five years later as I begin writing this, the prices for Gallardos, Murcielagos, Ferrari 360s, 550 Maranellos, and others were still higher than they could have been bought for back then. The market perceived this and individuals began purchasing once more. That implied my rental client base moved from individuals who were keenly beating the deterioration game into those whose credit was so awful they couldn't exploit the cheap vehicles that were broadly accessible in the commercial center. That lower type of individual implied the vehicles were done being dealt with well, assortment of installment was more troublesome, and appointments were significantly more last minute.

People take a gander at the everyday rental paces of outlandish vehicles and the ordinary money installments for a 60 or multi month term and accept the benefit should be insane.
They gauge that the vehicles should go out 10-20 days of the month so I probably been moving in the batter. Obviously, the genuine quantities of days out each month for most intriguing vehicle rental organizations is 3-8 so the edges remain decently slim.

The Georgia Tech Alumni Magazine named me one of the "30 Alumni under 30 Making a Name for Themselves." My employment was a long ways from anything requiring a Public Policy degree yet I valued that they observed my ongoing life circumstance sufficiently fascinating to promote. I outlined a duplicate and put it

in our office at the house. They had an extraordinary image of me before several the Ferraris and the yellow Lamborghini Gallardo. It was quick turning into an unexpected image.

Megan and I were battling monetarily and the nature of our marriage mirrored that. She could see the pressure the business was putting on me and had the insight to say the time had come to find a way out.

I was more obstinate. I removed an opportunity to do some composition, think about certain other options, and to attempt to sort out the correct heading to head. The Cannonball record could never have been further from my psyche since making the regularly scheduled installments on each of the vehicles previously felt like a considerable assignment. It was normal as far as we were concerned to end a long time with under ten dollars in our ledger. I had a few companions over to watch a ball game and in a real sense not having sufficient money in my wallet or ledger to get some food and lager. Something must change soon.

My standing inside the neighborhood vehicle scene was all the while hoisting in light of my industriousness inside the commercial center. I was a board individual from the neighborhood section of the Ferrari Owners Club of America. I was a successive appointed authority and attender of neighborhood vehicle shows. I was continuously looking for proprietors of these fascinating vehicles that really needed to drive them in lieu of basically leaving them in warmed carports and once in a while energizing the batteries back to make it to a show.

In the intriguing vehicle world you track down a lot of individuals with the cash to purchase cool vehicles yet the absence of ability or premium to drive them in fact. I generally observed this kind of individual to be horrendously dreary. I met a person named Tom Park who had moved on from Georgia Tech only a couple of years before me. He had made truly a framework for flipping vehicles and had bought his first Ferrari in quite a while 20's. I met him while selling a utilized Ferrari part on a message board we both regularly visited. He cherished driving out and about and track and was very skillful at doing as such. Tom transformed into an incredible companion and business friend throughout the next few years. He stays one of my number one and most respected friends.

I had for quite some time been pursued by both the Ferrari and Lamborghini showrooms in Atlanta to work together in some limit. I never believed that selling fascinating vehicles or selling any sort of vehicles seemed like a lot of tomfoolery. I recollected the

general spirit of individuals who I would bother mentioning test drives in these kinds of vehicles and it was nowhere near fortunate. As I took a gander at the Venn Diagram where circle one was great individuals and circle two was colorful vehicle proprietors I generally saw almost no crossing point. It seemed like I may very well be exchanging one unsavory client base for another.

As time drew on, the funds of Supercar Rentals got harder as opposed to simpler. I realized I needed to follow through with something. The income required was too high and my money saves were excessively low. An extremely terrible month could past injure. Moreover, as the credit markets had evaporated, the advances I had stopped by with such ease only a couple of years earlier were at this point not accessible. Losing the capacity to use my interest in the organization by utilizing a little initial installment and funding the vast majority of the vehicles moved the gamble into the unsuitable scope of even my persistently miscalibrated risk-o-meter. Megan thought selling extraordinary vehicles was really smart and I at last surrendered to give it a shot for at minimum a brief time frame. It seemed like I could enhance the income into Supercar Rentals and possibly track down a couple of clients to convert.

I was anticipating traveling every which way however i wanted proceed with the day to day working prerequisites of Supercar Rentals. That demonstrated incomprehensible. The vehicle deals business by and large involves a 100 percent commission based remuneration plan and there is an assumption that you are there at whatever point the entryways are open. As my vocation advanced I arrived at the place of understanding that it doesn't make any difference what amount of time you require off, it simply costs you a huge load of cash in lost or split deals.

It turned out vehicle deals was a ton like my encounters swimming seriously. I loathed it however I was very great at it. My capacity to talk and headway a discussion through an intentional rationale that made it simple for a client to concur with me and focus on a buy served me well in the business from the very beginning. I really sold a BMW 650i Convertible the principal day I worked there.

The showroom was an approved retailer for Lamborghini, Aston Martin, and Lotus and I decently fast accepted the seat as Sales Director for the Lamborghini brand. It sounds hotter than it is, at last a celebrated salesman. In the end we got McLaren too and I took care of that brand too.

Sales had battled seriously in the past several years with just 5 new Lamborghini vehicles sold in 2009. In 2010 we passed 15. 2011 was north of 20. 2012 was north of 30. In 2015 we were north of 50. I was finding a step and

relating great to the clients. My involvement with buying and managing these vehicles consistently was making very much a standing of ability. By 2012 more than 75% of my business was from rehash clients. As a matter of fact, I was developing a yield of clients that needed to buy vehicles similarly I generally had by and by - supporting however much as could reasonably be expected, a couple of years old, for certain miles, protected from deterioration, and pointed toward driving as opposed to parking.

It was a suddenly great relief from being a full time business visionary. I had none of the gamble, some extraordinary potential gain from a sensible commission structure, and free run of the current client base since no other person working there appeared to want to develop it. It didn't take long for it to remove my consideration from pushing the rental operation.

The pay was great and as reliable as is conceivable in the business however there was no time for Supercar Rentals. Obviously the scene for the plan of action wouldn't improve at any point in the near future. Recognizing what may be inevitable, I settled on the choice to close the business. It was a difficult concession however one I had the option to come to harmony with quicker than I had expected. The vehicle business in any structure isn't one that can be pussyfooted into. It always had to have a big business feel, even when it was just me. The 2010-12 monetary reality in America was not business visionary agreeable and everything was a waste your-time challenge.

I sold the client base to a person that I had assisted start a comparable business in Palm With grounding, Florida only a couple of years earlier. He was hoping to grow activities into the Atlanta market. It was anything but truckload of cash yet it perfectly shut that section of my life. I sold the vehicles separately all through the following year into 2011.

I appreciated investing energy getting to know the clients and driving them on drives to assist them with partaking in their vehicles. That was considerably more fun than the conditional part of the business. I discovered that rising the denominator being utilized while working out their own expenses of possession was the most ideal way to make them want more and more. I had restricted control on the top line of the situation, that being the number of dollars it cost them to claim the vehicle. Whenever I welcomed them to isolate that number by additional miles, companions, pictures, shows, drives, and occasions - the vehicles turned out to be more important and it was simpler to settle on the choice to move up to the following one.

I truly loved selling the kinds of vehicles that would engage me. I refer to them as "miscreant vehicles." They look just plain amazing yet they are modest comparative with the typical market for some explanation. It very well may be high mileage, mishap history, terrible varieties or choices, administration or support needs, and so forth. They are the sort of vehicles you can for the most part purchase, cruise all over for a little while, and afterward sell for almost what you paid for them. More often than not, they are not great enough for sellers searching for stock. That implies the check composing esteem is normally not exactly obvious discount. I was never in a position to own these cars when they were primed for depreciation but if the values were stable then I could make it work.

One way we got these vehicles as a showroom was by purchasing the press vehicles that the producers use for magazine tests and client occasions. One of the press vehicles we purchased as a showroom was a dark 2011 Lamborghini Gallardo LP570-4 Superleggera. It was a nicely optioned car that Lamborghini had used for some driving schools, car shows, and display events. It was an in fact intense life yet the cost reflected it. It was an Ed Bolian vehicle. No other person would have had an opportunity to get it in the event that I could endure dark vehicles. I drive them to an extreme and disdain tidying up after myself enough that dark vehicles are out. Splendid metallic tones don't show soil severely. This was the ideal vehicle for somebody hoping to extend into a Lamborghini that they typically probably won't have the option to afford.

Dave Black was a past worker of Apple who had moved to Atlanta and worked for the Intercontinental Hotel Group. He had bought a scarcely utilized Maserati GranTurismo Convertible several years earlier and thought it was the end all be all of auto flawlessness. I was coordinating drives toward the North Georgia mountains each a few months. I met Dave at our neighborhood vehicles and espresso get together and welcomed him to join. He went along and started to see how immense the hole in forceful road driving execution is between a Maserati fantastic visiting convertible and another Lamborghini.

Dave was really enveloped with The disintegration of his area of expertise at IHG and was going to go into independent counseling. The issue was that he presently had the Lamborghini bug. We took a gander at more seasoned Gallardos that would be more like an even exchange to his deteriorated Maserati however those simply didn't work. At the point when

we got the Superleggera press vehicle in, it was awesome. It was an extraordinary con artist vehicle that had a touch of paint work yet was under guarantee. The
disadvantage was somewhere close to low and non existent. Dave purchased the vehicle and joined our gathering of customary drivers. He had a first in class 2011 model at the cost of a 08-09 and it was all that he believed it should be. I don't know the seat at any point got cold.

I was no psych major except for I adored the psychological part of deals. The cycle was really elating to me. You pose driving inquiries, make it simple to say OK, and cautiously shape a rationale that prompts a choice. It is a style of spellbinding. I was bright green when I began yet the senior supervisor and team lead of the showroom appeared to see some guarantee. They concentrated intensely on showing me what they had realized in lengthy professions in the vehicle business. After a short time the word tracks streamed like honey and regardless of whether I loved it, I was a sales rep. I accepted that sooner rather than later I would foster that sparkle in my incisors each time I grinned. They say that mental cases exist most successfully as attorneys, lawmakers, or sales rep. Appears there is a reality to that notion.

I actually adored driving the vehicles however it was trying to surrender possession. It had been one of my #1 things about myself and keeping in mind that the triumphs at the showroom were great, it didn't come close to the pride I felt in possessing the rental business. Whenever a person is asked how he makes ends meet, the response matters. "I sell Lamborghinis" sounds cool however, "I own and work a fascinating vehicle rental organization that I began in school" sounded significantly better to me.

That was by no means the beginning or the end of my issues with pride. Lowliness and sports vehicles have somewhat of an oil and water relationship. Making its best was still kind of settling for the worse of the worst. That prompted a great deal of soul looking. I have generally observed myself to be great at things that you most likely ought not be great at. Assuming you let somebody know that you are profoundly adroit at pulling off things, bowing a problematic truth into an engaging reality, and defending overstepping the law; it doesn't necessarily in every case paint an appealing picture. It isn't the manner in which I believe that the world should see me yet it stays hard to escape.

Megan and I had bought our first house in a northern suburb of Atlanta late in 2010. It was not geologically near anything that I enjoyed going to yet she fell head over heels for the house and it was a forceful short deal so I concurred that we could get it. It was far from where we both

worked which made some pressure in the relationship. For all her astounding characteristics, comprehension of guides isn't Megan's solid suit. It additionally just had an enclosed carport which obliged the S55 and her Cayenne yet didn't welcome another colorful option to the family.

I attempted to inspire her to comprehend that a little carport was like just having one room. No space for youngsters. I surmise that implies we will not have any. She didn't appear to get it and, obviously, the house had four bedrooms.

I can't stand house purchasing. I think the extremity of my inclinations has generally made it simple to turn out to be nonsensically fixated on specific things not very many individuals even consideration about while having a lack of concern towards traditional objectives. The grass is generally greener however I think back on leasing and genuinely question why individuals are so fixated on claiming houses. Obviously those individuals who invest the entirety of their extra energy and cash dealing with their cherished house likely think, "For what reason does that dolt spend more on his vehicle than we spend on this delightful and fulfilling home we have here?" Touché hypothetical opponent.

Despite some monetary achievement and dependability I was very despondent. I never planned to think about separate as a choice in my marriage however we had totally various objectives and perspectives on what we maintained that our life should turn into. I had developed to energetically go against having kids. I missed my vehicles. I actually had the dark S55 yet Cannonball was a far off need. We were battling to observe a congregation that we could appreciate being a piece of. Her folks were not crazy about me and I was developing to mind less and less about their viewpoints. It was a genuinely dim spot beneath the outer layer of some at last quiet seas.

Over time I did whatever it takes to surrender the needs in my day to day existence that were keeping me from a blissful marriage and it started to move along. Megan and I started to give industriously to a congregation we had participated in Alpharetta and assisted start another Sunday With tutoring class for recently wedded couples. She and I were getting along better yet the remainder of my life actually felt pretty unfilled. I had carried on with my life up until marriage in an exceptionally narrow minded however compelling manner - bobbing from objective to achieved objective. That felt over.

The battles in marriage had removed a ton from me. I recall the day that I went with the choice that the main thing that made a difference to me was honoring
my pledge of marriage. That was a significantly more open finished reply than I was searching for. My marital promises to Megan were these:

I am not here since I love you

I am not here since you are the most astonishing individual I have

met I am not here since I need to use whatever remains of my

existence with you.

I am here since I know, without question, that God made

you for me.

All of those things are additionally obvious yet it is the
acknowledgment of God's plan
for our lives

that gives me certainty and delight to wed you.

So I truly do vow to adore you

From this day forward

Just as Christ cherishes His

Church For better or worse

In   infection   or

wellbeing For more

extravagant or less

fortunate Until death

do us part.

I knew that the "Similarly as Christ adores His Church" part would become an integral factor. Ephesians 5:25 orders us to do exactly that yet it is both an inconceivable norm and something we don't see play out frequently. Adoring somebody genuinely paying little heed to how they help you is hard however I gleaned tons of useful knowledge through attempting. I would remain with Megan and believe that God could fulfill me through that demonstration of steadfastness. I realized it implied proceeding to forfeit anything holding up traffic of our association. I genuinely let myself become involved with the possibility that assuming I continued through existence with that need first, I would discover an authentic sense of reconciliation and bliss than if I somehow managed to seek after the egotistical objectives that had pulled us separated from the get-go in our marriage. I had arrived at this determination after a ton of soul looking, supplication, mainstream mentoring, and Christian mentoring with the minister of the congregation that we experienced childhood in and who had hitched us simply a few brief years prior.

My God is one of unending elegance and dependability. I was in for a wild ride.

CHAPTER 7

A Prostitute And A Lamborghini

People get some information about what I look for from my life, how I need to be seen, what I could believe my inheritance should be. I need to be known as an ardent fervent Christian, a decent family man, and a reliable companion. I believe their questions are different though. To answer the genuine pith of the inquiries - I truly need to be the most fascinating man with regards to the world. Basically I need to be the most intriguing individual that individuals who know me know.

It doesn't matter to me how affluent I get, how instructed, how appreciated, or how famous I am. Those measurements are amazing yet when I examine knowing the past upon how I have settled on the choices that made me the most joyful, they were by and large pursuing thoughts that I thought would be fascinating to discuss later.

The means I had taken to balance out my marriage had bewildered a portion of my endeavors to do intriguing things however as the high level need further developed it started to feel more adequate to add back in certain things I was missing.

Early in 2011 I met one of the most fascinating individuals whom I have at any point known. A flatbed tow truck showed up at the showroom with a non-running Blue Caelum (metallic imperial blue) 2004 Gallardo. Each wheel was checked, the tires were bare, the grip was broiled, and it was pouring oil from wherever it could find. The entryway handles were severed and the inside smelled especially colorful. The two East Asian folks dropping it off didn't talk a lot of English. Best we could comprehend it, we were being approached to assemble a gauge of what it would take to make the vehicle back ready. With an incredible clothing list, the recovery came to right at $20,000.

We called the number they left and didn't find a solution. We had the vehicle all separated and didn't have anybody to pay for it. A man appeared two or after three days and let us know it had a place with his sweetheart's little girl and that she was exceptionally alluring. It was a bizarre spontaneous remark however he didn't introduce himself similar to the most socially adjusting kind of individual. She was in prison right now however would be out soon and presumably needed to sell the vehicle. My ears livened up.

The vehicle was too unpleasant to even consider evening discount. It required significantly more work than we expected she would have the option to bear so we stopped it out back and waited.

A couple of days after the fact I met Kimmi.

Kimmi is a whore. Wokeness could ask that I say Kimmi is a supposed whore yet that wouldn't be reasonable for the law enforcement framework that had previously indicted her for the charges multiple times in different metro Atlanta locales. While her mom's beau had suggested that she was in prison for speeding it was, truth be told, an expert appearance. Kimmi had paid $100,000 in real money for the vehicle in Miami around nine months before her latest imprisonment. While she was away a portion of her companions went driving around decently horrendously in the Gallardo and accordingly our ways started to cross.

We were right in expecting Kimmi was not in any kind of mood to keep in touch with us a check for the assistance so she inquired as to whether we would purchase the vehicle. There are never numerous bidders on a vehicle like this. You were unable to know what else it required until the first $20,000 was spent fixing the conspicuous things. The gamble made me the unparalleled admirer. I offered her $30,000. She needed $60,000 as it sat. We chose $30,000. I hoped for something else out of a profession negotiator.

I covered the assistance bill and stuck my detailers on it for seven days. It had a few infrequent electrical and mechanical peculiarities however it was an incredible vehicle. It likewise expressed Lamborghini on it and had cost me under another Hyundai.

Kimmi was half dark and half Vietnamese as best I could accumulate. She had blue and light hair and normally wore exceptionally close, nylon, creature print, short dresses. She had a great deal of tattoos and they were helpfully shown, even the ones in additional private regions. She wore some bizarre zombie-like light blue contacts with catseye understudies. Kimmi's most convincing and probably attractive component was her posterior. She had a sensibly proportioned, yet increased, middle however at that point she had 50" hips. I imply that she could enjoy reprieves while hula hooping. It was the sort of thing that you would look constantly at, regardless of it being stimulating to you. She was taller sitting in a chair.

The segment market for her specialty was a long ways from myself yet I viewed her as a sensationally fascinating individual. She needed a pink Bentley like the one Paris Hilton had on the TV. You can't buy a Bentley and paint it pink for the $30,000 I owed her for the Gallardo so we chose to check whether we could get her supported for the balance.

That implied Kimmi and I got to discuss her credit. I inquired as to whether she had at any point gotten a credit for anything and she said, "No." That would typically be a final knockout to a major vehicle advance however assuming she was funding half of a $60-70k Bentley we thought we had a shot. Past that, the discussion was an excess of amusing to stop. She took out her government managed retirement card which she clearly conveyed constantly and she gave me her driver's permit to duplicate. The location that was on it paired the title for the Gallardo that she had yet it was an abnormal area for a home. It was off a major street in the focal point of town so I Googled it. It was a foundation called the Gold Spa. She unashamedly affirmed that was correct.

I requested that Kimmi who list as her boss and she provided me with a name of a porn creation organization. She appeared to have her hand in an assortment of organizations. I asked her the amount she made and she said that it was between $10-50k each month, "So for what reason don't we simply say $500,000?" That was on the inconceivable side of the scale for a bank.

"What about this, what did you put on your latest government

form?" She shook her head.

"Does that mean it was not definitely or you haven't gotten around to filing."

"That." She said.

We estimated.

When we pulled her credit it was unusual. There were no records by any

stretch of the imagination.
She had never utilized her federal retirement aide number for anything. Not a wireless, library card, Mastercard, not so much as a financial balance. That turned out to be clear in the following step.

We had no banks that would move forward to be the principal credit proposing to Kimmi. Without a Bentley to apply it to, I told her we would give her a check for the Lambo. We printed it out, marked it, and gave it to her.

"How would I manage this?" She asked.

"You can store it or money it. Do you have a financial balance?" Head shakes. "Then, at that point, simply take it to our bank and they will give you cash." The specks were not connecting.

"Truly? Can you folks simply give me cash?" She was baffled. "No,

we don't keep that much money around. It is really simple, they are directly in the distance." I said. "Have you at any point
utilized a check?" She had not at any point seen one.

Kimmi went on her way and I possessed a whore's Gallardo. I had a bear of a time getting the second key from her though. I called, messaged, messaged, and had a go at all that to reach out to her to get it. I needed the subsequent key and wasn't excited about somebody in her calling keeping up with admittance to the vehicle - not judging.

One day she sends me a message message.

"It's my birthday tomorrow. Do you actually need that key?" she asked. Interesting mix of ideas.

"Most definitely. Would you bring it up here?" I asked.

"Might I at any point get $100 for it?" I shouldn't have been astounded given her ordinary pay procuring strategies.

"Sure. Get it here by 5 PM and I will give you $100." No reaction. No show by 5.

The following day similarly as we were going to close, Kimmi strolls in. The most ideal way to depict the dress that she was wearing is that it was a ball net. A bigger number of openings than stretchy white texture. It took a subtle approach with even less up than her typical closet. There was a lady with a little youngster at our administration counter. She saw Kimmi's dress, got the kid, and in a real sense ran shouting out of the building.

"What are all of you spruced up for Kimmi?" I inquired. She came over and embraced me. Kimmi was a hugger.

"Itsma birfday!"

"Well you are most of the way to that outfit, aren't you?" I am don't know

she got it. She gave me the key. I paid her the $100. Given her clothing I

felt like

the conspicuous inquiry was adequately fitting. My interest endured on a zoological level. Completely interesting. Seriously in spite of the fact that our neighborhood Atlanta, low spending plan embed installers need to brush up.

"Kimmi, do you have butt inserts?" I was at the edge of my seat.

She was glad to reply, "No. I got a fat rearrangement. They made me gain thirty pounds, and afterward they suck it out, and they infused it here." She highlighted the infusion site. They plainly utilized a turkey baster.

"Does it feel strange?"

"No. Feels typical." She appeared to be very satisfied with it. I was pleased to have lived to the point of experiencing the beneficiary of such a spearheading clinical procedure.

I haven't seen Kimmi from that point forward yet she truly does incidentally like and remark on a few online entertainment posts of mine. Now that is interesting.

I was extremely satisfied to by and by be an extraordinary vehicle proprietor and I drove the wheels off of it. As I said, the house that we had bought just had an extra wide carport. That really intended that there was no spot to put the Mercedes. I wound up partaking in the blue Gallardo as the primary fascinating that I had claimed that at long last had no surprises. One outcome of the rental business was a hyper-cognizance about the expense of driving them. It was $5.71 per mile on normal to drive a Ferrari 360 or Gallardo including the expense of consumable things, adjusting, deterioration, protection, cost of cash, and so on. With the monetary gamble eliminated from responsibility for Kimmi vehicle, It immediately graduated into everyday driver obligation. The lighthearted sensation of a vehicle that looks cool, is amusing to drive, and was just out of a beast administration was excellent.

Working 60-70 hours out of each week, attempting to develop a few reserve funds, chipping in a ton at chapel, and proceeding to chip away at my marriage implied that the Cannonball actually consumed a space somewhere close to a sideline and the least cupboard rack in the kitchen. However much I needed it and keeping in mind that the latrine was all the while running behind the scenes, time had just about run out or cash to distribute to it. I additionally had no clue about the amount it planned to cost to do. It is trying to spending plan for a mysterious expenditure.

I wasn't driving the S55 without a doubt and it was coming up on requiring a
ton of upkeep. It required a significant help, brakes, tires, a suspension/power guiding siphon, and a lot of other stuff I realized implied I was further from the record than I needed to be. Hesitantly, I recorded it available to be purchased on Craigslist and it sold rapidly. Rapidly truth be told. I got an approach the way to the air terminal from a truly closely involved individual. I was made a beeline for Las Vegas for a Lamborghini occasion so I let him know I would be back in a couple of days. He needed it now. "Well you can meet me at the air terminal parking area assuming you need." I told him, anticipating that that should end it.

"That works. See you in 15. Text me the part and section."

He arrived, consented to pay me what I needed, gave me half in real money, and we settled on the other half when I presented to him the title. I had Megan get the title and shot in the arm after my return trip into Hartsfield and we went to the purchaser's home to wrap it up.

The Gallardo was my main vehicle and I was very fine with that, in spite of the reality I didn't fit in the vehicle serenely. My knees often hit the wiper tail and my head was ordinarily against the main event. Jeremy Clarkson, who is just an inch more limited than I am, said all that needed to be said. "I can fit in any vehicle that I need to." I drove it as much as I could, putting over ten thousand miles on it in the next year. We wound up driving Megan's Cayenne at whatever point we required more space or comfort.

CHAPTER 8

Finalizing The Playbook

Time flew by however life actually felt cruelly exhausting. I needed energy, had no objectives, and had made a ton of materialistic penances for our marriage. Megan was cheerful however she was tingling hard to have children. I was not.

I was conversing with Chris Staschiak. With expanding extra charges, Gumball was presently too far for him too. The time had come to begin arranging the drive. Assuming we planned to take a stab at the Cannonball record we expected to quit taking reasons and begin moving toward getting something going. You can constantly determine common decency outside the edges of my intentional awareness by what I write down on the backs of and in the edges of paper left lying around my work area. Inside the earlier couple of weeks those spaces were brimming with shopping records and spending plans for radar indicators, laser jammers, CB radios, police scanners, and all the other things we wanted in light of the most recent nine years of planning.

Chris was penniless. He was exceptionally intrigued and prepared to drive when asked to however he couldn't contribute monetarily. I realized we had around ten thousand worth of gear to purchase I actually required a vehicle to do it in. I had sold the Gallardo several months earlier and was really driving a 2005 Porsche Cayenne S that had invested some genuine energy submerged. It had a Florida Certificate of Destruction instead of a typical vehicle title so we couldn't sell it as a showroom and just kept it around to get things done in. It had been an exchange on a Lotus Evora. You get unusual exchanges on Lotuses.

Cory Welles precipitously delivered the film that she had been dealing with for almost 10 years. It was called 32 Hours 7 Minutes and it chronicled the US Express occasions of the 1980s. It crossed from the beginning with Alex Roy. Alex had tracked down Cory mid-project and offered revenue, venture, and continuation. Cory was a companion of Doug Turner, a big part of the group that set the well established record in 1983. Their exceptional time was met with uncertainty and analysis by different US Express members. Her film set off to demonstrate the time was conceivable. Alex turned into her vessel of proof.

The film was splendid. It recounted to the story in an invigorating, generally important way. It kept on uncovering increasingly more about how Alex had broken the record also. This was a thought I saw as especially interesting. It filled in a portion of the holes left by his book. Seeing pieces of the drive on video was likewise incredible to assist with tending to the enormous unfamiliar obvious issue at hand of what the in-vehicle brain science of endeavoring this may be like.

I made a rundown of vehicles to consider. The Mercedes AMG vehicles were still numerically comparably great as it gets however they were going downhill. The high mileage ones were almost sufficiently modest to be expendable however they would require an unforeseeable measure of upkeep to prepare really to go. The fresher 6.2L AMG vehicles got awful gas mileage and were 200-300% the cost of the previous vehicles with next to no unmistakable benefit.

The 2010 Porsche Panamera Turbo was getting closer to affordability now that the Gallardo was out of the picture but based on the $16k I had paid for Megan's five-year-old Cayenne S just a couple of years prior I had a pretty good ghost-of-Christmas-future idea of what that $70k investment would turn into before too long. Likewise, when I put the energy units in the back hatch I would require new hotness safeguarding to safeguard the traveler regions because of the open design.

The 2004-2006 Bentley Continental GT had appeared to be intriguing 100% of the time. They were the equivalent $70k they had been for the earlier three years yet it nearly appeared to be worth the effort. The twin super 552 hp W12 was savage. It had a somewhat more bound back seat than a CL and an extremely confounded vacuum framework that could be hazardously costly to address assuming something turned out badly. Parts and upkeep made certain to be an issue. I would prefer to be related with breaking this record in a Bentley than a Mercedes assuming that counted for anything.

The Lotus Evora was the main vehicle fit for surpassing 150 mph and getting 30 mpg on the interstate. The North American central command was a little ways from the approved showroom I worked for. The rearward sitting arrangement is discretionary which is a different way to say futile. A third traveler was unrealistic and there was no extraordinary spot for the extra fuel.

A little on utilizing the 2005 Ferrari 612 from the rental armada. It had a few space for fuel and 532 hp out of a 5.75L V12. The vehicle was very agreeable and challenging to recognize by anybody yet a pass on hard lover. It didn't have journey control which appeared as though a gamble and I didn't know I could cut into the scramble for the entirety of the gadgets. I additionally had around 11 years and $198,000 worth of installments left on it. I was unable to envision having one more ten years of obligation commitment required just to keep the vehicle I came to value. Those excess installment coupons would add a ton of salt to the injury assuming the vehicle were seized or obliterated in the process.

Clearly I had never been one to save a vehicle for quite a while. I realize that it would be difficult to leave behind the vehicle that we broke the record in assuming everything went to design so vanity burdened the choice a piece. It would be the vehicle that I would show my grandchildren, the grandchildren I was obviously not going to have the option to try not to have in view of the diligence of my wife.

Life messed up my Cannonball-vehicle's way as a kryptonite vehicle. An Arancio Atlas 2008 Lamborghini Murcielago LP640 Roadster sprung up available with 24k miles. It had $80k in ongoing assistance history and was the least expensive one there had at any point been. It was my fantasy vehicle, in my number one tone, in the roofless design that would permit me to sit up straight for once. I needed to have it.

It radiated each certain feeling that had been inked on my cerebrum during that first Murcielago test drive as a seventeen year old, shrieking around a sluggish farm truck to the vexation and dread of the clueless sales rep. Getting a phantom confronted traveler petitioning God while his fingernails dove into the cowhide of a $300,000 Italian games vehicle isn't the evangelism that Matthew was discussing yet it should mean something. It was nirvana seeing an orange LP640, accepting that I could get supported for it, and having some exchange credits sitting at the showroom from past removal of the rental armada that I could use to keep away from any taxes.

Being around extraordinary vehicles the entire day represents a few issues in the individual inclination front. I clearly need essentially every one of them however I am compelled by spending plan and my capacity to back these vehicles. That set a few boundaries but since of having the enormous vehicle advances open for such a long time with Supercar Rentals, I would be wise to vehicle purchasing credit than everything except a modest bunch of my clients. The money terms were astounding. I don't put down anything, paid no deals charges because of the utilization of the 612 and the whore Gallardo as exchanges, supported the vehicle for a very long time/144 months, and had an installment of $1,799. It was perfection.

For me, however, the LP640 emphasis of the Murcielago is the benchmark.
It involves that $175-250k cost where you likewise find the Ferrari 458, McLaren 12C, Aston Martin Vanquish, a decent 599, and a few different choices. The thing about it is, they are only not generally so cool as the huge V12 doorstop-wedge-streamlined features Murcielago. It is the most futile vehicle at any point fabricated and it comes from a legacy of other totally pointless vehicles. You can't see out of it, the transmission scarcely works in rush hour gridlock or opposite, the motor is totally blocked off and should be taken out for most adjusting, the all wheel drive framework is tuned to work flawlessly at 200 mph and just imperceptibly at day to day speeds, it gets eight miles for every gallon more often than not and five when you are

having some good times, ladies can't get in any kind of mood without uncovering the shade of their undies, and it can scarcely go over a hindrance. Include the Roadster variable and you can't drive in the downpour, even with the rooftop on. It releases and the main windshield wiper hits the main edge of it each dip even after you've endured twenty minutes introducing it under a bridge. Envision a vehicle still worth the effort even after so much! It is the male form of a five-inch stiletto.
Worth each ounce of the aggravation for that look and performance.

Because I had bought the Murci, the more costly record vehicle choices were through the window. After five days I purchased a 2004 Mercedes CL55 AMG with 100k miles. It was a great vehicle with a little paint work, great choices, required a few tires, and some broad cleaning. I got it for $17,000.

The sensation of getting back on the pony with these two objectives of having a cool extraordinary vehicle and seeking after the Cannonball record was amazing. My life was at a mark of dependability with Megan and with our funds that these choices could be supported. I likewise went to our nearby reptile expo and bought a child Sunglow Albino Red Tail Boa Constrictor and named her Sunny the LamBoa. I assume while the idea had been to plunge a toe or two in the supposed pool of the indecencies I had been dismissing for a couple of years, this was presumably even more a cannonball.

It felt genuine this time. It was just about as close as it had at any point been. The discussions started to get more purposeful with the comrades I expected to make the drive a reality.

Through neighborhood vehicle occasions I had become old buddies with a person named Adam Kochanski. At the time he had an extraordinary vertical assortment of BMW
M3's. He had a 1995 Daytona Violet E36 M3 roadster, a Phoenix Yellow 2001 E46 M3 track vehicle, and an Alpine White 2008 E90 M3 Sedan. I get more dazzled than I presumably ought to by these kinds of in an upward direction generational vehicle assortments. It conveys a genuine authority status. I had long sought to storing up a comparably generational assortment of the V12 Lamborghini lineage.

I enlightened him regarding the arrangement to attempt to break the record and he was quickly interested by the thought. Like Chris, he was not in any kind of mood to contribute monetarily but rather he was accessible to drive or help depending on the situation. I really wanted a co-driver, support traveler, somebody to remain at home and screen climate, individuals to assist with establishment, and some assistance with confirmation. There would be bunches of jobs to carry out and he appeared to be equipped for bringing some solid ranges of abilities to the table. Adam had perused Alex's book and was energetic about the criminal specialty of crosscountry street racing.

Work kept on getting and I remained extremely occupied. I was completely partaking in the Murcielago and day to day driving the CL. Megan had driven the CL on one event and figured out how to run over something the size of a manufactured house park. It broke the undertray and one of the front wheels. I really wanted a bunch of extras in any case so I discovered some on eBay and ended up with 1.75 arrangements of AMG wheels for the vehicle. Fall was quick drawing closer and obviously there would be no way for a 2012 endeavor before the weather conditions got too risky.

I called Alex Roy to get up to speed. He was as yet occupied with a severe fight in court with Cory Welles where he asserted he had not approved the arrival of the film or the finished product. Instead of seeking after a dramatic or celebration discharge she had done a web directly to DVD discharge. I told him again that I was significant about an endeavor and just a tad about the scene of challengers he had looked since opening up to the world about his record five years prior.

He accepted that five to seven individuals each year endeavored the drive. He said in the time that he had held the record, he just accepted that three had a shot, me being one of them. That felt like very much an honor. We talked through my methodology, the vehicle that we were utilizing, course inclinations, authenticity, and check. It was an incredibly certain and accommodating discussion. He was a piece cagey about his endorsement of my choices, however I could see that he simply cherished discussing it. It resembled getting some information about her number one bathing suit bottoms - squarely in the wheelhouse.

I began building the conflict room in our work space. I met different times
over the colder time of year with the group of individuals that were keen in some capacity of inclusion in the task. I actually had nobody who was keen on or equipped for aiding me monetarily with the endeavor however I had sorted myself out to paying myself. The deadline now was May of 2013.

The vehicle was correct. It had 493 hp, an extraordinary benefit to the 400 that the M5 that Alex had utilized. The constrained acceptance would likewise assist with height variety and mileage. Fuel range was a gigantic issue. You need to go incredibly quick to compensate for each stop. Alex had utilized a helper sixteen gallon power module to expand his reach however he actually required six fuel stops. I needed to slice that to three. The simple math was 3000 miles = 4 tanks of gas = 750 mile range @ 15 mpg = 50 gallons required. The stock tank on the CL was 23 gallons so I really wanted basically another 27. Full exhausting was not likely so it was important to assemble a pad. Additionally, despite the fact that the genuine course was 2813 miles, efficiency would be under 15. I enrolled our inhabitant Lamborghini expert to assist me with obtaining and establishment. He was companions with Vincent Luongo, the Lamborghini professional who had introduced the power module in Dennis Collins' Ferrari.

That fuel would have been weighty. I wanted a customizable suspension to make up for the weight decrease over the long run as we consumed the fuel and to keep the vehicle level. Gas weighs around six pounds for each gallon so we would have a little more than 400 pounds of fuel on board when full. The tragic flaw of unwavering quality for that age of Mercedes was the Active Body Control pressure driven suspension. It was great however getting it completely functional at this age would have been a seriously costly endeavor. There could have been no more excellent choice out there. Likewise, the CL was at that point a weighty vehicle so the weight change was less inclined to modify the dealing with trademark than a more modest games vehicle. I would have been fine with a CL or a third S Class yet subsequent to burning through 10k miles driving this CL plainly the huge 2+2 roadster was a greatly improved dealing with vehicle than the S sedan.

Although 2003 was the main year of accessibility for this vehicle, it was graceful that it was a 2004 - the extended time of beginning of what I would consider expressly testing the record. In the event that I had limitless financing for the task back, I would have unquestionably meandered into a Mercedes display area and bought one spic and span. As a matter of fact, in 2004 I had imagined I planned to do precisely that and driven a $137,000 white variant of this vehicle that was currently being ready for electrical

analyzation. I think the reason I had used to keep away from a promise to buy at the time was a need to look at the recently delivered Bentley Continental GT prior to settling on a choice on which would make a superior crosscountry race car.

The rundown of countermeasures was developing. I had long utilized a Valentine 1 radar and laser finder. The positive surveys you find about the

V1 on the web are on the whole right. Forrest, the countermeasure devotee companion I had from Georgia Tech, and I went through the shopping rundown and we chose since the front facing gathering in the units were more grounded we expected to utilize another mounted in reverse on the back glass. His Bacon Blocker Radar Jammer stayed in the "approaching fruition" stage it had delighted in for three years.

For the purpose of overt repetitiveness we likewise needed to utilize the Passport/Escort locator framework for radar. That incorporated a front facing laser Jammer that had genuinely unfortunate surveys so I purchased a full Laser Interceptor framework to introduce for overt repetitiveness too. Route and documentation were vital and the ten year old framework in the Mercedes was pointless so I purchased two of the greatest and best appraised Garmin Nuvi frameworks with XM Traffic Data to utilize. I requested a Cobra 29, a completely flexible and programmable residents band radio with a K40 whip recieving wire. I likewise got a Uniden Bearcat Digital Trunking Police Scanner and its related GPS and radio recieving wires. I called up GeoForce, the following organization I had utilized for the rental vehicles, and asked them for one more unit with an observing arrangement. We began investigating strategies for improving the lighting of the vehicle too however battled to be intrigued by any suitable choices past a HID kit.

I constructed a shopping list for different supplies we would require for the vehicle - a jack, fire quencher, pee Bottles, chamber pots, pipe tape, electrical tape, twofold stick tape, spare wires, spare liquids, clasp, spotlights, optics, enjoyable nutrients (C, B, Multi), sustenance bars, treats, caffeinated drinks, unadulterated sugar sweets, sports refreshments with electrolytes, and filtered water. Bunches of time was spent gazing at the vehicle and the cockpit attempting to envision where everything could fit.

The greatest benefit that Alex and I had examined in doing this sort of thing in 2013 instead of 2006 was the commonness and capacity of cell phones. He had an early age Blackberry on his runs yet that was nothing contrasted with an iPhone and fastened iPad for applications like Waze, Trapster, and Google Maps. I made a point to load up on supports, chargers, and mounts for a considerable length of time and tablets. These were the main potential game changing variables that he saw somewhere in the range of 2006 and 2012-13.

Forrest was forging ahead with the Bacon Blocker and the MiRT. A MiRT is a traffic signal transformer as utilized by ambulances. Rawlings had utilized one of these too. The two of them were going along. He had the control board intended for the radar jammer and he asserted that the MiRT was a stroll in the park. We talked briefly about the punishments of utilizing each. It was illicit to utilize any dynamic radar jammer without FCC allowing. I hear that speeding is really illicit as well. Clearly our utilization didn't legitimacy such a grant. Infringement of those rules can bring about a one year least jail sentence and a $10,000 fine. The MiRT was lawful to claim however illicit to utilize or sell. We were great there since it wouldn't be being used during any weighty speeding.

We wanted an arrangement to control the wild factors. Climate, traffic, development, and mishaps could each toss gigantic wrenches into our time and progress along the course. Likewise new since Alex did the show was traffic data to satellite radio and by versatile web. Weather conditions was difficult to foresee extremely out of sight we realize that spring and fall were superior to summer. I additionally precluded summer because of the hotness and the probability that we wouldn't utilize the cooling during the ride to moderate power and efficiency. Later consideration and trial and error uncovered that utilizing the AC was an outright need and that other solace choices like windows/sunroof made substantially more parasitic drag.

Construction information was accessible by telephone for each state however not ordered in an entirely edible manner. Waze kept great information yet it was basically impossible to know the number of clients would be accessible in a given region as we went through. My arrangement became to send a few spotters up ahead. This would actually make our own custom Waze style network for individuals up ahead to make us aware of appropriate issues.

The course was additionally a test. As far as I might be concerned, the beginning and it were not difficult to end focuses. This had generally been the bone of conflict between Alex Roy and Richard Rawlings. Richard guaranteed a Cannonball Record, Alex asserted a cross-country record. In fact the course that Alex took was a couple of miles more limited however those miles were at the limits - the slowest partitions of

the excursion. His leave point from Manhattan could set aside to twenty minutes relying upon traffic and the leave point toward the finish of Route 66/the Santa Monica dock was navigationally considerably more basic. I essentially couldn't stomach utilizing a non-Cannonball recognition course founded on how the thought had created for me.

I tried to bind together the two records by breaking both while sticking to the Cannonball course of beginning at the Red Ball Parking Garage on E 31st Street, initially picked on the grounds that it was utilized to house the Car and Driver Magazine test armada and to complete at the Portofino Inn in

Redondo Beach which was currently called the Portofino Hotel and Marina.

The conventional course is to take the Jersey Turnpike to 70 and afterward drop down through St. Louis onto I-40. 20 and 80 were the hypothetical other options albeit the southern course utilizing I-20 was unreasonably lengthy and impractical. A portion of the Cannonballers had attempted it yet it had never been awfully effective. I viewed I-80 as convincing, especially because of the Iowa, Nebraska, Colorado, Utah part. It seemed like an extraordinary chance to place in a few high normal times. A portion of the others voiced worries about crossing the Rocky Mountains that far north yet it appeared to truly deserve thought. It would be a considerably more climate subordinate, gametime decision.

Timing was extreme. The most recent two days of every month are exceptionally difficult situations to take off in the vehicle business because of the bookkeeping system of shutting the books every month. Likewise, we should not mess with ourselves that being a cop is not normal for any exhibition based work. They have ticket standards to satisfy and the watching planned to increase close to the furthest limit of each month.

I went into this embracing the sobering reality that it would almost certainly take three or four endeavors. You can truly possibly attempt once each month while adapting to the planned operations of getting the vehicle home, re-overhauled, and back to Manhattan. Yet again it appeared to seem OK to go for Spring for a first endeavor so you would have the opportunity to attempt that year, probable in the Fall. There would be more downpour in the Spring however you would never realize when snow would introduce in the Northeast or Midwest constraining you to discount the remainder of the year. Each endeavor is likewise costly. Heaps of gas, flights, delivering, oil changes, tire substitution, and so forth. I had driven the vehicle hard however had scarcely provided it with a sample of the torment test to come. It was difficult to think about how the CL was going to react.

Verification was a not kidding issue. There was no sense in doing this and not having the option to demonstrate it convincingly. I maintained that there should be unnecessary overt repetitiveness around here. The satellite it was really to the point of GPS beacon. It couldn't be cheated by flying the vehicle however hypothetically it very well may be forged. The GPS trip information would be very important. The Garmin units had a screen that showed distance driven, normal speed, maximum velocity, time driven, time halted, and complete time. That would be the simplest method for showing the outcome to somebody in a bunch of pictures. The vast majority of conditional proof would be compelling.

The Mercedes on board PC was additionally incredible. It had a two screen framework. One showed the measurements since the vehicle was begun. The other showed them since a reset. I realized they would be valuable for the driver on every leg to assess how they were doing on a more quick premise so we made arrangements for those to be the resets. I anticipated the information "since start" to act as the excursion information. This expected that the motor not be stopped all through the excursion including during refueling. That wouldn't represent any mechanical issues other than popping a check motor light for an evaporative framework spill. While the additional fuel plumbing was not completely arranged, there was a really respectable possibility those codes would currently be available regardless.

Each screen would show all out time, all out distance, normal speed, and mileage normal. It was a delightful and comprehensive portrayal of this outing containing the employable factors in general. What's more, we would have cost records from the quick passes and Mastercard records for gas receipts. I felt like we had this region adequately covered.

The brain research and physiology of it was extremely hard to foresee. I had done significant distance drives, rallies, and rapid runs however it was absolutely impossible to estimate how the adrenaline planned to treat us during the drive. I was happy to have open to, massaging seats in the Mercedes and it was a relatively roomy car up front but would we be able to sleep? Would our eyesight suffer? Would we dehydrate badly? Would the onboard bathroom facilities be necessary? How should we eat? What should we eat? When should we eat? How do you pre-game for something like this? The litany of unanswerable questions was a real concern.

I concluded that a portion of those were essentially mysterious and I simply expected to acknowledge that as something that went with this investigated, however really uncharted

region. The primary endeavor should have been treated as an observation run in any case. Achievement was impossible and it would be the best way to gain proficiency with the solutions to a portion of these inquiries. It sure was some costly and unsafe research.

A more extensive inquiry was of driving conventions. What was the objective? My own objective, even before Alex and Richard laid out their records had been to break 30 hours. It seemed like the benchmark of the thought inside current mechanical boundaries. It was additionally an agreeable edge in front of Alex's 31:04 time where I would have the option to fall flat at my own objective while as yet breaking the record. 31 hours was a 91 normal. 30 hours required almost 94.

Estimating three fuel stops at ten minutes and four driver changes to uniformly partition each tank of gas at two minutes, 45 minutes halted appeared as though a decent supposition on the time that we wouldn't spend gaining ground. That increased the necessary typical speed to 93 mph for 31 hours and a little more than 96 for 30 hours. That was truly moving and really overwhelming from my perspective.

I took the CL out on a couple of excursions to attempt to perceive how long I could keep a typical like that up. The response was not extremely lengthy. The way of driving that would be required and ideally conceivable in this endeavor would be as a distinct difference to anything I did consistently. Rally driving is the main type of auto hustling where two individuals are effectively occupied with the most common way of driving. This is vital on the grounds that the course can't be retained and achievement requires going after the course like it is remembered. This requests consistent guidance. Keeping up with the velocities to be serious requires driving past what the driver can grasp without help from anyone else. Fast street driving is the same way. This sort of driving depended on the co-driver/pilot so the choice was basic. I wanted somebody who was however put resources into this filling in as I seemed to be. As the arrangement went on, I started to address if observing a helpful vehicle co-driver was really possible.

It was clear how a couple of long stretches of incredibly high midpoints (110-120) would enormously loosen up the expected speed until the end of the excursion. I had traveled 111 miles in a single hour during a leg of the AKA Rally back in 2004 and I had found the middle value of 85 miles each hour on one 600 mile trip from Palm Beach, Florida to Atlanta including every necessary stop. Those were quite far from what I really wanted here. The trump card was the co-driver. The speed that you accomplish and the mood you sunk into relied upon the solace level and certainty imparted by the individual giving orders. The driving conventions required to energize clear guidelines that would cultivate certainty and unwind the driver.

Alex had utilized two things I felt were gaudy yet pointless. He utilized a private plane to fly in front of him and watch out for cops. From what I could peruse and find in the narrative, it seemed to have had restricted use and the air to ground correspondence was troublesome. He additionally utilized a warm night vision camera. I talked with FLIR, Raytheon, and a few wholesalers of night vision frameworks and not a solitary one of them appeared to have sufficient reach to show anything the headlights wouldn't. Both of those howeverts likewise turned out to be restrictively costly for my ongoing position so they were rejected. It was great, though, to leave myself an outs in strategies to utilize in later endeavors as I would attempt to work on my time.

I had formed a decent playbook and the crates of instruments and treats came in throughout the following couple of weeks. As winter set in, life stood out started to meander. We had gotten very engaged with the congregation and were partaking in the associations being made there. It appeared as though there was a wedding, a birthday celebration, a couples shower for something, or a vehicle occasion each and every end of the week. It was simple for a really long time to pass by without me having a lot of time by any means to dedicate to the examination of and groundwork for the record. Different folks were not really much assistance in gaining ground. Business was great at the showroom and I was really developing more satisfied in the everyday issues where I had battled in the past.

CHAPTER 9

Becoming A Christian Outlaw

As a candid Christian, I am asked oftentimes the way that I accommodate lavish spending and working in such a materialistic industry with walking with confidence in a relationship with God. Mine is generally the main Lamborghini in our congregation parking area and I don't enroll a great deal of clients there. I don't really accept that that there is anything innately amiss with having or utilizing the capacity to purchase something costly however we will be generally called to deal with those buys sooner instead of later.

We do a ton of humanitarian effort through the congregation. One of my number one things is driving a teaching gathering of secondary school seniors each spring on an end of the week retreat. The adolescent clergymen love this is on the grounds that the children get eager to go spend time with Mr. Ed and I simply love getting to know them and sorting out what is happening in their lives.

The vehicle, the positions, the superstar clients, the online entertainment presence - everything assists me with getting to them and makes them drill down into what they battle with. In the event that keeping a major vehicle installment and pursuing insane dreams fills in as a way in to begin a discussion with one of these children about Jesus and how to offset existence with what is really significant then it merits each dime.

Showing individuals the amount you couldn't care less about your stuff is similarly essential to the amount you in all actuality do appreciate and deal with what you have. I'm never modest about allowing individuals to take pictures, sit in, and even drive my vehicles when circumstances grant. I can't teach that my fortune is in Heaven assuming I hop on top of each youngster that inclines toward my vehicle to take a selfie. It is a major box of carbon fiber and paint. It can be generally fixed and nobody would be more eager to call the AllState individuals than I would!

I get a ton of clients whose spouses and youngsters all can't stand their vehicles. They loathe the time and consideration the vehicles get and they are condemning of the prerequisite the vehicle stay in such immaculate condition. Folks stroll into my display area all an opportunity to exchange into their next vehicle. They won't let me know their ongoing one ever sees downpour, they go through days in the carport itemizing it after each drive and afterward they guarantee me that I won't track down an imperfection on it. It is

the cleanest one of all time! Woohoo.

Inevitably a remark comes up inside the following couple of minutes about how vexed their soul mate will be that they just expanded their interest in the sporting use office. I generally inquire, "Does she drive it?" and the response is dependably in actuality. At the point when I inquire as to whether they would like their spouses to drive, use, and partake in their vehicles close by them the response is by and large, "Yes."

The issue is, the wives are savvy to the point of realizing that it basically does not merit the gamble. They realize how crushed their significant other would be on the off chance that they returned home with a scraped guard, scratched wheel, or scratch. Their separation from the vehicle fills in as a safety effort to fortify or keep up with the prosperity of their relationship.

I let them know nothing new. Megan won't snatch the keys to the Lambo and go get espresso with a companion. She realizes that she is generally welcome to however she additionally realizes that you can't see out of it, the transmission is testing, and the parts are costly to the point of annoying her assuming we needed to supplant them. What she adores doing is driving the vehicle experiencing the same thing. My occupation as somebody believes that her should endure this fixation to set out these open doors for her.

I advised my clients to go on their spouses on a street outing some place sensibly close. 200-300 miles away is awesome. When you escape metropolitan regions bounce off an exit and switch seats. Anybody can drive one of these vehicles on the parkway. They figure out how the vehicle feels, how the controls work, and they settle in it. It is an incredible chance to give a few empowering words about how well she did, how fun it is, and how much her appreciating it adds to your pleasure in it. Outlandish vehicles - reinforcing relationships! I think there is a course series in there somewhere.

Once you get to the location, get out and let them know that it is so cool to see this delightful vehicle shrouded in bugs, brake dust, and loaded up with trash from the excursion. Be cheerful about utilizing the vehicle and clarify that the following stop doesn't need to be the detail shop. Show her that you are not saving it for the following proprietor to appreciate. You need to mess around with the vehicle and you are making her a piece of it.

After that you get to purchase anything vehicle you need!

I attempt to exhibit that mentality with each of the vehicles that I own and drive. They are exceptional things that don't need extraordinary treatment. Give kids rides. Allow them to take pictures. Answer their inquiries and show them you don't need to be Kanye West to have and appreciate something cool. As a matter of fact, our new political decision has demonstrated the way that you can be a multi-Lambo proprietor and proceed to become President of the United States. No matter what, cruising all over in a costly vehicle makes you a good example to a susceptible audience. Even however I offered a ton of vehicles to individuals who ought not be imitated, possession accompanies responsibility.

Over the beyond a decade I have claimed four Ferraris, six Lamborghinis, two Porsches, a Ruf, four AMG Mercedes, four Land Rovers, a BMW, and an Audi. The method involved with purchasing, driving them, and selling them has been loads of tomfoolery yet what I love most is offering them to individual vehicle fans. I believe that attracted me to the rental business the primary spot. Consistently I was giving somebody a supercar experience and making recollections they would have for an extremely lengthy time.

The moral inquiry relates to the record along these lines. Was the record my golden calf? Was overstepping the law wicked? Is it true or not that i was jeopardizing individuals? Every one of those questions merit some discussion.

We serve an astonishing God that fabricated a perfectly mind boggling world for us to hang out in while we get to know Him. The possibility of a record is a festival of such countless things about creation. It encapsulates the cutthroat soul of humankind and the drive that permits us to endeavor something remarkable. It shows the way that gatherings can meet up to altogether seek after and achieve something really special.

The beauty of God permits us to partake presently here, to win things, to put forth objectives, and the have loads of fun en route. I love my God for that. What is considerably cooler is that since I set this standard - you just got to peruse those words from me. Whatever we do can become a platform for a message that is much, much greater.

Is it corrupt? At the point when I was consulted on the TODAY Show, the hosts asked how I could accommodate being a Sunday School educator with violating such countless regulations. I let them know this was an illustration of objective setting, arranging a plan to completion and being who you need to be. The genuine response is fairly more profound than that and it was something that I spent this whole excursion attempting to make sense of. The "Why?" question is piercingly difficult to answer.

The security question is also troublesome and unwinnable. As I pondered endeavoring this record obviously there was a component of risk and that I expected to comprehend what the genuine dangers were. I would in any case have to gloss over them for Megan and my other loved ones, however I should have been straightforward with myself about what was on the line.

As the Spring moved nearer I controlled more discussions toward the record. The possibility of responsibility was something I needed. Assuming that a year passed and I was no place nearer to having this done then I wanted somebody to call me out on it.

Throughout my life, I had never been bashful about making my objectives understood and afterward following through on them. This felt different though. The more extended my companions heard me discuss it the higher their insight on my own interest in it went. Adding embarrassment to the destruction of disappointment was a blade that cuts both ways. It pushed me harder however it added an enthusiastic strain and fear to the thought. I have generally said I am not scared of something besides insects. I don't actually count the bugs since everybody ought to can't stand insects. They are slippery and they tear into you. I assume as I consider it I fear the day that I figure out I can't accomplish something that I genuinely needed to do and what individuals around me could imagine that.

At that point the gathering helping me comprised of Chris Staschiak (co-driver choice #1), Adam Kochanski (co-driver choice #2), Taylor Clark (support traveler choice #1), and Forrest Sibley (professional and backing traveler choice #2). Taylor Clark was an incredible companion, clerk for my colorful vehicle rental business [read "masochist"], and a genuine wellspring of a word of wisdom. I figured he would be an exceptionally huge resource for offer the conversation starters concerning how hard I was pushing such that I could not promptly reject outright.

Starting in 2012 I shaped a gathering of ten companions that I periodically met with to conceptualize enterprising thoughts and ventures. The gathering included Tom Park, Taylor Clark, and a few others who had some awareness of my advantage in breaking the record. One of them carried Dan Huang to a gathering we had about an intriguing vehicle track driving experience idea. We really engaged utilizing the Cannonball World Record project as a business attempt yet the adaptation viewpoint is so troublesome/incomprehensible it felt too risky

as a benefit looking for business.

I had not addressed Dan in excess of a modest bunch of times since school. We had discussed several vehicles he was keen on and he had shown up on two or three our drives. He would before long turn out to be very important.

I let Forrest know that we needed to make an endeavor in the spring so he expected to get the Radar Jammer functional. The Bacon Blocker had two or three months from fulfillment for around four years. Strangely, his mission to fabricate the gadget and my journey to break the record were basically the same in span and cost. Forrest was likewise fabricating me the MIRT which was nearer to completion.

From Forrest Sibley, Countermeasure Expert

Our testing of countermeasures returns to 2009 when Ed was currently at Supercar Rentals. We talked about a few choices for mask. Ed had a white Mercedes at that point and had the plan to rebadge the front and back of it with something like an Audi symbol toward the front and a Lexus insignia on the back. I recollect plainly that Ed needed to have BMW hubcaps or focus covers on the wheels since it is a conspicuous logo when the wheels are turning and the blue tone is as yet perceivable at speed.

We were clearly extremely worried about speed estimating gadgets. The two principle gadgets utilized today are radar and lidar. There are a couple of different techniques utilized for estimating speed, to be specific the stopwatch strategy (VASCAR), however there isn't a lot of that should be possible for this other than banging on the brakes. There were a few choices accessible for lidar. One was latent assurance. This includes diminishing the optical impression of a laser pillar being pointed at the vehicle.

Ed and I discussed various methods of doing this such as painting the car black, putting a dull vinyl bra on the front, and wrapping the car. I observed an infrared-retaining polymer that could go on the most intelligent pieces of the vehicle: the headlights and tag. A green powder costs more by weight than Heroin, a few hundred dollars for a couple grams.

I observed a dissolvable for it that would break up in auto clear coat and wound up with a lidar-spongy green clear coat. I bought an enhance with Photoshop and splashed down my tag, headlights, and a piece of test plexiglass. The outcomes were brilliant. The reflectivity of anything that it was covered in was nothing. I was struggling with getting readings off my vehicle at significant distances with my lidar weapon. Nonetheless, everything was green, and in no time, daylight annihilated the polymer, the thing turned clear, and the covered things became intelligent once more. This wouldn't work in the long haul, thus we deserted the thought. For lidar, Ed bought a bunch of Laser Interceptor jammers which I had a great deal of achievement with. That dealt with that problem.

As for radar, I had something in progress and had been chipping away at it for a couple of years at the time that I met Ed. It's my drawn out leisure activity project, and

I can't discuss it, yet we should simply say that they would struggle with getting a speed perusing with their radar firearms. At the hour of the principal run, the primary circuit board was being delivered in New Jersey. We were expecting the principal rush to simply be a trial and planned to do it without dynamic radar insurance. I had seven of these sheets delivered, front and back each for six vehicles in addition to one extra. I have the extra holding tight the divider in my office. Since we were anticipating utilizing one of these gadgets on the run, I put a Mercedes logo on the base to make it match the vehicle. We would have had focuses for style assuming we had utilized this. All things considered, we went with two or three Valentine One radar identifiers. One pointed through the back window and one pointed through the front windshield. Ed and I checked with one of my radar firearms to be certain that the indicators would be able "see" through the metallic covering on the windshield after he brought up the weak trapezoidal gap at the base. The finders functioned admirably for the little that we tried them in this design. This was all there was to it for radar.

Ed and I examined two strategies for radio correspondence: a police scanner and a CB radio. Ed had me select the best scanner that cash could purchase, I tracked down it, and he requested it right away. The equivalent went with the CB. Not exactly seven days before Ed made the run, I headed toward his place, and both of us went through a long time going through the street chart book of the course state by state, province by region, and city by city. I picked frequencies to transfer to the scanner as Ed poured over the street map book and named the geographic areas. A significant number of the frequencies had GPS metadata appended to them with the goal that the scanner would naturally get them as we moved toward the specific districts. Practically speaking, there were an excessive number of frequencies without GPS information that the scanner needed to go through constantly for our arranging to be of any utilization, and the scanner was so stalled that it did no decent during the run. Hello, this is the thing trials are for, right?

The CB radio was one more significant thing that Ed and I chipped away at. We settled on the best in class Cobra 29 radio, and he went with the K40 recieving wire since that was what I had utilized previously. The recieving wire was a piece on the huge size, and when I had one on my vehicle, everybody alluded to it as "the lightning bar." We generally disliked the radio being packed once again into the scramble. Whenever Ed got the vehicle back from the installer, he saw that he had no gathering on the pristine radio. The installer had pushed the CB enough to break the connector from the coaxial link. Gathering was maybe

great for two or three hundred yards, and the VSWRs were through the rooftop. I requested a 90-degree point connector to make more space behind the radio and introduced it the next week. It appeared to get the job done, the VSWRs dipped under 2:1, and we lacked the opportunity before the hurry to get another crease connector in the event that the connector was downright horrendous. A few days after the fact - and I don't know whether this was before the run or during it- - the association was awful once more, and the CB was performing decently badly.

A couple of months before the run, Ed got some information about controlling traffic signals. A couple of years earlier, I had assembled a gadget that could do this on unencoded frameworks. It comprised of an infrared light source constrained by a microcontroller that beat it around 10 Hz. It chipped away at certain lights and was a "ideal to have," however I don't imagine that Ed at any point utilized it. (Incidentally, Ed, in the event that you at any point take out all of the "great stuff" or sell the vehicle, I need this thing back!)

CHAPTER 10

The Criminal In The Mirror

Spring immediately became Summer and I was not prepared. The other colleagues were not really accessible and I was incredibly occupied. The vehicle actually required its clothing rundown of administration things and I didn't have the money to pay for that.
Megan and I were doing great in our marriage yet she was annoyingly restless to have a kid.

I concurred in the long run I would bounce on board the multiplication train however I told her that I needed to break the record first. Our office was loaded with an adequate number of gadgets that she realize that it was close enough for that condition to be acceptable.
She was at long last egging me on to finish it in the near future. The clock was ticking in additional ways than one.

That Summer I took care of business and purchased the remainder of the countermeasure things I really wanted. My confidence was disappearing however I needed to ensure I essentially had one endeavor in before the year's over. I realized the enormous development projects in Oklahoma and New Mexico had gotten done and I was running out of excuses.

Every discussion I had with arranged co-driver Chris, however, was not exactly uplifting. He was occupied with work, his sweetheart at the time had some medical problems, and he was making it sound like he wouldn't come through. Every responsibility accompanied some sort of way out.

Backup co-driver Adam's better half got pregnant. She had reveled both of us in accepting she was alright with him taking part yet when little man began baking she was out so he was consigned to the sidelines. It was rapidly turning out to be clear I probably won't have a co-driver. It was likewise turning out to be evident that assuming somebody had a lot of chance to ponder the cornucopia of catastrophe that could emerge out of endeavoring this run, it very well could make it inconceivable for somebody to stay occupied with the task.

In a similar summer of 2013 I sold Dave Black a second Lamborghini. He was appreciating driving his Superleggera yet he needed a convertible. He had been driving the previous press vehicle extremely hard and it really had transmission disappointment. I involved that mechanical difficulty as an influence with the Lamborghini production line to assist with getting him an incredible arrangement on another vehicle. Throughout the span of half a month I ironed out the subtleties for him to purchase another Lamborghini Gallardo LP570-4 Performante Edizione Tecnica at an attractive markdown. I put the 2011 Superleggera with a West Coast distributer who gave him $20k more than he had paid us for it nine months and 5,000 miles earlier. This was one of the last extraordinary versions of the Gallardo and a genuinely novel vehicle for him. Dave was invigorated; still jobless, yet excited.

He had a ton of available energy on his hands. He would track down minor flaws in the vehicle and get it for us to fix it. He lives around two miles from the showroom so I would see him shout by in the vehicle consistently en route to QuikTrip to purchase the biggest cup of wellspring soft drink that he could convey. He would drop the vehicle off and afterward make sense of how adaptable and obliging he would be in respecting our timing to fix it. Then he would stop in every day once or twice to check on progress. Dave declared himself to be the most laid back client of all time. The incongruity stuck and he procured himself the epithet Laid Back Dave Black or LBDB for short.

During one of our discussions Dave referenced that he had seen a film as of late called 32 Hours 7 Minutes. This was the narrative by Cory Welles about the US Express and Alex Roy's record breaking endeavors. He read the article in Wired Magazine about Alex and the readiness that he had done to the vehicle back in 2007 when the news had broken about the record. He thought it was a particularly cool thought. He needed to sort out a screening and needed to converse with me about the achievability of getting sorted out a race along a similar course today. Obviously I knew about the case among Alex and Cory and I was not hoping to embrace Cory in that battle. I actually needed Alex's affirmation of my record when I set it.

I additionally clarified that due for the manner in which tortious suit works there was genuinely no decent method for getting sorted out a race on open streets. It had been attempted, neglected to send off, and was by and large socially unsatisfactory. There couldn't be anybody on Earth more keen on beginning or taking part in a race of that sort than me yet it just wasn't possible. I let him know to that end each of the new endeavors were single vehicle, one-off efforts.

I discreetly uncovered to Dave I was currently breaking that record. That implied setting up an evaluating for a film that would be the previous information before too appallingly lengthy probably won't be the best utilization of his time.

It blew him away. He was exceptionally energized and inquired as to whether there was any assistance he could offer. At the time I had a group together and was holding out hopeful expectation that they could really come through so I didn't play a part for him to play. I let him know the CL was at that point at CarTunes getting everything introduced and Charles was preparing to construct the fuel framework. He proposed to lead me out of Manhattan on the off chance that I needed. I let him know that would be great.

It was a troublesome discussion to have on the grounds that I could perceive how genuinely invigorated he was about the thought. By memorable point of reference and I am certain by his own confirmation, Dave was a long way from the best individual to do this. In one of my discussions with Alex Roy he referenced that he felt the best age to attempt this was 28-35. I was 28 when I made it happen. Alex was 35. Dave was 45. He had a 15 year old little girl. He actually required future managers not to mark him as a criminal. He was well external anything thin segment of blockheads I exist inside that permits me to stomach the dangers of doing this.

Obviously, I would never blame anybody for an interest in the thought yet when I pondered the individual sitting in the front seat close to me the psychological picture was unique. There is a pomposity reared by the preparation of this sort of thing. To accept I had what it would take to challenge this record, I expected to persuade myself that there was some part of my range of abilities and capacities that pursues me settle on preferred decisions over the competition.
Without such a qualification, how might I feel equipped for success?

That implied when somebody offered all around planned counsel or an option in contrast to the bearing I was going it was extremely challenging for me to acknowledge it. My personality defects are ample. They make me who I am. Settled among the rebellion, excessive pride, and fake relief pushing charm is a piece of me that similarly gauges all impediments among me and an objective. Capture, my own gamble of death, and monetary ruin kept equivalent ground with the climate and traffic patterns.

This is as great a period as any to specify this - there was a second only a couple of months before the endeavor where I had a disrupting mental breakthrough. It was presumably while heading to work, cleaning my teeth, or selling a $500,000 vehicle - some careless assignment. There was a moment where it hit me. I'm a criminal.

Throughout my life I had seen numerous conditions where I genuinely respected criminal venture. It very well may be the Guy Ritchie motion pictures talking or the passionate psychopathy carrying on yet I had generally seen a more prominent allure there than it felt mindful to concede. It might have been the restless evenings in school exploring the complexities of duplicating money, getting altogether too made up for lost time in thinking how intriguing an advanced existence of theft may be (eyepatch-aaaargh! theft, not Napster robbery), or the adrenal requirement for incidental justified abnormality yet I generally felt like I would be a decent lawbreaker. I in all actuality do adore pyramid schemes.

I had generally seen Christianity as a restricting power to this and I had never distinguished myself as a possibility for an existence of wrongdoing. Then it hit me. I was a crook. I was, and had been for a long while, arranging an intricate plan to overstep the law. As an expert defense advisor I invest a ton of energy telling individuals scratching that tingle and venture out into a lavish purchase is alright. I obviously do it to myself too.

One obstacle that I generally had with the possibility of Christian salvation was my requirement for Jesus. I never felt that similar as a delinquent, essentially I convinced myself to feel that my transgressions were alright comparative all the others'. At some point, however, it hit me. God sees each of our careless activities with a similar weight. The same way all that could turn out badly on this drive had a similar measure of land in the "con" segment, all disappointments were something very similar to him.

Saying you ate one Oreo when it was as a matter of fact every one of them was equivalent to being a hatchet killer of infants. We as a whole plainly sin and from that point, the unconquerable idea of compromise to God separated from a simply penance in Jesus made sense.

Obviously, nine years of arranging into a thought that was illicit, when an acknowledgment like that hits you, it can cause some sort of a situation. Really it didn't. Perhaps it was the reality I was not doing it for any private monetary benefit, to acquire an unreasonable benefit over anybody, or to hurt anybody. I was not doing it for a specific explanation. It had quite recently turned into the most recent score on the fixation belt. That next look into a mirror felt very strange.

From Dave Black, Co-Outlaw

June 19, 1981 was not only my thirteenth birthday celebration, it was the delivery date of The Cannonball Run film. My sibling and his companions saw it before me. They returned discussing a vehicle called a "Lamborghini." Up until this point, I had just had some significant awareness of Ferraris and Maseratis - particularly the 308 GTS driven on Magnum PI. The following morning, I rode my bicycle to the theater and watched the early show. The film blurs in with a dark screen and an astounding exhaust note to uncover a dark Lamborghini Countach driving across a stretch of desert expressway. My jaw dropped - it was the most astonishing thing I had at any point seen. The other 308 GTS driven by Sammy Davis Jr. and Dean Martin was virtually invisible compared to the Lamborghini. In the wake of watching the film, I needed to see the vehicle once more. I slipped into the adjoining hall and sat tight for 15 minutes until the following one started, and snuck back in. I rehashed this multiple times, and got back with a companion the following day to watch it two additional times. At the point when we at last leased the film on VHS, I most likely watched it twelve more times.

I was a crazed car enthusiast. I liked cars and loved driving. My first car was a canary yellow '79 Camaro (hand-me-down from my sister) that I totaled while racing a friend on an empty, rural Texas highway at 2 am. My second car was a charcoal grey '83 Firebird. I drove this to college for a couple years before trading in for a new, red VW 16-valve GLI Jetta that I totally abused. Within the life of this car, I had been pulled over by police over twenty times, and I developed a first-name relationship with my traffic ticket attorney. While I had always tried to achieve high average speeds during my commutes to college, spring breaks, etc.; I eventually got a job taking photos at gymnastics schools around the country. It was during this time that I checked off 30k miles of interstate and developed a "sense" for highway driving where I could avoid tickets while going fast.

When I turned 25, I exchanged the GLI for a new, green '93 Jeep Grand Cherokee, followed decade after the fact with another in 2003 that I kept until 2010 when I purchased a diesel Jetta station cart. I was appreciating being ticket and mishap free, and having affordable vehicles that upheld my mountain-trekking hobby.

In 2005, my family moved to Beijing China where we resided for a very long time. I purchased a Tian Qi Mei Ya TM6500 or Tian Qi Bing which means "vehicle of the sky...great champion" - a Chinese Mitsubishi 4 chamber manual shitbucket of a SUV. Driving in China can be drawn nearer with two outlooks - 1: "OMG...look out...these individuals are insane," or 2: "Damnation ya!...this is the means by which I've without exception needed to drive."

I was #2 and had some good times driving on controls, administration paths, and approaching vehicles. The mark foolishness is at left turn paths where individuals lock guards and never let approaching vehicles through. In the event that I were attempting to go through the crossing point, I would go max throttle at this vehicles as a risky game and would inspire them to open up a space until the end of the traffic to move through. It didn't hurt that I had introduced enormous steel bull bars on the facade of the vehicle my family named "the soldier."

I drove the diesel Jetta to San Francisco and kept up with my most elevated record to Dallas from Atlanta - 83 mph incorporating stops with a moving normal of 86, totally stunning my mom when I showed up 4 hours sooner than anticipated. While the vehicle was an incredible vehicle, the diesel Jetta started to press a few wrong fastens - it was excessively little, excessively pragmatic, and too...um...dorky - like a couple of orthotic shoes. Twenty plus years of suppressing my love of cars combined with a 100x increase in value of my company's stock options became the fuel and air that would soon ignite an intense emotional fire for something more "me."

Christmas 2010, I was strolling through Phipps Plaza shopping center in Atlanta with my family when I happened upon a Black Maserati GranTurismo in plain view. It left me cold speechless. My family proceeded to go out on the town to shop while I strolled around the vehicle entranced. It was funny...from my childhood to youthful adulthood, I battled with being materialistic and desirous of others' things - the consequence of being the most youthful of three kin. But once I hit my 40s, I learned to live rather practically...just give me a decent PC, a decent bike, and a modest rooftop over my head and I was content. This was unique - it was whenever that an actual article first had me. For the following nine months, I designed this vehicle online more than ten times, had screensavers of it, and continued to look online at it.

Then, at some point, I saw that our neighborhood seller had a pre-owned one in a variety combo that I preferred. I went to the showroom, test-drove it, and found myself

amidst an existential emergency about the importance of life. I couldn't resist - I went to the bank, got a clerk's check, returned and got it. I figured I ought to win an honor for the most wonderful emotional meltdown ever.

As somebody who has been a voyaging advisor for a whole profession, I had no neighborhood Atlanta companions. My whole informal organization was in San Francisco, South East Asia, and Europe, and my companions were not generally "vehicle folks." I ended up searching for bunch vehicle occasions and coincidentally found Caffeine and Octane. I awkwardly attended my first one, then a second one. During one of them, I saw a Lambo, and several Aston Martins pull in. It was Ed, his better half Megan, and some others. They appeared to be a scary bundle - youthful, appealing, and driving vehicles that cost two times as much as mine, however the C&O show was an agreeable spot where I could visit with other vehicle individuals and not feel like the main blockhead who leaves behind a decent part of his abundance on a vehicle. The following C&O, I associated with a person from Maseratilife (an internet based Maserati Forum) - Scott Shetler who brought his Verde Ithaca Gallardo. While chatting with him, Ed drew closer and we were presented. The scary air was gone.

Ed welcomed me to go on a mountain drive and a couple of months after the fact welcomed me to a supercar proprietors' supper. These were an impact and throughout this time, I got to realize Ed better. Perhaps the earliest time I met with him at the showroom, he said "you know...a GT vehicle like a Maserati is a 'entryway vehicle.' You'll either go with more extravagance like a Bentley, or more execution like a Lambo."

"I see what you're doing there...you're attempting to sow a seed in my mind," I said. "But I'm cool with this car...if I sell, it will be to the furthest limit of my introduction to vehicles through and through." But after some time, I valued that Ed had a profound comprehension of the connection between an individual's brain research and the characteristics of a vehicle - it's image/plan language, sound, and other instinctive characteristics. Ed impressed be the main vehicle seller I've at any point met who could support a discussion at this level.

A couple of months after the fact, I was taking a gander at utilized Maseratis on the web and saw that my vehicle was devastatingly deteriorating. A companion of mine recommended that I get a Lambo, and even had a line on one that would be a good worth. It was whenever I first genuinely pondered claiming one - it would be another renowned Italian marque...a checkbox. I didn't cherish the possibility of such an unreasonable vehicle, yet for of remaining in the vehicle side interest somewhat longer, it checked out. I began getting into genuine conversations with Ed about a purchasing a Lambo - searching for one that would cost about equivalent to my Maserati.

That implied a Gallardo five years more established with double the miles. I actually didn't figure I would really purchase one...yes, it would be cool, yet no, I shouldn't. Eventually, I thought I had a "off button" to keep me from really getting one - my absurdly steep driveway.

I let Ed know this, who immediately answered, "We should attempt it." So we did, and at the right point, we had the option to climb the carport without scratching the front. To see a Lamborghini in my carport made it happen - I planned to get one. The following couple of days were depleting, I was unable to rest. I at long last chosen to go to the showroom and purchase the vehicle we had test driven - it was near the cost of the Maserati and would check out financially.

When I showed up at the showroom, Ed did the "let me show you something different" stunt (which I currently appreciate). He took me to their back parcel, showed me an alternate one - a dark 2011 Superleggera that was still under guarantee. It was a press vehicle that had been marginally manhandled, however the value was to such an extent that I could possess it without losing cash - it just required an essentially higher payment.

Sure, why for heaven's sake not? Inside the initial not many long stretches of possession, I was taking a gander at some photographs I had taken of this dark monster. It hit me - the wing, the dark, the large air admissions - it was what could be compared to the dark Countach in Cannonball Run. Understanding this touched off the thirteen year old in me. It's presumably why I appreciated showing it, and giving rides to adolescent vehicle aficionados - I was remembering my young years through their enthusiasm.

My organization laid off my group the following month. Jobless, I ended up endeavoring another startup. My everyday custom to clear my head, was to go to QuickTrip for a pop. The QuickTrip is across the road from the Lamborghini showroom. As often as possible, I'd stop in to take a gander at the fresh debuts by cruising all over the parking garage, and regularly, I'd head inside and express greetings to Ed and everybody. Without a task, they endured the worst part of my need to get an everyday fix of human interaction.

Ed lIkewise coordinated an excursion to Palm Beach, Florida for the Lamborghini Esperienza track preparing occasion. I drove my SUV while Ed and others tracked with in Lambos and different supercars. I would have driven mine, however I was excessively tall and got continuous back torments while driving brief distances. I found the middle value of somewhere in the range of 85 and 95 mph, and would travel ahead a couple of miles, spot for police, then get back to the gathering to continue. In the span of a moment, they'd blow past me, dialing back, allowing me to pass to rehash it. On one especially void stretch of the expressway traveled south I opened up a couple of miles of room and Ed began shutting the hole rapidly in his orange Murcielago LP640 Roadster. He blew past me so quick I didn't know his tires were still on the ground. I approached the two way radio to perceive how quick he had gotten and he shared with me "194." I made him rehash that a couple times.

The Lamborghini preparing occasion was loads of tomfoolery and provided me with a ton of certainty at higher paces, in any event, when the brakes were blurring the tires were delicate to such an extent that they felt like sponges.

April 27th, I got the DVD "32 Hours 7 Minutes" - a narrative about the cross-country races and speed records. It lighted something in me - the craving to escape with an amazing street trip...check, the longing to speed...check, the craving to look down on regulations plainly intended for the most reduced normal denominator...check, and utilizing innovation and development to get it done? CHECK! i.e., it resounded firmly with me. But seeing Alex Roy break the record, all his expense and preparation made me shy away from the idea of wanting to do the NY to LA Cannonball. This was plainly not something that could be nonchalantly drawn closer. All things being equal, I began plotting out a more drawn out course from Seattle to Key West - the corner-to-corner run - significantly longer than the Cannonball, and something that could be laid out as a new record.

During one of my visits to the showroom, I imparted this rally thought to Ed. He referenced that it's an awful thought in this legitimate environment to advance a race. Untimed rallies are alright, however when a clock reached out, the coordinator could end up horrendous broke or in prison. I was frustrated, yet it likewise made sense of why Cannonball races don't occur any longer. Given the lively drives I had joined Ed on in the earlier months, That's what I trusted assuming there were a method for getting sorted out an enormous scope Cannonball race today, he would have figured it out.

At this point, he motioned that we ought to stroll into the other display area away from different workers. He put on his genuine face and turned down the volume. Having encountered this previously, I realized this would have been great. "Might you at any point leave well enough alone?" He inquired. Amazing, it will be genuine good.

"Absolutely," I answered. "Working for Apple for a long time requires

it." "Alright, you can't perceive anybody everything that I'm going to

say you."

"Alright," I replied...this *is* genuine. I was beginning to believe that he planned to educate me some succulent tattle concerning somebody I knew, or offer a business recommendation, or let me know he planned to begin his own showroom - something big.

"I will break the Cannonball Run record," he said gravely. I almost stifled with giggling on the water I was drinking.

"Bologna," I replied.

"Nope...I'm Serious...I have a vehicle at CarTunes getting furnished with everything...I'm going to do this in the following couple months."

"Alright," I thought...I began to accept him and it began soaking in. Then, moved by the phantom of the young form of myself, I quickly answered "DO YOU HAVE A CO-DRIVER?!!!!!" It was a shot time second where I envisioned that the whole "secretive mystery" was a preface to him requesting that I be his co-driver.

I was imagining the following second where he would agree "that is the very thing I'm conversing with you about", however rather it was "No doubt, I have this person in Ohio..."

I was unable to hear anything more after that point. I was so bummed...all these boo inciting showy behaviors prompting an all out setback. Notwithstanding my failure, I answered "Hello, I absolutely need to be a piece of this somehow...let me know whether I can help." Ed made sense of that he could require some assistance escaping New York. "I'd thoroughly assist you with that...just let me know and I'll fly up, lease a vehicle and destroy it on the interstate" - this presumably came from watching Smokey and the Bandit many times.

I returned home and swore Lisa to mystery prior to telling her the news. She had known me when we were young people so she got the meaning of this to me. Dissimilar to my experience only several hours earlier, when she felt that the following component of the story may be me telling her that I was co-driving with Ed, she was feeling quite a bit better instead of crushed as I was.

Months passed. I saw the prepared vehicle at the showroom one day and once more, I was battling with my desire over being important for the endeavor. Be that as it may, I

recently continued quiet...waiting for the call to fly up to NY to help. The main issue was that I had been jobless such an extremely long time, and flights, tickets, and expanded insurance installments were beginning to seem to be genuine cash. I wasn't entirely certain I would be in a situation to help.

CHAPTER 11

Assembling The Bomb

There are very few positions where the compatibility of this record wouldn't represent a difficult issue and undermine the eventual fate of your work. In the event that I were a grade teacher like my significant other, a government official, or a cop; this sporting action would be disliked. Luckily in the vehicle business, it works. My chief and the proprietor of our showroom were uncertain of regardless of whether or not they would in any case have the option to have me on our insurance contract a while later yet they didn't even try to impart that worry to me. They thought it was extraordinary thought and Brandon, our senior supervisor, really consented to have the store contribute $5,000 to the undertaking. It was a unimaginable assistance at a second when I didn't know where the last money mixtures planned to come from.

I was pot dedicated now. I was past the reason behind counting receipts and keeping an awareness of what this work was setting me back. On the off chance that I wanted it and had the cash it was coming. Notwithstanding the monetary help, the showroom had allowed me to suggestion our twenty-year tenured ace Lambo tech into concocting a fuel framework for the vehicle as a side job.

Charles gave me a shopping list for the JEGS inventory and I requested two extra 22 gallon energy components with siphons and tubing. Charles formulated an exchange siphon procedure to take the fuel through the manufacturing plant gas cap into the current filler neck. The more modest cell in Alex's vehicle was gravity taken care of in light of the fact that BMW puts their gas tanks under the floor of the storage compartment on a 5 Series. Mercedes puts the tank upstanding, between the back seats and the storage compartment. I enjoyed this since it implied that the production line heat protecting was among me and the additional 44 gallons of fuel.

Charles' technique kept the check motor light on for an evaporative framework spill yet it was rich in its effortlessness. He talked for a long time to Michael Luongo who was the Ferrari specialist that Rawlings and Collins had used to introduce their energy unit in the 550. It worked in basically the same manner to our own however was more modest in limit. I would say specialists love looking at working on vehicles more than really dealing with

vehicles. This was the kind of undertaking that you
got a few miles out of talking about.

From Charles Carden, Master Lamborghini Technician

There is just a single Lamborghini expert still at a seller in the US that has a more drawn out residency with the brand than I do. In the twenty years that I have been with Lamborghini Atlanta, the main individual who has shown up with as solid a fondness for the brand as I have is Ed Bolian.

Ed was recruited as a deals fellow a couple of years prior yet we realized Ed well through adjusting the vehicles for his rental organization. We looked as his initial Gallardo hit a deer toward the start of groove one year, turned an interfacing pole bearing and sent cylinders through the two sides of the square because of oil starvation, and required a couple of paint fixes going from a wheel scrape to crashing into a Ferrari.

When Ed came on, he truly caused a ruckus. Our new vehicle deals detonated and our clients turned into much more dynamic. That helps me since we began to see significantly more clients really overhauling their vehicles. At the point when life disrupts everything, dismissing the consideration of your supercar rushes to occur. Ed seemed like the sort of fellow that could offer ice to an eskimo and afterward some way or another get that eskimo to return a half year and exchange for some more pleasant ice. He was pushing vehicles out quicker than we had since the prime of the intriguing vehicle industry in 2007. Ed additionally constructed truly a brand for himself. Individuals came from everywhere the nation and web to purchase vehicles from him.

He was never timid about gathering miles on the vehicles. He is the main deals fellow I have at any point seen care anything about possessing the vehicles himself. Even after he was finished with the rental business, Ed would always wander back to my corner of the shop and ask for my advice on cars to buy, issues to look out for, and my thoughts on the significance of each model. We both developed worried about the fates of a portion of the innovations that were being added to our most loved supercars. Those discussions would likewise sporadically float something different engaging - Cannonball.

I am mature enough to be Ed's dad so I recall the stories of fugitives dashing the nation over, no limits, ocean to sparkling ocean. I remain nearby the hustling local area and carry on with two or three miles from Road Atlanta, a circuit utilized yearly however many top dashing associations. My child, Casey, is the head

teacher at Skip Barber Racing School. They are the inhabitant that supplanted the Audi/Panoz Racing School Ed let me know he had worked at quite a while back. My ends of the week are generally spent re-building Vespas or race vehicles with my son.

Watching him grown up from Karts to high even out dashing seats has been perhaps my proudest accomplishment. Right off the bat in 2013 Ed moved toward me to begin gaining ground towards his own cutthroat driving goal.

Ed informed me regarding his arrangements to break the Cannonball Run record around 2010. It was plainly something that he had been chipping away at and pondering for quite a long time. Having watched many dashing endeavors require a long time to create, this was not new yet the setting was certainly curious. I had seen Richard Rawlings on Fast and Loud gloating about his lower arm tattoo and discussing his 31:59 time yet I asked Ed the number of individuals were really attempting to do this. He informed me concerning Alex Roy and a portion of the other history that existed in the hole starting around 1979. It was entrancing stuff, especially when it came to furnishing the car.

In 2012 Ed showed me the blue-ish CL55 after he had gotten it and he ran down the rundown of contraptions that he had fit to be introduced. Obviously he had placed a ton of thought into this thought yet there was something else about Ed. Ordinarily the person oozes certainty like 9 bar blended coffee however I could detect the anxiety in his voice. The stakes were different than his normal half a million dollar car transactions. This made a difference. He requested my assistance in gear up the helper fuel framework. We discussed the reach that he was searching for and how the bundling expected to work.

Ed let me know that he never minded if the vehicle would be returned to stock however I really wanted to imagine that even our godlike sales rep may be in a tight spot with this one. it appeared to be a disgrace to assemble something onto this Mercedes that couldn't ultimately be taken out. That was likewise logical superfluous in light of the fact that there was obviously not going to be any simple to way to gravity feed the cell into the principle tank because of the height of the manufacturing plant tank inside the vehicle. Assuming there was truly anything Ed needed, it was surely not certainty but rather the parent in me tries constantly to be the capable advisor.

One Saturday I took the Mercedes up to our shop, opened an instance of lager and just gazed at the open trunk, lining eliminated. I read about the folks who had designed an arrangement of 55 gallon drums inside the structure of a plane and utilized careful tubing to take care of the fuel into the wing tanks as they flew as far as possible all over the planet. I called Mike Luongo who I knew from Lambo preparing in years past. He had moved over to Ferrari and afterward began an autonomous shop. My idea had been some low strain move siphons emerging from every cell and T-ing into a line going through the gas cap. He affirmed that their methodology was comparable. I gave Ed a shopping list and a JEGS catalog.

I designed a section to connect across the extra tire well under the industrial facility trunk floor that would uphold the heaviness of the tank. I mounted the cells, plumbed in the lines, got capacity to the siphons, manipulated up certain measures for the tanks and mounted them on the scramble, and made a 180 degree turn that would keep the industrial facility gas cap cover set up. It was removable during the refueling system so Ed could utilize two siphons simultaneously to fill the three tanks. Ed purchased an extra manufacturing plant gas cap and I cut into the old one.

The folks from CarTunes, our nearby sound system and post-retail gadgets masters, had wired a switch for the exchange siphons into a custom board where the vehicle's ashtray used to be. It had controls for a portion of the radar and laser frameworks, an off button to the transfers sequenced into all of the wiring for the back lights, and a traffic signal transformer that one of Ed's Georgia Tech companions had manipulated up for them. The checks were not exceptionally exact yet seat testing uncovered that it was moving about a gallon at regular intervals. Whenever Ed and I tried the exchange, the idleness of both the helper checks and the stock measure was huge so I advised him to move multiple times for fifteen minutes to deplete the tanks. Each move meeting ought to have moved around ten gallons of the 44 that he would have. It was a straightforward enough system.

At least I suspected as much until I got a call from Ed while heading to New York letting me know that they had quite recently showered gas all around a silver Impala that was following them on the highway...

CHAPTER 12

The Nine Thousand Dollar Tune Up

It took CarTunes around three weeks to introduce everything in the CL. The form had more gadgets drawing more power from additional areas than they had at any point placed in a vehicle. It accompanied a limited work rate and a serious disclaimer that if this skunkworks project went sideways it was as yet my inoperable hill buggy and they were repaid. I was not by and large consoled by that admonition however I realized Monty was their best installer and he was on the job.

The successful vehicle turns into the prize so I invested a great deal of energy contemplating what I believed it should resemble on the opposite finish of this entire experience, keeping up with at minimum some similarity to good faith. On one hand you need to have a clean introduce without wires running all over and each of the gadgets got into a pleasant, perfect spot. On the other you need something that can depict the coarseness of the street and the bootstrapping soul of a very long term purposeful venture. The vehicle was the vessel to get done with the responsibility yet additionally recounted the story. I trusted it would be a period container of a genuine high point in my life.

If everything worked out positively, a long time from that point when my grandchildren were understanding this, the carport where I kept the vehicle would be the following stop. It should have been something to see. The dated route hardware, the recieving wires, the gas tanks, it was generally going to give them a brief look into what those two or three days in October felt like.

Sales at the showroom were not easing up. I sold half a larger number of vehicles in 2013 than I had in 2012. It kept me so bustling I addressed if I have opportunity and energy to do this. Taylor Clark, the Supercar Rentals bookkeeper and voice of excursion reason, found another line of work and couldn't get some much needed rest to act as the help traveler and rude awakening in the vehicle. Gumball Chris was out with work and sweetheart issues, Adam's developing child actually kept him out. Forrest had been called up to the A group upon small scale Adam's origination however he was working crazy hours at an examination lab and he didn't know whether he would have the option to get some much needed rest. Without him, the Bacon Blocker was a no-
go. Any usefulness he could accomplish wouldn't be usable by any other individual who was new to the internal activities. I continued to push forward yet the result was considerably a greater amount of an unknown.

Money was still close in spite of my achievements in selling vehicles. I really wanted a couple of additional gadgets and countermeasures. I was searching for something to sell. I tracked down the thing - my $50,000

Lamborghini motor square espresso table.

In January of 2007 I was dining with an individual understudy from Tech.

I recall the seat I was sitting in at one of my number one Mongolian eateries. We were talking about if these new cell phones planned to get on. I got a call from a companion in south Florida saying, "I saw your Gallardo on a flatbed heading down I-95. It seemed as though it was not doing so well." As the Atlanta rental market had calmed for the colder time of year, I leased the vehicle to a person in Palm Beach that was advancing an intriguing vehicle show. I attempted to call the rental client. He didn't answer.

My heart sank. The following morning I started calling around to the extraordinary vehicle shops in South Florida that were possible objections for a wrecked Lamborghini. I tracked down the vehicle at Lamborghini Miami. The determination was "horrendous motor harm." The vehicle had tossed one and a half associating bars, the vast majority of a cylinder, and a pole confirming the two sides of the motor block. Their primer parts gauge was $56,000.

This was an impossible catastrophe for a youthful understudy business person. The business had been doing great yet this would have been a tremendous opening to climb right out of. The client was somebody whom I had known for a really long time and who knew not to abuse a vehicle like that. He had been paying me by the mile for his utilization of the vehicle yet in this latest charging window had driven the vehicle almost 3,000 miles including some extremely harmful low speed moves. This had run almost out of oil and the supported high RPMs had popped the motor.

I wound up observing a motor in Europe that had been removed from one more early Gallardo which had been engaged with a front end crash. It was $15,000 and I had it sent to the seller in Miami for introduce. Another grasp, seals, and work was another $15k or thereabouts. A month or so later I got the vehicle home and started the claim against the client. It yielded nothing past proceeded with cerebral pain, sorrow, and the legitimate bills.

I wound up with an exceptionally cool looking blown Gallardo motor. I purchased a substantial cart from the nearby tool store and a major piece of reinforced glass to put on top of it. It turned into the focal point in the client holding up region where I put away the vehicles. It likewise filled in as a decent advance notice to clients not to manhandle the cars.

I had really sold the motor two or three years before that highlight an organization designing super frameworks for Gallardos. They had stripped it

down, involved the heads for a venture and they were left with an exceptionally spotless aluminum motor square. That was uniquely of scrap an incentive for them so I inquired as to whether they would transport it back to me. Indeed they did. It was an incredible momento to the rental organization that was currently a couple of years in the rearview reflect yet the Cannonball objective was close and I really wanted the money. I sold the embellishing motor square for
$3,000 and submitted the request for the couple of remaining supplies.

The rundown of things introduced in the vehicle wound up being:

- Valentine 1 Radar/Laser Detector x 2

- Passport/Escort Radar/Laser Detector and Diffuser

- Laser Interceptor Laser Diffuser/Jammer

- 2 x Garmin GPS Units with XM Traffic

- 3 x iPhone Cradles with Chargers

- iPad Cradle and Charger

- GeoForce Satellite Tracking Device

- Uniden Police Scanner with GPS and Radio Antenna

- Cobra 29 CB Radio with K40 Antenna

- Toll passes for the appropriate areas

- 2 x 22 Gallon Auxiliary Fuel Cells with Transfer Pumps

- Custom Switch Panel with off button for back lights, fuel siphon control, oversee capacity to all gadgets, Passport and Laser Interceptor Controls

- Power Inverter with Outlets in Center Console

- MiRT - traffic signal changer

- Full Size Spare

- Fire Extinguisher

- Full Size Hydraulic Jack

- 2 sets of optics - 8x and 10x

- 3 computerized timers

- Cooler

The fuel framework was done. Overhauling the vehicle was the last advance leftover to be prepared to press the GO button. The outing planned to force more weight on the vehicle than I could expect. I additionally realize that Alex Roy's most encouraging endeavor went off track by a stopped up fuel channel and siphon gathering in Oklahoma. His M5 was six years of age at the hour of his run. My CL55 was nine years of age with almost double the miles. I needed to ensure the vehicle got a comprehensive tech investigation and a needlessly physician's approval before departure.

One of the explanations behind picking the Mercedes was the overflow of free help choices. I expected I would observe a shop that thought the thought was intriguing and they would twist around in reverse to get the business. I wasn't right. Many were frightened. I was unclear about the motivation behind the vehicle. It was essentially only a solicitation to supplant each liquid, channel, consumable thing, and to address the suspension issues. The best assistance proposition and statement really came from one of our nearby approved sellers - RBM North in Alpharetta, GA.

We had quite recently employed perhaps their best deal folks to come and work with us at Motorcars of Georgia. It is entirely expected for recently added team members at the showroom to do something excessive to praise their new position. The messed up record banality is purchasing a cruiser. The primary week that Nick was at our store he took conveyance of another Victory Motorcycle. In Georgia, you need to take a class to get a cruiser permit. You should give your own bike to step through the examination to get your permit. You must have a bike permit to purchase cruiser protection. You don't need to show verification of protection to purchase and take conveyance of a bicycle. You might be seeing a sequencing issue here. He was anticipating making the mindful moves to possession like purchasing a cap, taking the class, and getting protection inside the approaching months.

One of our different representatives planned to move the recently conveyed bicycle into our shop for safety's sake. Scratch, the new person, requested to sit on his bicycle briefly. He then grew bold and decided he would try to see if he could make it move. He did and figured out how to hang on for around thirty feet straight into the rear of a Porsche Panamera. He broke the back hatch glass with his un-helmeted face.

I was on the telephone attempting to purchase a Bugatti for a client when I heard the accident. I went outside to find blood spilling out of Nick's face. It was a scene that would make a hatchet killer squeamish. The remainder of our group at Motorcars of Georgia appeared to be genuinely puzzled by the entire thing so I assumed responsibility for getting our new man some appropriate clinical consideration. They were scrambling to get the bicycle, discover the degree of the harm to both Porsche and Nick, and for the most part going ballistic. I left, got Nick by his shoulders, grinned, and said "We are in for a long night!"

I stacked Nick into Megan's Cayenne, which was at the showroom for reasons unknown. Luckily, it had a few huge moving Blankets inside that I used to cover the calfskin seats from the unspeakable measure of blood all over him. I took him to the trauma center and watched the A, B, and C groups take an interest in sewing his face up. It was something like eighty facial lines. At a certain point, the specialist pulled back a free fold of skin and an insect left Nick's face. I recounted to him that anything stories we got from today, they could never measure up to everything that subterranean insect got to say to the following grasshopper he ran into. "I was staying out of other people's affairs, hanging out on this bulbous Porsche station cart thing when all of a sudden..."

He had not been working at the showroom adequately long to have medical coverage so before we left the ER I did some haggling with the monetary instructor. We got his $8k greenback down to $800 or somewhere in the vicinity. I took him to a drug store to get his solutions filled and got him home. The experience made me seem to be an extraordinary companion and procured me a few blessings. I traded a couple out on assist arranging this help with his previous business. Peculiar method for procuring a limited work rate however I really do partake in the story.

I dropped the vehicle off at RBM North Mercedes-Benz in Alpharetta. My directions were genuinely straightforward. The assistance consultant Nick had alluded me to knew about the thing I was doing however the specialists were not at first. Fix or supplant all that needs it or could require it and afterward look the vehicle over so I can

drive it without stressing. The last option was the issue. The 115k mile CL55 was not without needs in the help department.

They replaced the tires, brakes, fluids, and filters like I asked but it also required spark plugs and wires, two shocks, some other suspension components, motor mounts, a new battery, something called a flex disk, we agreed to do all bulbs, etc. for a retail total of over $17k and a discounted price to me of $8,800. The technicians and the shop foreman were very intrigued by the project but they looked at me like I was crazy when I proposed it. The car was barely worth the price of the service bill and it was obviously not the type of request they expected to encounter in their careers of servicing daily use cars for businessmen and their overly entitled wives.

Even however I had been expecting something nearer to a large portion of that, it was a reasonable arrangement. That being said, I was still short from having the option to pay for it. A couple of months earlier I had run over a youthful person whose father claimed an espresso developing activity in South America. He was utilizing his innovative chops to extend the business into a packaged, prepared to serve, chilled espresso drink. The organization is called Blue Donkey Iced Coffee. He felt like the vehicle fellow market was extraordinary for his item and he inquired as to whether I may be keen on some promoting help for one of my occasions. He showed up on a mountain drive and we discussed a couple of different thoughts. Whenever I referenced that I was attempting to break this record he thought it was terrific.
Driving for quite a while with caffeine needs equalled his item to him. It came pre-blended in with milk yet I won't contend. He came through with the last $2,500 that I expected to complete the process of covering off my AMEX bill after the Mercedes service.

There were a ton of different alterations I had investigated doing to the vehicle preceding the drive. The objective was clearly to make the vehicle quicker yet additionally to further develop the efficiency. A famous bundle of adjustments for that kind of supercharged AMG motor was a blend of a more modest pulley for the supercharger, headers, exhaust, higher streaming air channels, and an ECU tune.

The Initial not many of those would have been useful to me yet the ECU tunes that were accessible were not intended for this sort of drive. They were delineated to change the air fuel proportions to cause the vehicle to speed up quicker from zero to sixty and further develop the quarter mile time. I talked with the three significant Mercedes Benz alteration houses - RennTech, Kleeman, and Carlsson. I
updated them on my goals and all concurred that it was hypothetically conceivable yet they were don't know when they would have the option to convey it. Whenever I had felt I expected to draw nearer to 15 mpg this was essential. In light of how much fuel I was wanting to convey by then, this appeared to be superfluous. It was added to the heap of thoughts to be utilized assuming we wound up making our first altercation 32-35 hours and required ways of enhancing the time significantly.

I additionally chose to save the vehicle as stock as workable with the end goal of dependability. While it is well known to alter and customize a vehicle to suit the requirements or needs of every client, the mechanical parts of the vehicle were best passed on to the first specialists at Mercedes as I would see it. It was easy to make a car go faster for a short time but building an engine that was still capable of doing this drive seemed best left up to Marco Weissgerber when he signed the hand assembled AMG engine in the first place.

Throughout that mid year the sheer monstrosity of the undertaking had begun to set in. It was at long last working out and this was really the most hazardous thing that I had at any point done. That was a new and extremely odd acknowledgment. I could see that my mind was advising my unpreventable longing to do this that it was actually a quite poorly conceived notion. It seemed similar to smoking with a name that says it will kill you, or purchasing a pet tiger, or dating a lady who undermined another person with you. You realize the chances say what is going on won't end well yet you perceive how cool, fun, and provocative it tends to be as sane estimation simply flies through the window at 150 mph.

I purchased a $2 million extra security strategy. It appeared to be really smart given the improvements in arranging and the advent of the main endeavor. It likewise might be the main thing I could possibly do that did right by my father by marriage. We had no undesirable measure of obligation at that point yet it actually felt like a decent bet.

From David "Klink" Kalinkiewicz, Former Master Technician At Mercedes Benz Of Alpharetta

I truly didn't have the foggiest idea what to think about this person.

I first met Ed Bolian in late 2012. I was then serving as a general "go to guy" in the service department at a Mercedes Benz dealer in metro Atlanta. I was told that he had recently purchased a 2004 Mercedes-Benz CL55 AMG and that he had a question or two about it.

I was predisposed to dislike him. I was told that he was "some kind of sales guy at the Lamborghini dealer." Yes, I realize that my mental imagery was out of date, possibly by decades, but perhaps you'll forgive me if I admit that I was expecting to see verdant waves of chest hair circled by loops of gold chain, and a huge ring on one hand counterbalanced on the other by an oversized watch so encrusted in diamonds that the hands could not be viewed without polarized sunglasses. I was kind of hoping that his inevitably white shoes would be marred by our usually, and in that moment unfortunately, immaculate shop floor.

The Ed Bolian that I was introduced to was not that guy. The guy I met had probably never even seen a prostitute, much less aspirated the cocaine off the thigh of a very expensive one with a Giorgio Moroder soundtrack pounding in the background. Maybe this was only the gofer that the "Lambo person" sent to drop off an MB trade-in, that for some reason they weren't simply auctioning off? This fellow was remarkably unremarkable; Mr. Rogers, noT Mr. T. He could have been a Sunday school teacher.

He certainly did not seem like the kind of guy that could be making a living by fogging dodgy six-figure lease arrangements and balloon notes past gullible finance company agents before an inevitable appearance in the collateral confrontation scene on an episode of "Airplane Repo."

The man I met was calm, polite, thoughtful and articulate, with knowledge of automobiles that went to a much greater depth than my unfair biases had predicted, or that his obvious youth made likely. I was starting to like this guy, but then again, my pre-meeting prejudices had set such a low bar.

At least he had good taste in cars. The one he had chosen to spend his own money on was everything that high-line cars attempt to be but often aren't: responsive, fast, stable, comfortable, durable, even reliable if maintained, and with a restrained industrial design aesthetic that emphasized form over contrivance. Like many of the big Mercedes-Benz coupes from the '60s to the present, this car has a look that is now lost on a generation raised on Ritalin, particularly so in its rainy day blue/gray hue - Granite Gray.

Ed told me that he had experience with Mercedes-Benz cars, and the rest of our conversation bore this out. He expressed his desire to keep this car for some period of time.

I had no idea what mission this car was being prepared for. I also never would have guessed that this much younger gentleman would become a personal hero of mine in just a few months.

In March 2013, Ed brought his MB to our shop for a few repairs and a routine maintenance service. I was happy to see that his "new old car" appeared to be working out for him and that possibly through, or maybe only in spite of our conversations, we had earned a chance at some business his employer was more than capable of providing. We performed an "A" service and generally looked the car over.

Well, we must have done well enough on that visit, because in early October 2013, Ed again brought his CL55 to us, this time for a strangely comprehensive preventive maintenance…

Ed's instructions were to change every fluid, filter, and consumable maintenance item. He asked us to carefully inspect the suspension in particular, and to address anything else that we saw. This was a change of pace in this new age of all show/no dough customers. It is not uncommon to get carte blanche to make a newer S65 perfect again after some unfortunate accident, or to bring great-grandad's 1964 230SL back to road worthiness, but this was a somewhat alien request for a high mile CL55, a car that by this point was usually in the loose and uncaring grip of its insolvent third owner.

And this CL had definitely accumulated some life experience. The bones were alright but it had clearly received a bit of paint work. The mechanicals of the car were pretty sound, but as happens with complicated cars, the "what you really should do if you're serious about keeping and DRIVING this thing" list was growing.

We knew that Ed had negotiated some discounted pricing, but even considering that, this was going to get spendy. When we went over the list, Ed said, "I want to be able to drive this across the country without ANY trouble. Do whatever it takes to make that a certainty."

We all wondered what possible future this newly revived car would have. At this visit, the car was already full of radio gear, tablet computers, GPS screens, jacks, tools, spare wheels, and had 2 huge fuel cells in the trunk. Why the hell someone would muck up a perfectly serviceable CL like this, I had no idea.

Someone muttered, "Maybe we should call Homeland Security" and they were serious. Those of us that knew better could tell that this wasn't the way one would package fuel if he was actually planning on blowing it up. Then someone said, "I heard he's doing some kind of gumball thing…"

Now it finally made some sense to me. This guy was cobbling up some kind of servicing vehicle to chase after and care for his customers, some of whom were obviously about to commit some sort of exhibitionistic misallocation of wealth, youth, and hedonism while they still had some of each to spare.

The following is a compilation of the so called "nine-thousand-dollar tune-up" that at least one media account had mentioned. It should have been the "ten to eleven thousand dollar tune up" but of course the "Lamborghini guy" negotiated a substantial discount. I remember thinking that this was a lot of money to invest in a somewhat impractical douche-hoon ambulance on call for people "doing some kind of gumball thing." If nothing else, he was going a long extra mile trying to take care of and entertain his customers, and it was certainly interesting looking.

Ok, now there was work to do. The work was performed by one of our most respected technicians, the relentless perfectionist, Ralph Mandoeng. Don't look for Ralph there anymore. He has since defected to Tesla.

On this job, Ralph was managed and assisted by his shop foreman, Mr. Bill Peek. Bill is a legend well known to most of us that work on these things for a living and even to many who don't. There is no way to overstate the esteem and respect that this man has engendered in so many of us, and I wanted to take this opportunity to thank him for his outsized positive influence on me and so many others. The success of Ed, Dave, and Dan's excellent adventure owes so very much to Ralph and Bill's dedication and fastidiousness.

The pre "gumball thing" work performed at RBM of Alpharetta included:

- Automatic transmission fluid/filter change. No abnormal wear particles or debris were found in the transmission fluid pan or filter

- Brake fluid change

- Brake pads and rotors

- The inner elastic bushings of the front axle rear lower control arms ("spring links" in MB jargon) were worn and cracking through. They were replaced.

- 4-wheel alignment

- Install 4 Michelin Pilot Super Sport tires - Tires are arguably the most important part of any car. This tire was then, and still is, an overall performance benchmark.

- The left front wheel had a slight bend that was repaired before the new tires were installed.

- A fuel filter replacement was done. It is also a specified maintenance item at every 60,000 miles or 5 years. At 114,106 miles, it was near the end of its service life.

- Coolant flush and pressure test

- Engine air filters

- Cabin air filters

- Replace all light bulbs

- Replace wiper blades

- Replace key batteries

- Oil change - Mobil 1 Formula M 5W-40. This is a version of Mobil 1 that is sold to M-B dealers in the USA. It is labeled to meet only one engine oil specification, that being MB 229.5, which was at the time, and currently still is the highest specification for MB and AMG specified gasoline engine oils. It is essentially the same as the readily available Mobil 1 0W-40 "European Formula" except with 5W base viscosity. While any oil meeting 229.5 is fully up to any possible road use conditions, including the German autobahns, if I had known that these guys were planning an actual full-on Cannonball, I may have suggested the similar MB and Porsche dealer sold Mobil 1 5W-50, or the readily available at parts stores 15W-50 for possible lower oil consumption at speed. Most engines develop an appetite for oil at extended high speeds and loads, and these are no exception. Needing to make oil stops between the fuel stops could knock an average speed down considerably.

- The inoperative windshield washer fluid pump was replaced.

- Replaced the ABC (Active Body Control) high pressure hose/metal line assembly that carries the pressure from the hydraulic pump to the main pressure regulating valve of the system. A gas pressurized diaphragm type pulsation/noise damper was also replaced. This damper protects the system from those same pump pressure pulses.

- Both right side ABC suspension spring struts were replaced due to slight leakage. This was one of the only areas of the preparation where Ed showed any financial restraint. We suggested replacement of all four struts because replacing one of an axle pair on a car that has already developed a strut fault is a little like replacing one shoe. While there can always be more wear and tear on one side relative to the other, it is reasonable to assume that one could expire not long after the other. This small gamble proved to be well played. Other than the high pressure pump developing a nasty noise near the completion of the trip, no ABC related failures occurred.

- ABC hydraulic fluid system was flushed out and filled with new oil.

- The hydraulic ABC oil filter was also replaced.

- The seeping valve cover gaskets were replaced.

- The crankcase vapor separator chambers on the tops of the valve covers were resealed.

- The spark plugs and wires replaced.

- There is a wound/woven fiber reinforced flexible rubber joint disc at each end of the driveshaft. The rear disc was showing some wear and crack formation, so we replaced it. The front disc on these cars usually shows deterioration sooner than the rear disc, yet it was in perfect condition, so it was safe to assume that it was recently replaced.

- The expired original motor mounts were replaced.

- The original battery from the 46th week of 2003 was still fitted. We replaced it.

- The most favorable of the removed tires and Ed supplied an additional wheel that we used to create an non-speed-limited spare.

- And everyone can breathe easier, because, yes, the Georgia state emission inspection required for renewal of the license and registration was passed.

The completed vehicle left our shop, and neither I nor anyone else had another thought about it.

Not that you should care, but here's why I love this. Maybe some of it resonates for you, too. I hope so.

I grew up in a small town where all acceptable recreational activities ended in "-ball." For reasons that I still don't fully understand, and certainly didn't choose, I didn't fit in. I was the geeky kid that took my dad's power tools and my mom's appliances apart. Later I could put them back together, too.

I was fortunate enough to be raised in a time when my rampant ADD wasn't simply medicated away and I became attracted to order as an antidote to the chaos in my head. Not social order, but mechanical order. As a young child I had two obsessions. I loved fans. The big window fans that were ubiquitous before even the poorest among us became wealthy enough to have air conditioning were the best. My grandparents had the best one, their belt driven type being more interesting and making better sounds than the direct drive one we had at home, which was still, quite literally to me, awesome. The love of fans beget the second obsession.

I was around three or four years old when this happened, and I remember this like it was an hour ago. My dad picked me up and held me over the open engine compartment of his 1959 Impala coupe to show me that the car's engine also had a fan. A nice big noisy fan! And with belts! Cars, places, motion, fans, fun!

From that day, I was obsessed with cars. To paraphrase another Cannonballer, "cars became the monocle through which I viewed the world." My mother would bribe me to go to school by offering to buy another quart of oil to add to my collection after I got back home. I was lucky enough to ride in the trifecta of the 260, 289, and 427 Shelby/AC Cobras. God bless America, and save the queen while you're at it. The guy with the 260 powered car actually gave the best rides. He thought nothing of driving it sideways in the rain while somehow never spilling the open bottle of Iron City that he kept wedged between his legs. If my mom had known, she would have beaten the both of us comprehensively senseless.

The car became my vision of a better future, and by extension, even my present got a little better. From the time I could read, I devoured everything automotive related that I could. This was the sixties, and the "muscle car" era was in full flower. I was also fortunate enough to have a service station at the corner entrance to our neighborhood, and this station was the "hangout" for many of the local hot-rodders, street racers, bikers and motorcyclists (yes, there's usually a difference). I got to sit in, ride in, and "help" wash, wax and fix just about every American muscle car, '62, through '69, and even a few of those odd ball fancy "furrin" cars.

And some of those were where it coalesced for me, this combination of order and precision along with visions of freedom and fun, the adult and the juvenile seemingly integrated without conflict. I became fascinated with the deliberateness of German cars, and the most deliberate of all German cars were those from Mercedes-Benz. I admired their fearless embrace of complexity, especially since it was usually tempered with just enough practicality to actually work most of the time. I loved how nearly everything had a purpose and could be explained. I liked that modern materials and manufacturing methods were not eschewed in the superficial service of tradition, yet this company had a pedigree without peer. Still later I got to appreciate that unlike with some other engineering heavy makes, little of that heavy engineering was needed to mollify those characteristics that were the inevitable result of overall bad design. To have this precision, order, practicality and excellence marshalled to serve the ideal of unlimited operation at top speed? Well, at least for me, it just didn't get any better.

What could have seemed better was the spirit of the times. The malaise that gave the era its name was really starting to take hold. Though short in reality, the years that I had left to stay in school felt like a death sentence. The political and intellectual war against private transportation had recently started anew, but in that dismal zeitgeist, it was fashionably fresh and unquestioned. The future of private motoring was going to be bleak, and an armada of technocrats and authoritarians was hell-bent on creating that reality. The same people that couldn't make a single show about animals without attempting to convince everyone watching that they were somehow personally responsible for killing them all were now going after the device of my obsession. This was personal now, dammit!

Too young to protest myself, I absolutely rejoiced and reveled in the exploits of Brock Yates and his Cannonball Baker Sea to Shining Sea Memorial Trophy Dash. A lot of name for such a simple idea: drive across this country as fast as you can "without so much as messing up anyone's hair."

Much is made about the flouting of the law in this questionable exercise, but the people that think that's what it's all about are the same people that think racing fans enjoy watching accidents. How fast is too fast? Any answer is hopelessly arbitrary.

Why do we drive so slowly here in the land of the free where everyone is supposedly so pressed for time that vacations are minimal? My personal opinion is that speed limits (and driving standards) are kept so ridiculously low so that the hapless American motorist can remain an endless source of revenue to be used for anything other than supporting your right to go wherever the hell you want, whenever you want, and often to projects aimed precisely against those rights.

We toil in a world that wants to make sure that everyone and everything lives forever as it also deliberately works to deprive us of any joy that could possibly make that life worth living. We are sanitized, pasteurized, processed, surveyed, droned, and surveilled. We have "trigger words" now, the entire concept implying that a person having heard one has no power over his response to it. Everyone needs a "safe space." Young people are told that they can't possibly have any control over what becomes of their individual lives while simultaneously being taught that they are somehow in control of the weather. And the poor things seem to readily accept both.

Nurse Ratched is here with your pills! Yum yum! Down the hatch. You little darlings all be good, now. No wonder they are so miserable. We have actually allowed our breath to be classified as a "regulatable pollutant." The bumper stickers that used to say "Question authority!" now sheepishly plead for hope and some spare change. People act as if second-hand smoke from a car window four lengths ahead of them is poisoning them to the marrow while thinking nothing of subjecting themselves to an evening of debauchery that would have made Caligula wretch.

The leader of our ostensibly-still-free world somehow thought that it was ok to be seen riding a bicycle in one of those ridiculous foam rubber safety hats! What the hell was he thinking would happen after the world saw that?

I can't believe how much this decade is feeling like the 1970s. Our betters tell us that lackluster is the "new normal" but as I write this we see daily changes in this attitude. It seems that radical chic is chic again. The children of the sixties have even managed to bring back the street riots that they always seemed to feel so sentimental about. I'm feeling sentimental, too. There's a new Cannonball record!

I don't remember the exact date or time I heard about the Cannonball record being shattered by Ed, Dave, and Dan; but it wasn't long afterwards. I can only report accurately my reaction to it. Please excuse my (by now you can tell…) irrational exuberance, but I was just reveling in a tsunami of positive emotion.

I felt younger. I felt vindicated. A cosmic wrong seemed to have been righted. Some larger part of our, or at least my universe was vibrating at a sweeter frequency. This was no mere rich idiot "gumball thing." These guys did a full-on Cannonball! And Hosanna in the Highest, they did the holiest of holies, the Red Ball to Portofino run! I swear I could hear the pealing of bells. The backside of this recently reincarnated cultural revolution of joyless nanny-ism had just been given a rough, unlubricated finger.

The Cannonball record, that most venerated festivity of individual transportation opportunity, a definitive American excursion had been broken and set presumably unrealistically high by individuals I truly like. And best of all for me, they did it in a Mercedes-Benz! For a marque fanatic like me, that's the home team winning the championship. You generally realized they were awesome, and presently, at last, affirmation.

For at minimum that second, everything was solidly in my reality. To have been involved, even in such an honest and digressive way has been an interminable wellspring of pleasure and motivation. A debt of gratitude is in order for tuning in, to my continuing, and gratitude to Ed, Dave, and Dan. On the off chance that it could never have been me, I'm so happy it was them.

CHAPTER 13

The Co-Driver Draft

The issue stayed that I didn't have anybody to go with me. Chris was still out yet he was ready to help scout for us through Ohio. Adam was prepared at the controls on the home front as an eye-overhead outsider observer however up and coming paternity actually kept him out of the vehicle. Forrest moved summoned to explode things in Arizona for the public authority. Taylor remained neck somewhere down in work with the new position. It was September and it was certainly now or one year from now. It might have been currently or never.

It was an ideal opportunity to continue on toward plan G or anything letter I was on by then. I had met a person named Doug Demuro a couple of years earlier. He went to Emory University, extremely near Georgia Tech, and was a not kidding vehicle aficionado. He imparted a cling to me and with the majority of my clients where we spend a totally ridiculous part of our pay on four wheeled pursuits. He had claimed numerous intriguing games vehicles and was never reserved about involving them in fascinating ways.

At the time Doug had an incredibly interesting Mercedes Benz E63 AMG Wagon. He showed up with us on two or three our energetic North Georgia Mountain drives. On one late drive he had said without sales, "I nearly didn't come today. I was attempting to get somebody to come up to New York with me, purchase a BMW 335i at Carmax, drive it to LA, break Alex Roy's record, and afterward return the BMW at a Carmax out there under their multi day test drive policy."

Blank stare.

"Entertaining you ought to specify that. We want to have a discussion this week." Doug had worked for Porsche already yet was presently cutting an effective way as a pseudo-independent car columnist. His mind, encounters, and keenness were cutting out an extraordinary space with a few online publishers.

Ed, meet Ed following a marginally unique way in life.

I called him later in the week and updated him on where I was with the project. He was intrigued. To him the over the top excess preparing procedure had been pointless however the more we talked, the more, "No doubt I suppose you truly do require that," reactions he gave. I let him know that I thought my co-driver planned to go missing and I would like him to go with me. His underlying reaction was exceptionally sure. He said that he expected to clear it with the vitally editorial outlets he worked for in light of the fact that he was concerned they probably won't have the option to show him on their approaches assuming he became known for having done this. Such a setback would hold him back from having the option to take care of his business testing the vehicles and composing play on words filled accounts about them. I most likely ought to have heard that and verified whether I would have a similar issue however I didn't. Truth be told, losing my employment was on the table of satisfactory penances to make this work.

We additionally discussed how it read according to his point of view. It is intriguing that individuals who seek after this as a fantasy are recorded concurrently as their co-driver. Dan Gurney came in without a second to spare to co-drive with Yates. In any remaining endeavors Yates battled to observe individuals he considered satisfactory co-drivers or travelers that were able to partake. Diem and Turner were the most viable group that I read about. Alex Roy and Richard Rawlings are the most candid of their groups and more answerable for the preparation than their partners so they have lolled in a large portion of anything greatness can be acquired from this sort of attempt. For Roy's situation, that is despite the way that his co-driver, Dave Maher, kept up with cruising midpoints that were 10-20 mph quicker than his own. Dennis Collins was the cash behind their drive however got undeniably less attention.

I didn't utilize that comprehension to seek after a specific co-driver yet it was some reassurance as the people who had even more a hand in arranging (and meriting the related recognition) demonstrated inaccessible. There is an inevitable degree of self-centeredness that accompanies attempting to break any world record and it seems this one specifically caters more to an individual instead of a group. My advantage in the pursuit was not essentially consideration chasing however I don't wish to imagine it was anything but a factor.

For Doug, and the equivalent would have been valid for me assuming the jobs had been switched, this was the kind of thing that he needed to do himself. It had not involved his awareness for most of 10 years earlier however it was a section of Automotive Americana that he cherished and needed to connect himself with one day. While I can't envision having the option to say "no" to this

stumble on any level, this would have been the main grounds where I could think about it. I provide Doug with a great deal of credit for having the option to express no to a show up and drive program. Not certain I might have done that.

Doug actually needs to attempt it. I don't figure he would see any problems not breaking the record but rather he observes the set of experiences also convincing to the manner in which I check it out. He accepts that there are still privileged insights out there that will open minutes and perhaps hours from the current times. He needs to do it based on his conditions, utilizing his methodology, and for his own reasons. It would be hard for me by and by to track down a more noteworthy motivation to regard someone.

I began going through my contacts attempting to observe anybody I felt was an adequately capable driver to co-pilot and another person whose presence was average to the point of riding in the rearward sitting arrangement, considerably less be valuable. This was introducing a surprising obstruction to my arrangements I had not expected. Assuming you ask anybody near me, they all knew sooner or later an endeavor planned to occur. I can't envision that the chances cast for my prosperity were ever exceptionally high. It had made for some fascinating supper discussions over the years.
Most individuals had extremely sure view of the thought in principle. I'm certain they figured the execution would ultimately bomb in some fascinating way.

People had generally rushed to say they would be glad to go with me on the outing. They actually are right up 'til today. When confronted with driving 130-150 mph for over a day with no genuine security from prison or episode, they find something different they need to do that end of the week. It could be pawned off on work, family, planning, a crisis yearly physical, or a hard to reschedule hair style yet it is simply dread. This is a mysterious encounter until you are in it and the vast majority of individuals around me were basically adequately shrewd to understand that this is essentially only a terrible idea.

I was grappling with the possibility that individuals in the vehicle with me were likely not going to be the gathering who had arranged and mulled over this thought with me for these years. I understood they most likely wouldn't be completely mindful of every one of the dangers implied. That represented a couple of dangers in itself. They could pull out of the blue and they probably won't respond as I would trust in a most dire outcome imaginable. That implied it was the ideal opportunity for one more call to the credulous protection man. $2 million general responsibility umbrella - check!

Over the years Kevin, Chris, Forrest and I had invested a great deal of energy talking

about tricks, masks, and ploys that may be helpful in the excursion. Getting pulled over in a vehicle furnished like this planned to bring up a couple of issues and it appeared to be mindful to have a few responses. Rawlings didn't have much in such manner yet Alex had invested some genuine energy and arranging into it.

He had equipped the vehicle with a couple of additional things to make the presence of being a tempest chaser. He tracked down that the rundown of required contraptions for barreling into the focal point of a twister is shockingly like what you could pack to go out and attempt to break a crosscountry prohibit record. He had stickers and shirts made alongside extraordinary marks for all of his hardware with weather conditions related names. Alex Roy is the Brick Tamland of fugitive crosscountry road racers.

Obviously the sacred goal of Cannonball stratagems was the phony emergency vehicle utilized by the group of Brock Yates and Hal Needham in 1979. This was not pragmatic in light of the bearing that we were going in vehicle determination. At the point when my planning had warmed up in 2008, I had called up a nearby pig slaughterhouse and obtained two currently frozen pig hearts. I did a few light illustrations configuration work and concocted a sweet TransCon TransPlant TransPort Logo and was going to fab up some administrative work making sense of why this relocate heart must be moved via vehicle. Danger of sore emission appeared appropriate.

We had discussed distractions, blinding LED back confronting lights, and loads of other stuff. One Gumball member used to sidestep police by tossing basic food item packs loaded up with 500 one dollar notes out of the highest point of his Ferrari F50. Individuals would stop their vehicles and attempt to get the cash, blocking the streets for pursuit. Less parkway than surface road common sense however intriguing nonetheless.

I had seen variety changing choices. The picture of the development laborers washing the brief white paint off of the Countach in Cannonball Run II was obviously going through my cerebrum. I thought about a couple of conceivable outcomes. One was to change the shade of half of the vehicle

with a line askew from the front right corner to the back left. That way the
car would appear to be a different color when seen from the front than from
the back.
Another was to involve low glue or static grip vinyl in dark that could be
eliminated headed straight toward uncover the stock paint tone. The Plasti-Dip
sprayable vinyl items were likewise going onto the scene and those were
worth investigating. Eventually I wound up not utilizing any of those
thoughts because of cost and timing however they were loads of amusing to
contemplate.

Around a similar time as my advantage in the Cannonball was aroused,
I educated a reality in a social examinations class that was genuinely
fascinating. I was as a 18 year old sitting in an Advanced Placement
American Government Class. My instructor was floating through the US
Constitution as it related the Article that administered treatment and honors
of legislators and representatives. It said in Article 1 Section 6 that:

"The Senators and Representatives will get a remuneration for their
administrations, to be determined by regulation, and paid out of the depository
of the United States. They will in all cases, with the exception of treachery,
lawful offense and break of the harmony, be advantaged from capture during
their participation at the meeting of their particular Houses, and in going to
and getting back from something very similar; and for any discourse or
discussion in one or the other House, they will not be addressed in some other
place."

Privileged from capture? That sounded astonishing. Knowing how hard
strategic plates and honors were to get, this appeared to be inside the
domain of practicality. On the off chance that I could get chosen for state or
government Congressional seat and view an explanation as in Los Angeles,
hypothetically I wouldn't confront any ramifications for speeding whenever
pulled over. That relied on the cop knowing the US Constitution and on
them not discovering a good method for upping the ante into lawful offense
peril or avoidance. Fun as it very well may be, that thought got scratched.

Years sooner I had a companion with government associations in
Nigeria get me a Nigerian Driver's License with a going with International
Driving Permit. That's what I figured assuming I needed to give up it the
punishments may be less serious and the documentation probably won't
advance back to Georgia. The companions of mine that progressed forward to
graduate school assisted with edifying me concerning what an impractical
notion utilizing it was.

Police pantomime is a well known trick in conversation. Like consideration/execution improving medications I considered guising the vehicle as a cop vehicle to be beyond the soul of the activity. There had not been any phony police vehicles in Cannonball or US Express and it seemed like a bearing that I would have rather not gone in. Alex had dressed the M5 up in different policing for Gumball and different occasions yet he too chose against

utilizing even the strobe lights in his drive.

With a group that was probably not going to hold up a transfer trick and a financial plan previously tapped, the time had come to continue with the original arrangement of just not getting found out. Alex had invested a great deal of energy pouring over the regulations and punishments of speeding in every ward that the course takes you through. I realize that speeding was disliked and I realize that you could wind up going to prison for it. That being said, the truth of getting found going 150 and 110 is for the most part something similar so there was very little else to think about.
Without a recon hurry to go from, my arrangement was to drive as quick I could all over and see where it got me. I had the hardware to make it as protected from the result of capture as I believed I could.

Most individuals who knew enough about the record to comprehend the trouble, myself included, questioned the chance of breaking it on the principal endeavor. I'm certain a considerable lot of them were enthusiastically expecting the potential chance to go next time and to benefit from the illustrations learned in the principal disappointment. I realize it was Tom Park's reason. I positively can't fault him. Prior that year when my timetable had gotten too full I had considered attempting to get another person to do the first recon race to try out the vehicle and let me know how things were functioning. Obviously that couldn't have ever worked.

Forrest and the Bacon Blocker were an all inclusive bundle because of control usefulness. He was near having it prepared however it was not prepared for use in 2013. It became pseudo-functional around a month after we returned from the outing, complete with "Mercedes Benz Active Cruise Control and Accident Avoidance System PROTOTYPE" screen imprinted on the control board. As far as anyone is concerned it is the most developed dynamic radar jammer for police radar frequencies in non military personnel presence today.

Alex Roy had broken the record on Columbus Day which was the conventional date for the US Express in the mid 1980's. That happened to fall on my birthday in 2013 and it was unclear if the car would be ready by then. Additionally, spending my 28th birthday celebration in prison sounded terrible. I would have rather not endeavored it on the last few days of the month due to the expanded watching of parkways as various portions were attempting to be met.

The 19-21st turned into the deadline. The dates are generally a multi day window because of the time change and the way that you would rather not show up in LA whenever other than the center of the night.

I would pass on Manhattan at 10 PM and expect to show up in Redondo Beach by 1 AM neighborhood time for a 30 hour slipped by time. This provided me with a pleasant edge of disappointment that actually established achievement. I expected to arrive before 2:04 AM to break the record. I implored it wouldn't be a near disaster in one or the other bearing. Assuming that I just beat it by two or three minutes I needed to accept that it would cause truly a battle about precision of estimation. I realized I could win such a contention yet I would have liked to keep away from it. Questions and allegations of deceptive nature feel like they demean the pursuit. On the off chance that I was a couple of moments more slow yet adhered to the genuine course I would feel like I had the right to guarantee the record even with a more drawn out time. The vehicle was done in support and CarTunes was doing some last moment dabbling with the CB and Scanner.

I called Alex half a month prior to we left. I knew that to keep away from a portion of the rules of impediment, Alex had held up a year to approach and guarantee the record. I expected to be that in the event that another person had broken the record as of late they would have called him regardless of whether they wouldn't guarantee it freely. He said that he didn't know about any other person attempting to break the record at that point. I let him know I was anticipating attempting it soon and he advised me about running out of ends of the week. It was unexpectedly warm in New York yet that will undoubtedly change at any time.

He raised a fascinating point, somebody had as of late done me the blessing of testing the public reaction to openly overstepping transit regulations. Adam Tang, going by the name AfroDuck, had as of late broken a record that Alex had held quite a while earlier - the lap around Manhattan.

It went poorly. It might have been a long time since 9/11 yet the hunger for showing a capacity to beat an administration framework in New York City without being contained by the current guard conventions was not the bruised eye that NYPD needed. The public clamor had been serious and policing taken a few inconceivably drastic actions to track down him and capture him. This was fairly unique with no genuine positive verifiable point of reference to stick to or any redemptive social worth in that drive. Pot Kettle issues understood.

At least there was no picture of two wonderful young ladies getting out of a Countach wearing spandex dashing suits spraypainting across a sign in Manhattan saying No Right on Red. Then who could oppose disproving the framework? That Cannonball Countach picture was as always emblazoned in my memory as it was for the beneficiary of my next telephone call.

It was Wednesday, October 16, 2013.

I got into work and concluded the time had come. I got back to Laid Dave Black. I helped him to remember our discussion half a month earlier, a region where his memory required priceless little shaking. It was clear he thought I was going to request that he fly to New York, lease a vehicle, and lead us out Manhattan. He was retreating on his unique proposal as his psychological individual bookkeeping math began kicking in. Dave was as yet jobless and dealing with some web advancement projects. It was hard to the point of excusing his month to month Lamborghini installment, considerably less burning through $1,000 on an up and back excursion to help and abet.

"I believe that you should be my co-driver." I told him.

"[expletive] yes. I'm in." He answered as a reflex. a couple of moments later his mind started to process the request.

I advised him to meet me the following evening at my home so we could get together a few things and plan for the outing. We were leaving Friday morning.

As soon as he hung up the telephone I got an instant message. "I ought to likely ask Lisa."

There goes the area. Luckily, Dave didn't know anything about the record other than Burt Reynolds and 32 Hours 7 Minutes. Lisa, his better half, knew even less. Neither had perused Alex's book, they had close to zero insight into Rawlings, and had never known about Brock Yates.

Dave was a decent driver. He could hang with me in the mountains and we had done a few Lamborghini track occasions together. He is incredibly smart yet he over-thinks most things. Having worked for Apple, he was incredibly technically knowledgeable and he processes data rapidly. Notwithstanding hypothetical models and presentations, he was an extraordinary contender to be a co-driver.

I had gone through my free day sooner that week looking for provisions, pressing my toothbrush, and going through the frameworks on the vehicle for usefulness. I went to Bass Pro Shops to purchase two sets of the best [returnable] optics that they had and made a point to keep the receipt.

Their deals fellow asked me, "What might I do for you?"

"I'm searching several arrangements of optics for an

excursion." "Gracious definitely, where are you

headed?" He asked.

I replied. "Sort of out of control. I want to spots bears. Likely from 1,000-1,500 yards. Also, out of a moving vehicle."

"That is quite intense without adjustment. We don't sell those." He was not hopeful. He showed that two of the plans were great. I let him know I would attempt them both out and perceive how they functioned. I checked the lunar stage for the approaching end of the week and it would have been an almost full moon which implied evening perceivability ought to be excellent.

I am 6'5". Dave is 6'2". That really intended that there was no help for anybody sitting behind both of us. On the Thursday before we left I was getting frantic, calling individuals I had not addressed in years and requesting that they ride with me. I was near getting Megan to go however I was as yet rational enough to realize that was an ill-conceived notion. My more youthful sibling was a short flight away yet I Saving-Private-Ryan-ed him out of thought before our folks would have done the same.

I considered Dan Huang. He was little, savvy, and preferred vehicles. However, i didn't have his PDA number. I sent him a message through Facebook. "Do you have any plans this end of the week? Call me." I left him my telephone number.

He called several hours after the fact. The discussion was brief. He consented to go. It was a sufficiently fast reaction that I didn't know he comprehended what we were doing. I wanted to explain the idea of the solicitation yet the sales rep in me knew all around ok to stop while I was ahead.

Dan is several years more youthful than I am, appropriately measured for secondary lounge CL riding, Chinese, incredibly tech skillful, and simple to get along with.
Come to figure out he was additionally truly adept at keeping up quiet superficial presentations when he was pretty gone crazy within. Dan had

bobbed around from one startup to another since leaving Georgia Tech and offered the benefit of checking out at the world in a fundamentally the same as way to Dave and I. Our moved extra tire which presently refreshed behind the driver's seat would be in great company.

The compatibility of this record was an exceptionally innovative activity. It had each component of a new company just without the possible potential for productivity. I get asked this frequently and I realize that Alex has also - How would you bring in cash from holding the record?

You don't. Richard has done well with the reestablishment and continuation of Fast and Loud however that is because of his character and the showcasing of the Discovery Channel. The tattoo on his arm perusing 31:59 has assisted with the history however it isn't the genuine justification behind his success.

I needed to characterize our objective/market, sort out what capital costs were required, oversee costs, take care of issues, oversee adverse results, fabricate a helpful group, and execute. The business arranging of Great White Reptiles, Supercar Rentals, and building the Lamborghini proprietor information base had served me well. Anything equation for progress might exist, I felt like we had it.

I made a last staple run before the excursion. I purchased water, Red Bull, Gatorade, Nutrition Bars, Dried Fruits, Candy Bars, enjoyable nutrients (C, Multi, Zinc, B12), facial cleaning materials, hand sanitizer, paper items, urinal bottles, chamber pots, wire ties, each sort of tape, electric lamps, etc.

Finally I had our driving group. On Thursday night we as a whole met at my home. Dave and Dan appeared. Adam came too. This was whenever that they first had all seen the vehicle in its done state and one another. I would have wanted to completely get what was going through their heads at that point.
They were both obviously apprehensive and the state of mind was one of serious confusion.

I need to accept that they were expecting a genuinely easygoing excursion. It was a sensible allowance in light of the way that I had requested their help. How might somebody be treating this in a serious way and have to ask two individuals totally irrelevant to the task to come on at the last conceivable moment?

Adam had approached see everybody. Adam is every last trace of 6'10". Whenever Dave appeared straightaway, he took a gander at Adam and expected he was our third. The heaping on concern was all the while entertaining and telling. He was obviously anxious. Adam was developing less and less remorseful on the open door that he was forgoing.

Dan pulled up. Dave murmured in alleviation. Adam hadn't seemed to be a Huang. "You should be Dan?" Dave said.

"No doubt, Dave?" Dan asked to confirm.

"Yes. I advertised. This is Adam. He will utilize the GPS beacon to screen progress and beware of climate." Introductions with anticipation are better.

The vehicle changed the discussion from easygoing to extreme. My orange LP640 had never been more neglected since it had left the processing plant in Sant A'gata. Whenever they glimpsed inside the CL and saw all of the gear that had been introduced and came to see the value in the speculation that I had made in the thought, it began to turn out to be more not kidding. The openings in the scramble, fuel tanks in the storage compartment, wires run all over, and latrine offices ready - it was clear I implied business.

CHAPTER 14

You're Leaking Gas

Some of the coordinated operations stayed open finished. The takeoff time represented somewhat of an issue. Dave and Dan were not of a mentality or position to contend with anything I was proposing. I had chosen the best opportunity to leave was somewhere in the range of 9 and 11 PM on a Saturday night. That implied we would overcome the Midwest before individuals began awakening to go to chapel on Sunday. Sunday was definitely going to be the most minimal traffic day so we needed to amplify the Sunday driving.

Leaving Manhattan at 10 PM in the wake of getting some genuine rest the day of flight was extreme. I had wanted to drive from Atlanta to Washington, DC on Friday, remain the evening, go into New York City by early afternoon on Saturday and afterward get a lodging to get around five hours of rest prior to making a beeline for the Red Ball.

That was easier said than done. Look at was at 11 wherever in Manhattan and check in was no sooner than 4. I would need to get the space for the night prior and the following evening, accessibility was low and cost was restrictively high.

Ash Majid was a companion of mine who had as of late moved from Atlanta to Manhattan and his condo turned out to be straightforwardly opposite the it were beginning to stop carport where we. I sent him the initial not many turns as we were arranging the course out of the city and he answered, "I imagine that could really be right across the road from me."

He had consented to see us off on Saturday night and offered us some guidance on where to remain. The Manhattan inns all had stopping accessible yet it was generally underground valet parcels that felt hazardous. It was difficult to eliminate all of the gear from the vehicle and a burglary of any of it, but far-fetched, was not an OK gamble to take. Substitution was conceivable. Arriving again to attempt after re-buy and re-establishment was not. Debris advised us to take a gander at remaining in Jersey City. It would be less expensive, more straightforward, and the stopping accessibility was much better.

Dave, Dan, and I had a conversation where they essentially gestured their heads and vacantly gazed in shock and dread at what they didn't know they had found themselves mixed up with. We concluded the best calculated game plan was to make the whole drive up the main day and to get into Jersey City late Friday night or right off the bat Saturday morning. That way we could rest until early afternoon or so and afterward go accomplish some recon work on the best leave way out of the city. We consented to renounce the stop in DC and make the whole crash up into New Jersey on Friday. The arrangement was to reconvene at my home around 9 AM on Friday morning to go out in the wake of morning heavy traffic faded away in Atlanta.

I didn't rest a lot of Thursday night and I question different folks did by the same token. Lamborghini had planned a seller meeting at Fontana Speedway in California for the approaching end of the week so Brandon, our GM, went rather than me. Everybody asked where I was and they were very eager to hear what the better deal had been. The possibility of Cannonball never neglects to inspire a really compelling passionate reaction from a gathering of vehicle folks. The colossal allure of this objective to individuals I stick around consistently was something incredible. You can't adore vehicles and not love Cannonball. Significant distance colorful vehicle travels rest close to the highest point of most petrolhead lists of must-dos. The most elevated evaluated Top Gear episodes were generally their amazing street trips.

The staff of Top Gear Magazine really made a Cannonball endeavor around 2006. They went on 2 Jaguars on an outing from New York to Los Angeles yet halted around evening time to rest, halting the clock as they did.

They were captured close to the Eastern California line for speeding in spite of the fact that their typical moving velocities were no greater than those of the top Cannonball and US Express times. The peruser remarks were reproachful of their pitiful halting system and they immediately brought the article down from their web site.

As I proceeded to look at and assess my own inspiration for doing this, the designated advertising part of the uncover was a significant expert all of the time. I have never been any great at isolating work from my own life. Each characterizes the other. That has been simple on the grounds that each occupation I have held spun around an individual interest. I never expected to quit working and begin it was never obvious to play in light of the fact that the boundary. The working was a piece less satisfying and the playing was significantly more costly however to an external spectator I would envision it is an intense qualification to make.

Most individuals at the showroom were not aware of what I was doing. The greater part of my companions didn't know about the thing I was doing. As a matter of fact, basically my close, two or three individuals from work who I expected to clear the downtime with, and the developing rundown of dynamic confederates it took to pull it off were the ones in particular who realized what was happening that weekend.

I wanted to keep the circle near the chest was significant. It only took one person who knew someone that knew a cop along the route that could get wind of one of the biggest catches of his life coming through town to really throw a wrench into the plan. It additionally felt genuinely more secure for me to have a more modest gathering to make sense of this for in the occasion I bombed on this attempt.

I realized I was more ready to do this than anybody at any point had been. We had the unfathomable advantage of having two groups freely break the record in the earlier ten years. I had perused and once again read Alex's book, Brock Yates' book, and each of the tales about Rawlings' outing. The vehicle was prepared, running great, and it appeared as though the wild factors were taken care of. However long we hit no significant traffic we got an opportunity. I assessed our possibilities breaking the record at 30% and our possibilities completing around 70%. I felt that those were higher than anybody had at any point had since Yates did the recon run in May of 1971.

Assuming you are a fit driver and you have an adequately pre-arranged vehicle to dependably convey you the nation over, its vast majority is out of your hands after you get to New York. I have utilized the illustration of a Hot Wheels Track like we used to play with as kids. When you let a vehicle go from the highest point of the track, it is out of your control.

You inactive before the Red Ball and you pull the switch on a gigantic infinitely wise gaming machine. The main wheel uncovers the climate, the second reveals development and street terminations, the third police action, a fourth shows you the traffic, regardless a fifth exists there as a boogeyman. It very well may be a deer, a pothole, a meteor. There are simply such a large number of conceivable outcomes to foresee.
You realize you have no control over them. Two 7's strength get you under 34 hours. Three could get you in yelling distance of 31. Four places 30 in your sights. Nobody knew or had felt what it would resemble for every one of the five to turn up 7's.

I invested a ton of energy in supplication that evening. I don't see regulation breaking
cross country records as a God thing but I do believe in his ability to protect me even when I do some stupid things. Petitioning God is significant to me in its ability to assist me with placing my own interests and issues into viewpoint and to perceive where readiness perpetually meets an edge that is beyond our reach. That is the way the week had felt. Who might have speculated the most troublesome aspect of this whole cycle would have been tracking down somebody to clasp into the safety belt close to you?

This was one of those minutes where I got to gaze at the roof and contemplate what was happening in my life. I understood this fantasy, despite how ridiculous and incredible it very well may be, was a tremendous honor. Individuals spend their whole lives attempting and never have an opportunity to pursue something this hard. I had cut to the chase of genuinely taking the necessary steps to make this a reality.

There was not a point in my life that I could review needing something so severely and taking such measures to accomplish it. It was positively elevated to accept I was able. I could say that my readiness was comparable to the people who had preceded me. I had not a great explanation to accept I was less proficient than they were as drivers. I did, notwithstanding, realize what portion of my success was outside of my control and I recognized that I was trying to do something that hundreds if not thousands of people had been trying to accomplish for over forty years. It was astonishing organization to be in yet I was unable to shake the inclination that I probably won't have a place there.

I in the long run snoozed off, still inquisitive what this all should feel like according to the point of view of Dave and Dan. I came to figure out later, in his own apprehension about the monstrosity of the endeavor, Dave had let his significant other know that he would drive with me to New York and on the off chance that it didn't feel right, he would forsake the excursion and fly home. Dan's position was very similar.

The thought asks inquiries concerning the dynamic and the redirections inside the vehicle. What did you play on the radio? How was the casual conversation? Was there a ton of I Spy?

The real drive was all business. The drive to New York was all schooling. As Dave and Dan had no genuine thought of what's in store, there was an important acclimation and trial and error stage that was required. We expected to foster specialized techniques, conventions, and gain what to anticipate from one another to make the drive work. Dave was very useful in such manner. A lot of his work at IHG was in client points of interaction and encounters. He talked a lot about zen mental focus jargon and other things that might have normally warranted a punch in the face but without someone else on deck I endured the psycho-philosophical mumbo jumbo about hierarchies of needs and idea flows.

We repositioned a portion of the telephones, iPads, and different gadgets to make them more usable. We tried the specialized gadgets and attempted to sort out some way to make the following two days of our lives really agreeable. I additionally invested a reasonable setup of energy making sense of for them what we were doing - Cannonball 101 if you will.

I let them know the historical backdrop of Cannonball. We discussed what was practical out of the films and what was improved. We discussed our own driving encounters and about what I had gained from the accounts of past contenders. I updated them on how long I had spent dealing with this and attempted to inspire them to see exactly how it affected me. They posed a great deal of inquiries that began with "Why...?"

I cleared up for them the decision of the vehicle. They were far fetched of the capability of a 2004 CL55 AMG yet I went through the rationale. High power for maximum velocity. Diesels could never have cut it. Constrained acceptance for elevation and efficiency. The variety was somewhere between blue and dim which made vagueness. If somebody somehow managed to call the police they could report it as either.
When a cop was searching for the vehicle he could decipher it as either.

Keeping the powertrain stock was for dependability and not forfeiting efficiency. Dave was extremely pleased with the couple of moments that he had spent over 175 mph in his Performante, and addressed why I had not eliminated the stock electronic limiter on the ECU at 155 mph. The simple response was on the grounds that the ECU streaks cost you efficiency since they accompany more power we didn't require. The more substantial response was weariness. However fun as it seems to be to pursue 200 mph in a road vehicle it is extremely challenging to process as a driver. The psychological decompression time expected subsequent to burning through 5-30 seconds over 150 is long.

We would have been hitting 175 mph for 30 seconds and then spending the next two minutes at 90 feeling proud of ourselves and letting our brains recover. We could have spent that same 150 seconds traveling at 130 and felt fine. In the first scenario you travel 4.46 miles in 2.5 minutes. In the second you go 5.41 miles. It not by and large a turtle rabbit peculiarities yet to a greater extent a bunny versus more intelligent rabbit strategy.

Extra fuel implied additional weight that changed as we consumed it. This bring forth the requirement for a functioning suspension. The Mercedes Active Body Control framework estimated and evened out each side of the vehicle on numerous occasions each second and was the most ideal choice in the business paying little mind to cost. It was known to be the tragic flaw of unwavering quality so it represented a huge piece of the new upkeep cost. As Dave had been partaking in the guarantee status of his Gallardo that was only a couple of months old, the possibility of a $8,800 cost in upkeep on an it was puzzling to work vehicle. Quit worrying about the level of the vehicle's worth that bill represented.

The deceived out inside with all of the toys was exceptionally fascinating to my technically knowledgeable comrades. As a matter of fact, I had done next to no testing of the frameworks. The CB and Scanner were not getting a lot but rather there was very little driver traffic around us so it appeared to be reasonable. I had not modified the frequencies for the Eastern Seaboard states into the dynamic scanner bank so it was unrealistic to test it. I needed to invest some energy trying out the fuel framework on the drive up. They were quick to perceive how it filled in as well.

We had two extra 22 gallon power modules mounted in the storage compartment. Each extra tank had a siphon with a result line that y-ed together and took care of into a 180 degree transform under the fuel filler cover and down into the filler neck through a changed cap. The stream rate was deliberately genuinely delayed to keep away from expected reinforcements, pressure related holes, or timing issues. Charles had determined it to be around a gallon at regular intervals. We were sending the fuel into a 23 gallon primary tank. The stock fuel measure actually worked and there was a check for every one of the two tanks mounted to the scramble. They were exact just on an exceptionally fundamental level.

The arrangement was to move around ten gallons between the tanks multiple times and for that to consume the space between 1/4 tank and 3/4 on the plant measure. Each move ought to require fifteen minutes by Charles' math. On our way up through North Carolina we attempted this for the first time.

The change to control the fuel siphons was on a custom board CarTunes had manufactured to supplant the previous ashtray on the mid control area. It likewise had a change to kill the back lights as a whole, the actuation button for the MiRT, the power controls for the Laser Interceptor, and the control board for the

Passport system.

Around the time our exchange clock got to fourteen minutes a vehicle behind us started blazing its lights and attempting to pull up close to us. An irate driver was not a frightfully new or unforeseen peculiarities so I just anticipated that he should lash out at us for passing excessively close, going excessively quick, or simply being Ed.

As he pulled close by us he motioned to move the window down. Dave was driving so I obliged him from the front seat. He hollered, "That is no joke!"

Our aggregate mental picture quickly went to a mushroom haze of flares inescapably emitting from the rear of our quickly moving vehicle. Dave began blowing a gasket and I advised him to find the following way out or open shoulder with the goal that we could research. We cut the exchange siphons and out of nowhere the fuel check went from a large portion of the entire way to the furthest reaches of its reportable range.
There was obviously an inactivity in its capacity to measure.

During move there was an extremely impressive smell of gas beyond the vehicle. It didn't actually saturate the lodge while driving however because of the manner in which the vents work it is obvious to an external eyewitness there is something peculiar happening in the background. The storage compartment smelled firmly of fuel and that was where the little baggage that we had pressed was. We had enveloped it by garbage sacks to help yet I realized any flooded fuel would have likely run over and through our packs on out of the vehicle and onto this great Samaritan's windshield.

We promptly left and found a service station and Dan had sorted out some way to eliminate the wellbeing tab from the fire douser wedged within the extra wheel possessing the seat behind Dave. We leaped out of the vehicle and opened the storage compartment. There was fuel trickling through the bumper liner and it possessed a scent like the superiority of a Derek Zoolander episode yet there was no fire to suppress. It had not filled the remainder of the storage compartment space with fuel so we were as yet furnished with a usable difference in garments. We were unable to tell precisely how much fuel had spilled yet it was something like five gallons. We concluded that our real exchange rate was a piece north of one gallon for each minute.

After the pressure at long last left our nerves we got back in the vehicle. Dan set the fire douser back straight and we as a whole gazed at one another attempting to accept we were not as out of our profundity as the beyond five minutes would have

demonstrated. Every illustration in Cannonball 101 I had instructed to Dave and Dan on the way up was a Jenga block. Encounters like this fuel emergency were eliminating blocks line by column and compromising our steadiness collectively. I recently trusted that we would have the option to keep the pinnacle standing to the point of getting to Redondo Beach.

We talked about the course and how I had shown up at the navigational methodology. I had invested a ton of energy in Google Maps taking a gander at a harmony between the numerically briefest way and a hypothetical quickest course while adjusting the unmistakable inclination for roadway driving and limiting the quantity of turns. Each navigational guidance was a chance to get lost and that was something I was really apprehensive of.

Dave was a tremendous defender of Waze. Waze is an online entertainment navigational application that utilizes the movement information from different clients to alter directional guidelines and accelerate drive times. It additionally permits clients to report traffic issues, police movement, and different deterrents to advance. He accepted this could be all you want to break this record. With enough clients ahead it could take care of all of the data that we could require. Obviously, the objective of the flight procedure was to limit cooperation with other street clients so we were circularly debilitating the ease of use of this instrument. More Waze clients rises to more traffic. Sadly the unavoidable driver traffic has been delayed to embrace Waze, sticking to the social communication and junk talking chance of the residents band radio.

There would obviously be times when the Waze, Google, and Garmin navigational models would vary and we expected to make a convention for managing those occasions. Google and Garmin utilized authorized phone information from AT&T to characterize traffic designs. Waze was substantially more progressed (this was preceding the Google securing). On the off chance that it let you know there was traffic ahead it was bound to be right. That being expressed, the nav frameworks were not generally designed to comprehend how we were driving. Crisscrossing through a modern park might function admirably in midtown Atlanta to get around a gas principle break however in this style of drive, the tension of having no clue about where you are going could wind up harming more than helping.

During the drive North to the beginning, we got an opportunity to test this. Waze said there was traffic up ahead while we were in Virginia. Clients were going 7-12 mph. It encouraged us to take an exit, go through a little surface street,
make a lot of turns, run along a frontage road corresponding to a tad, and afterward reappear the highway.

We did. It was insane. We were unable to see to turn, the other nav frameworks were shouting "Recalculating" continually, and the streets were horrible to speed on. Dave concurred tolerating those sorts of instructions was best not. Limiting pressure and nervousness merited several minutes sitting in rush hour gridlock as opposed to battling to track down another strategy for getting around it. The "keep it straightforward, moronic" mantra was coming into play.

As well as spending the days preceding takeoff arranging individuals to be in the vehicle with me, I had invested a lot of energy chipping away at something different I thought really could give us an upper hand. I had set up for various individuals all through the course to drive in front of us by 75 to 150 miles. They would have the option to give us continuous data on climate, traffic, mishaps, speed traps, and different issues. The correspondence would likewise be an invigorating bind to the world beyond the vehicle. As far as anyone is concerned, this was something neither Alex Roy nor Richard Rawlings had accomplished for any significant piece of their runs. Alex had investigates of NYC and Richard professed to have employed a group of limo drivers to obstruct crossing points. Both had partners lead them into Los Angeles. I needed to take that to the following level.

During the drive up to New York we called the companions we knew along the course to affirm their eagerness to act as spotters for their legs of the outing. Debris Majid planned to see us off from Manhattan. We planned to organize in the impermanent stopping region before his place, utilize the bathroom, clean our teeth, and change garments there before leaving.

Danny Landoni would leave from the Eastern Pennsylvania line when we left the Red Ball and lead us across the state. I didn't know Danny and had just spoken with him on the telephone once. He was a companion of Cody Heron who I knew through Lamborghini proprietorship. At the time Cody had a M5, Ferrari 458, Lamborghini Aventador, and had requested a Huracan from me.
He thought the thought was fabulous however was summoned on business so he designated the undertaking to Danny who demonstrated both incredibly skilled and eager to take part.

Chris Staschiak planned to leave from the Pennsylvania/West Virginia boundary and lead us through Ohio. He was as yet upset to not be riding shotgun

yet eager to be a piece of the activity at any rate. David Wiggins planned to lead from Columbus on yet he got seasonal influenza. He had bought a Ferrari 458, Lamborghini Gallardo LP550-2 Bicolore, and a Lamborghini Murcielago LP670 SuperVeloce from me in the earlier years and I was eager to fly by him for once yet sadly he couldn't go along with us. Chris wound up going on through the areas where Wiggins would have been useful.

Tom Greulich, one of the contenders from the 2004 AKA Rally, planned to lead us through Missouri starting upper east of St Louis. Jules Doty was a companion of Dave's and would lead us through New Mexico. Scratch Reid was investigating the course into LA yet was expected in court later Monday morning and was inaccessible during the genuine arrival.

REMARKS

From Nick Reid, Los Angeles Scout

Ed and I met on a crosscountry street rally from New York City, NY to Los Angeles, CA around a decade prior. Both Ed and I utilized AWD super vehicles for the excursion. Over that week, Ed and I became companions. For years we continued to talk to each other about our similar interests in cars and long trips even though we lived a thousand miles apart.

Eventually Ed would proceed to work for Lamborghini and I started delivering secondary selling parts for Lamborghinis. We both now own almost indistinguishable Lamborghini's. I have the main Grigio Telesto 6 speed manual Murcielago LP640 they brought to the US. Ed has the main Grigio Telesto 6 speed manual Murcielago LP640 unique shipped off Canada. The flawless part is we both drive our vehicles frequently, and drive them significant distances, which is exceptional in the outlandish vehicle local area. Ed and I have an affection for street trips.

I called Ed in mid-2013. Around then Ed indicated that he would endeavor the New York to California run and inquired as to whether I might want to help. I readily concurred. Half a month after the fact Ed called and expressed that inside a couple of hours he would set off from New York. Sadly I couldn't lead Ed into Los Angeles as expected, however I had the option to assist with affirming Ed's arranged course as the most productive way to the coast and to stay away from conceivable traffic delays.

During the opportunity Ed was coming into Los Angeles I was remaining optimistic for him. I had not heard any updates of how their advancement was.
However, they well-known axiom "no news is uplifting news" was going through my brain. Then it happened, late at night, a text came through from Ed, "we did it." I knew no subtleties for the run with the exception of the way that Ed did it on the main attempt. I was exceptionally energized for everybody included on the grounds that this was an incredible feat.

In the next few weeks subtleties of the run were delivered. Ed was extremely energetic about everybody that assisted him with accomplishing this extraordinary accomplishment. While perusing the rundown of "much obliged's" sent by Ed, I saw that there were numerous shared companions from that crosscountry rally we went to 10 years prior on the rundown. Ed's fantasy to establish the standard from New York to Los Angeles was an extraordinary accomplishment, yet it united companions. Companions that have the same

normal love for travels. Ed's fantasy united us all once more, and accidentally we as a whole were important for an incredible record that we won't ever forget.

CHAPTER 15

Pulled Over In NYC

We didn't mean to set any records driving up to New Jersey that Friday yet assuming we had, we would have been disheartened. Traffic was troublesome, we were not conveying well indeed, we were frightened of getting captured, and the streets were not helpful for the sorts of velocities we were arranging. Even without the concerted effort to average more than ninety it was pretty demoralizing to see the average plummeting well below eighty. I was doing my best not to add a lot to it but rather I was winding up excessively effortlessly disappointed with Dave and genuinely worried that the result of the following day would be a remarkable joke.

We halted for supper in Tyson's Corner, Virginia at a Maggiano's Italian eatery. It was a weird state of mind at the table. The sluggish applaud of progress to New York was acquiring recurrence and we were all attempting to sort out what 24 hours from that point would resemble. As we had driven North, Dave and Dan had the option to extend how they might interpret what's in store yet their tutelage was coming from me, somebody who had no direct thought of what's in store. Different folks were obviously attempting to foster a coordinated restroom routine to convey them into the following day.

As I was driving, Dave observed a four star lodging on a movement markdown site and booked it. It ended up being the Hyatt in Jersey City, an extraordinary lodging delightfully disregarding the Hudson River and Freedom Tower. We got in there around 1:00 AM on Saturday. Dave was not happy sharing a room so he booked an additional a one. Dan and I remained in the other one. There was a road level valet. I tipped the orderly $20 and requested that he keep the vehicle out front. That would make it more straightforward for the following evening when we would arrange for takeoff. The valet took a gander at the vehicle dubiously and obliged.

I was really worried that I would get a call or instant message at any second from Alex Roy. The beginning of distrustfulness was an abnormal sensation. Being an inhabitant of Manhattan, we were on his home turf. Assuming a vehicle like this, obviously ready to challenge his record, was cruising around the neighborhood doubtlessly there would be associates in and out of town who would

alert him to tHe danger. Every one of the discussions that I had with Alex were altogether genial and accommodating yet I had purposely tried not to let him know which dates we were anticipating driving. I would have rather not troubled him with the ethical issue of treachery. He, himself had let me know that his attorneys restricted him from seeing some other runs and exhorted me not to tell him (or anybody) precisely when we would make the run.

I had gotten us a late checkout so we had sufficient opportunity to get some rest. I advised everybody to attempt to remain in bed until at minimum early afternoon. Dan was the only one fit for this. I awakened at around 10:30 and remained in bed until around 11. I messaged Dave. He had been up since 7.

Dave and I circumvented the corner to a bistro to get some morning meal. We let Dan continue to rest. He appeared to have a low caloric admission need in any case. I had the drive plan with me. This was whenever that Dave first had seen it. It by and large illustrated the windows for driver changes, assessed normal rates, and some designated spot times through significant urban areas and navigational guidelines. The objective time stayed 30 hours. Dave recorded 31:04 on a napkin as he attempted to envision the objective. We snacked at our morning meal and kept on discussing what the drive could feel like. That was the most un-comprehensible aspect of the undertaking and I felt a lot of like an authority driving the team into fight with just a somewhat preferable vantage point over they enjoyed.

I got several packaged natural product juice smoothies to drink en route. Obviously they were $5 each in this bistro/general store rather than $2 at home yet I was blissful realizing that I had somewhere around 1,500 short-lived calories to appreciate all through the drive as expected. I recollected the manifest of Brock Yates' Moon Trash Van with sandwiches, apples, and customary food. Other Cannonballers had set off loaded down with customary Italian home cooking. The division between those outings and what we were going to set out on started to remain as a glaring difference. It was not need to feel superior that had gotten me to this mark of arrangement and hypothesis yet rather it was the continually spearheading soul of gearheads and cutting edge travelers making bold strides to work on the time.

Given the edges of progress through history we as a whole concurred that there were huge gains still to be had. The wild factors plainly came into play.

1971	40:51	Smith/Williams/Yates/Yates Jr	Dodge Sportsman Van
1971	35:54	Yates/Gurney	Ferrari 365 Daytona
1975	35:53	May/Cline	Ferrari Dino 246 GTS
1979	32:51	Heinz/Yarborough	Jaguar XJS
1983	32:07	Diem/Turner	Ferrari 308 GTS
2007	31:59	Rawlings/Collins	Ferrari 550 Maranello
2006	31:04	Roy/Maher/Welles	BMW M5

The edges of progress had been enormous. Alex accused a short tempest and traffic in New Mexico for at minimum a thirty-minute postponement. The crosscountry drive contained such countless individual issues to address and a competitor really needed to vanquish them all to be in conflict. We had the vehicle, we had the drivers, we had the stuff, yet could we have the karma? An opportunity to pull the arm of the legendary gambling machine was nearing.

Dave and I strolled back to the lodging and awakened Dan. We left the rooms and got the provisions commonly organized in the vehicle. I called Ash to let him know that we were going his direction. The arrangement was to investigate the Red Ball and assess the best course out of the city. Roy and Rawlings had utilized the Holland Tunnel. I likewise needed to take a gander at the New York Classic Car Club area that Alex Roy had left from to perceive the amount of a benefit that appeared to be. Now, Dave didn't have an enthusiasm for the passionate meaning of the Red Ball to the record so he was keen on the quickest way out that would allow us the best opportunity of breaking any record.

I had driven in Manhattan multiple times and for the most part tracked down it to stream well, remain occupied however moderate, and remain genuinely sensible as long as you were certain and continued to push ahead in similar soul as the cabbies around you. That was not true that Saturday. It was totally nuts. We came to the Red Ball to observe the whole stretch of E 31st Street destroyed in a repaving project. In view of the signs and work designs it seemed as though the street could really be shut at the principal convergence that we would need to go through. We met with Ash and talked for a couple of moments about methodology. He had left his Laguna Seca Blue E46 M3 in Atlanta and utilized the Subway to get to work so his experience driving in region was decently limited.

I asked the orderly at the Red Ball carport assuming he at any point had anybody appear there referencing Cannonball in vehicles seeming to be our own with additional screens inside and recieving wires mounted to the trunks. He said, "No," and saw me like I was an appropriate moron.

We outfitted up and made an exit. We mimicked resetting all of the outing information on the vehicle and GPS frameworks. We began the clocks and advanced out of the parking structure which was an incredible whirlwind of button pressing.
Following the GPS exhortation and the drive plan that I had recently formed I guided us away to a more extensive, hypothetically quicker moving, go across road. It wasn't. We endlessly sat. The navigational guidelines were hard to comprehend and Dave knee-jolted to Waze to endeavor a re-route.

We at long last got to the Lincoln burrow and could see the entry to it. Dave saw that Waze said a fast Left Right-Left would sidestep the stop ahead. Hesitantly I consented to attempt it. I made the left uniquely to hit another jam. I got to the front and made a directly through the red light. That was contrary to the guidelines in Manhattan and the cop who turned out to be right behind me chose to carry it to my attention.

He popped on his lights and pulled me over. The street I turned onto as I obliged the capture quickly split. The right seemed to be a parking area so I picked the left. It was a road that goes only one direction and I had driven this cop down it going the incorrect way. It would have been unsafe assuming that there were any vehicles coming. Fortunately, there were not and I had the option to pivot and get back to the legitimate bearing of traffic stream with the most likely astounded cop not far behind me.

Dave felt awful. I felt distraught. Dan dreaded for his own security. The cop was genuinely bewildered by the entire thing. He approached the vehicle and requested my permit and protection. You don't need to convey a legitimate protection card in Georgia since all records are put away in an administration open framework in light of your driver's permit. That implies that the one involving my wallet turned out to be a couple of recharging cycles terminated. I offered it and he was not intrigued. Some way or another he oversaw not to get some information about the wheel in the back with Dan, radio wires on the decklid, and extra screens in the cockpit. I think he had proactively arranged us into some not-from-around-here simpletons who might have been wearing aluminum foil caps on the off chance that they didn't block our vision for driving. I did all that I could to regretfully build up that deduction.

He consented to let me off with an advance notice and provided me with a ton of room to approach my way.

I communicated my disappointment with Dave and offered a harsh admonition that assuming he counseled Waze again among now and our appearance in Redondo Beach I would cast off his telephone from the vehicle. Dan was the main individual with authorization to involve Waze for navigational purposes. Both acknowledged this new functional reality.

The work torments at long last stopped as we birthed ourselves from Manhattan by means of the Lincoln Tunnel and explored our direction through the exchanges that got us onto the Jersey Turnpike/78. All things considered, nearly. Dave was safeguarding his activities and I was being vulgar and annoying so we both figured out how to miss the navigational guidance for the turn. It took us thirty minutes to get back on track.

We had plainly passed up this great opportunity on this leave technique. We returned into the city and concluded we ought to attempt to observe the New York Classic Car Club.
There are two of them. We went to some unacceptable one. It was obviously not a benefit so we left and precluded that. The one that we didn't go to was the one that Alex utilized, further examination showed. It would have been more straightforward and reasonable enticing as our navigational certainty faded so it was great that we didn't figure that out.

We contemplated Times Square. It was notable and dispensed with about portion of the driving distance on the island of Manhattan. Assuming one were beginning an occasion today that was the consistent spot to start. The AKA Rally, GoldRush, and Gumball had done that in their visits to NYC.

Ultimately we settled the first choice of the Red Ball actually seemed OK. Assuming we ended up missing the mark by under twenty minutes maybe we could pound ourselves for it however we trusted it wouldn't be the situation. I chose if we could get city in under twenty minutes it would worth proceed. Whatever more drawn out and we might return again and restart. I had never talked about the restarting procedure with any other person yet I thought it appeared to be legit. I also decided based on the fact that 31st eventually ran into the Lincoln Tunnel it would be best for us to simply endure the slower movement on that road and stay relaxed than to weave around searching for a few seconds here or there.

Upon arriving at that choice I expected to escape the city. We expected to gas up and in the wake of cruising all over Manhattan for two and half hours I expected to rest, de-pressurize intellectually, and be still for a brief period. We drove off of the island and into New Jersey, followed the course to 78 and tracked down an exit. It was getting into center of-no place zone so the main sensible eating foundation we could find was a TGI Fridays.

In the ordinary course of our lives, not a single one of us could at any point have paid the an unwelcome visit of a TGI Fridays again however in this situation it some way or another appeared to be legit. Straightforward menu, simple stopping, no psychological strain in requesting. Following a tenser day than any of us had believed it should be, this was great. It was intriguing to see what comprised solace food on such an event - not all that much, the same old thing. Simply whatever got us taken care of without causing us to apply any psychological energy on something besides what the following day and a half was going to entail.

I let Dave and Dan stroll inside and get us a table. Prior to separating I let Dan know that assuming I needed to kill Dave tomorrow and cover him in the desert that he would never express an expression of it. He gestured his head and took a gander at me with the absolute perfect measure of vulnerability in regards to my reality at the moment.

I called Megan. I was depleted, broken, and debilitated. I questioned Dave's capacity to help explore and our ability to work collectively. The cooperation expected to genuinely challenge this record appeared to be a long ways past us.

I told her it was basically impossible that we planned to break it. She could hear in my voice how squashed I was and it was the main time she at any point said that I ought to anticipate attempting it once more. Her recommendation was awesome, to regard it as an activity and to improve the following one. It quieted me down and I had the option to return inside with some similarity to a grin. I actually expected that we would get into Illinois or Missouri, acknowledge how distant speed we were, and ask the nav frameworks to just bring us back home humiliated. I was at that point thinking about the pessimist text I could draft to Alex Roy. Despite lessening certainty, we had overcome much to quit attempting now.

Each of us ate boring food and a few vegetables. It was a quiet dinner where we were all obviously attempting to diminish our circulatory strain and heart rates
from the nervousness. Subsequently we searched for a spot around us to go endure an hour unwinding and extending our legs a piece. There turned out to be a Target with a Starbucks within it only a couple of miles away in Watchung, NJ. We went that way.

There is a point in the 32 hours 7 minutes narrative where Alex Roy is talking with his companion and co-driver in his first genuine endeavor to break the record (he attempted multiple times). He examines setting up his Last Will and Testament before the drive. He talks with one of his co-drivers about the possibility that he is ready to bite the dust in doing this and afterward they invest some energy examining the meaning of that idea.

I wouldn't agree that I was able to kick the bucket to do this. That is moreso a reasoning for decision making inside a test than an acknowledgment before attempted a mission. I did, notwithstanding, perceive that this was the most perilous action I had at any point embraced. Attempting to surpass 200 mph on open streets, perusing a text returning from work, eating hamburger tartare, and hair bringing school stunts withered up in contrast with the gamble I felt in this movement. I realized we had made however many strides as we could to expand the wellbeing of the excursion and I thought we had limited the gamble. It actually existed to a degree moving toward my edge of decency. Anybody who knows me or has perused this far can see the value in my gamble resistance is absurdly high.

This acknowledgment kept on reminding me exactly that I was so lucky to be at that time. Whether or not or not it very well may be soundly defended by even another individual on Earth, I was pushing at maximum speed into the tempest of a test that was proceeding to characterize me. The honor of arriving and figuring out exactly how far I could propel myself was something I realized a great many people never got to see and feel. As mysterious as things were, my eyes were totally open and I was all set. Many individuals in the forty years earlier had faced similar challenges attempting to rope a similar unicorn I was hunting. Just seven had held the record.

When we got to the Target we started pulling the rubbish, void containers, coverings, and general excursion shrapnel out of the vehicle. We disposed of the food and hydration supplies that we had over pressed. There were a couple of things that every one of us perceived that we had neglected so we went in to get them. I wanted some greasing up eye drops. I have been myopic with a slight astigmatism since Middle School and I realize that I would have to switch

among contacts and glasses two or multiple times through the drive to keep my vision functional.

I had truly considered finishing a Lasik technique before the outing yet perhaps the most well-known aftereffect is a corona glare around lights while driving around evening time. This chance was less adequate than the burden of exchanging among contacts and glasses. I wound up making it happen a couple of months after we returned home and it has been phenomenal. I presently have vision somewhere close to 20-10 and 20-15. The night glare went on about a month and presently it is over and above anyone's expectations. Looking back it would have been exceptionally great to have managed preceding the drive.

Over the course of around a half year, I fostered a trigger like colonic reaction to coffee utilizing the Lamborghini Dealership corporate character espresso machine that involved the focal point of our display area. Several shots without help from anyone else or as the items in a milk containing drink and it was working out. I approached the Target Starbucks counter and requested an enormous/grande/whatever Cafe Mocha and plunked down to allow it to work. Perfect timing. Yet again different folks attempted to no end to deal with something similar without success.

The entrail trigger prep showed Dan how this venture affected me. I later figured out he was so anxious by then paving the way to takeoff that he scarcely tried not to articulate his aim to flag down a taxi and discover some way to LaGuardia and back home. Luckily he remained. We perused around just a little and afterward did some last association of the items in the car.

We left looking for certain gas. At 8 PM it was far beyond the waking long periods of Wherever, New Jersey we were. We figured out how to track down a station. We pulled up to their air blower and evened out the tires as a whole. Aside from the capacity to change a wheel I had no locally available capacity to re-expand a tire. That would be the last they were checked before California so we invested energy endeavoring precision.

News to us: you can't siphon your own gas in any kind of mood of New Jersey.
We pulled up to the siphon and opened our trunk. The game plan that I had permitted us to fill the two tanks in the storage compartment with the close to side spout of a two sided siphon and afterward pull the contrary side spout around and fill into the fundamental tank at the same time. That was very bewildering to the specialist at this

Exxon station. After a few odd gazes and exchange he consented to return inside and let us siphon our own gas.

I let Dave drive back to the beginning line. I got toward the rear of the CL to shut just a tad and rest before flight. Debris welcomed us to come up to his condominium to change garments once and for all, clean our teeth, and prepare for liftoff.

The inclination was that of being on a high plunging board. You don't have the foggiest idea how high it is. You can't determine whether the pool is full. It could simply be loaded up with Jell-o as water. You have just caught wind of individuals making it happen however you can't see anybody toward any path. Scaling was a haze and you have no clue about what's in store on the way down. All you know is...you are going to jump.

From Dan Huang, Navigator And Support Passenger

It was slow Thursday evening. I was over at my sweetheart's place when I got the Facebook message from Ed. It basically came these lines: "Hello man. Call me at (770) 633-XXXX whenever you get an opportunity. I was unable to view as your number." I was interested and in no time, we were on the telephone. I was hoping to hear that he had a vehicle in stock that I may be keen on. At that point, I was

thinking about an Evora, that is until I figured out how horrendous they really are. All things being equal, the discussion got some information about my arrangements for the following two or three days, which appeared to be unusual to me.
Finally, he lets me know his well conceived plan - stretching out a greeting for me to participate in it.

The main issue? We planned to leave tomorrow first thing. I had under twelve hours to choose. Assuming I were intrigued, I would drop by his home to look at the vehicle that evening. I needed more chance to deal with the gamble or check what I was finding myself mixed up with. In the wake of getting off the telephone, I asked my sweetheart for direction: "What do I do?" I asked, while going over every one of the unpleasant conceivable outcomes that could happen.

I clearly recollect her response, "I know whether you don't do this, you will think twice about it." She expressed it such that main a strong soul mates could have - by having my childish cravings as a primary concern while her eyes loaded up with stress. Subsequent to hearing her response, I messaged Ed that I'll be by this evening to look at the car.

It was my first time visiting Ed's place. The second I saw the CL, I couldn't have cared less about the shocking Orange LP640 Roadster that was all there was to it stablemate. I looked over all the planning and difficult work that went into the vehicle. The cockpit seemed to be mission control. It had this multitude of gadgets that I had practically zero clue about how to work. Ed consoled me that it was easy to use and that we'd get to know it on our way up. I still had my doubts though. In the wake of doing some test fitting and acquaintance, I consented to show up Friday morning for our excursion up, still ignorant about the risks. I simply figured it would be a tomfoolery and intriguing method for spending the weekend.

My first genuine alarm (which addressed what I was doing) occurred with the fuel spill. Whenever the vehicle pulled up close to us shouting "You're not kidding!" everybody in the vehicle (counting me) went into a controlled frenzy mode. We needed to get off the highway and quick. Everybody was alloted an errand when the vehicle would stop. Fortunately it was undramatic when we examined what happened.

While still traveling up to NJ, I was able to watch at least half of

32:07 on the iPad, which felt like I was cramming for a test. I didn't know the history and significance of the Cannonball Run, US Express, etc. so I learned as much as I could as we headed for the start line. Seeing how much prep past Cannonballers did made me realize how insane this endeavour was.

When we got to NJ, we remained at an amazing lodging right on the Hudson.
It was dreamlike to leave around evening time and see the NYC cityscape when ATL rural areas was the last thing I saw. It was an unusual inclination to imagine that we were so near NYC just to leave it the following day. This excursion didn't feel like a get-away any longer - it turned into a mission.

After all the training runs endeavoring to leave the city we had been awake for ten hours as of now. Depleted from the dissatisfactions of how the roads of New York City had treated us and the misgivings of our route capacities, I had no clue about how we planned to deal with the 30+ hour long distance race in front of us. Our spirit was low. I recall Ed getting out of TGIF to settle on a telephone decision to his significant other, definitely to make sense of how horrible the excursion had been going.

When we got to the Target, things weren't greatly improved. Now, I understood that every one of my assets were in a basic knapsack and I could just Uber my way to the air terminal to hang tight for the following trip to ATL. Nonetheless, since we made it this far, notwithstanding the entirety of our mishaps, I ought to at minimum try it out. This was the least piece of the outing for me, on the grounds that the longing to bail was most prominent. In any case, similarly as things would unwind, they generally appeared to make themselves barely enough to permit us to keep up with forward progress.

I viewed it as an extraordinary help to spend time with Ash and his companions prior to beginning our legendary excursion. They were truly neighborly and provided us with an increase in certainty minutes before flight. All the concern I had developed blurred subsequent to putting shortly in their organization and exquisite apartment.

Since I'm so used to telecommuting, bathroom use was never an issue. Be that as it may, when you are in a vehicle for 30+ hours, you want to remain hydrated and you can't utilize the bathroom any time you need. I apportioned my water admission so I didn't utilize an excess or utilize the bathroom as much of the time. I attempted to utilize the bathroom on the shoulder once, yet I suppose i'm too modest to even consider getting it going on the freeway.

An anonymous transportation organization's 18-wheeler nearly ran us off the street. As we were going to make our pass on the left, the truck began moving into our path. Ed performed admirably even when two of the CL's wheels were kissing unpaved road. All of this occurred at speeds my Volkswagen GTI would finish out at. I really thought it was over by then, and in addition to the race.

Many times when I was enticed to shut my eyes. I contemplated whether I could at any point open them again.

CHAPTER 16

Down The Hot Wheels Track

At 9:55 PM on Saturday, October 19, 2013 Dave Black, Dan Huang and I left from the entry to the Red Ball Parking Garage at 142 E 31st Street and traveled West. I was driving. The odometer of the 2004 Mercedes Benz CL55 AMG that we were in perused simply over 115k miles and the vehicle was loaded up with each enemy of police contraption that we could gather. We had 67 gallons of fuel on board alongside the entirety of the food and supplies we expected to require for the following day and a half. There was no aim of halting whenever soon.

Our objective was to honor the exemplary Cannonball Run course. That would limit possible issue with the record and feel more genuine to us. Dave really downloaded Yates' book on his Kindle App as we were exploring around Manhattan before that day and read the initial not many pages. He had been inclining towards casting a ballot Times Square previously yet he right away and earnestly moved his inclination to the Red Ball. Obviously I needed to prevent him from attempting to peruse the whole book in the two or three hours we had left prior to leaving. I was OK with his precise degree of misconception of what the evening and following day could seem to be. There was no advantage in making it any more clear at this point.

Around the very time that we left the Red Ball, Danny Landoni left the eastern line of Pennsylvania. This put him around seventy miles in front of us and he started taking care of us status reports by call and text. The Garmin route framework wouldn't handle the whole course the entire way to the Portofino so we had moved toward programming in steady designated spots around the meeting focuses with the lead vehicles. Obviously that main covered a fifth of the excursion. The route for this drive didn't need many turns and I had every guidance separated plainly in the drive plan accounting sheets arranged months prior.

We left and quickly ended up in gridlocked Manhattan traffic. However troublesome as it seemed to be, we had all consented to resist the urge to panic even with such a situation. It worked. We glanced around by any stretch of the imagination of the clocks, trip PCs, and nav screens counting and proceeded with the ceaseless process

of adapting ourselves to the mentality of the drive.

We left the Lincoln Tunnel shortly. That was in front of our twenty moment "pivot and restart" time limit. We explored through two cost trades utilizing our EZ Pass and got onto 78. Seventy miles into the excursion we were into Pennsylvania. That first stretch had taken us one hour and four minutes bringing our normal almost to as far as possible scarcely into the excursion. The streets were unpleasant and traffic was thick yet we were stringing needles through it without breaking a sweat and little show. I had stressed over what amount of time it could require to get our normal up to a level allowing good faith however this felt amazing.

With the Danny-revealed coast being clear, I pushed through Pennsylvania hard. The segment through the Allegheny Mountains was a finished exciting ride. It was plainly stamped however the street wound through the territory like an event congregation ride. The couple of other street clients were for the most part logging and transport trucks.

It is hard to portray the fervor of really being at speed on a genuine endeavor. Despite the fact that my nerves were all the while terminating to some degree unusually, the soothing surge of foothold toward the well cleared PA streets as well as my 10 years of dreaming was mind blowing. The enormous rise changes, long passages, and disregard sees were likely beautiful.

We were not focusing on those perspectives and it was dim other than the astounding amount of reflectors out and about. A couple of moments into the state I was cruising reliably at north of 140 miles each hour and Dan said his first expressions of the outing. "Is it true or not that you are significant? This is truly the way in which we will drive?" He said that 130 was the quickest that he had at any point been in a vehicle. That was evolving. It was additionally not true.

Apparently, Dan had shut out the last time that he had ridden in a vehicle with me. Years earlier I had a daily practice of meeting a gathering of clients at the showroom almost immediately Sunday mornings for a gathering takeoff to our month to month vehicles and espresso gathering. We would shout onto State Route 400 traveled North to the scene. It is a suburbanite thruway so toward the end of the week mornings it is normally unfilled. Multi week Dan had inquired as to whether he could follow along and ride with me to the forthcoming show. I obliged him and he went along with me in a dark 2008 Lamborghini Gallardo Spyder that we had available to be purchased at the dealership.
This probably been in late 2010 in light of the fact that it was before I purchased the blue
Gallardo from Kimmi the prostitute.

When we proceeded onto 400 it was a phantom town. I sped up and tracked down no real explanations to let off. Whenever I peered down at the speedometer not long prior to letting off the choke we were doing a showed 180 mph. That look all over in the back view reflection of the CL as we tore through Pennsylvania was not altogether new to me.

There are not many likenesses between how we drove on this outing and any customary driving consistently. That is the essence of incongruence between the basic public view of security and the truth of being in the vehicle.
Peculiarly, this is the absolute most secure inclination driving I have at any point done. Whenever I go on an excursion with Megan, she is on her telephone, playing with the radio, plotting the following decade of our lives, or doing 100 different things to occupy me from the street. Whenever I drive while heading to work I am as yet tired, enticed to get to the dozen instant messages that come in, and carelessly continuing through a course I could drive in my sleep.

This dislike that by any means. It was simply past 12 PM and we could never have been more ready. Further, my attention was totally on controlling the vehicle. The approaching information, telephone discussions with Danny, understanding of street conditions, and even minds my own prosperity were being finished by Dave and Dan. We were our own main goal control, analyzing each conceivable part of auto activity with at least some expectations of simply enduring the following twist a piece quicker.

There was almost no traffic out and about. We were passing a vehicle each 5-10 minutes and there was a lot of room. We would ease back to 100-125 relying upon the range of a turn yet progress was extraordinary. The demeanor in the vehicle was a lot more settled than I had expected and the goal situated conversation was incredibly efficient.

There were times when obviously we were all kind of flabbergasted with the rates. I moved my hands along the controlling haggle that I was holding it so hard my palms were it was enveloped by to scrape the cowhide it. It was a decent suggestion to inhale, unwind, and change my seating position. My prescription school companions had encouraged me that each fifteen to thirty minutes we ought to siphon our legs and move our middles to invigorate blood stream and limit the dangers of blood clusters. The layers of novel issues to tackle in this challenge never stopped to amaze.

It was 322 surprising miles across Pennsylvania and I found the middle value of just over 100.6 mph. That was a normal of 35 to 45 mph over as far as possible in the state. We were totally amazed. There was nothing on the scanner, nothing on the CB to dial us back. Waze had no clients ahead, Trapster didn't announce anything. Danny was correct. Other than some early sprinkling precipitation we endured the Turnpike trade onto 470 and afterward to 70 with next to no real excuse to lift. Without the introduction of the perpetually potential motivations to dial back, not a solitary one of us could truly envision some best approach any quicker than we had been. The Pennsylvania streets were nowhere near straight. How quick might we at any point hope to go once the streets really began to smooth out?

When we hummed past Danny in his Volkswagen I had no clue the greatness of how he had quite recently helped us. We were in a real sense going 20-30 miles each hour quicker than I was hoping to on the high side and despite the fact that we really dropped into the high 80's and low 90's while passing a couple of vehicles and exploring a portion of the harrier twists, it seemed like we probably been averaging 150.

From Danny Landoni, Pennsylvania Scout

Who doesn't cherish a Cannonball Run? Whenever I got a call from one of my most regular accomplices in car wrongdoing that he really wanted me to fill in as a scout for a NY to LA record endeavor it didn't take long to reply in the positive. I didn't have to know what its identity was. It didn't make any difference how late it would be. I was there.

I addressed Ed on the telephone for around five minutes the Tuesday night before the run and he made sense of what he was searching for. Drive as far as possible or anyway quick I wanted to and let him know as to whether I saw any police, awful climate, traffic, or development. We would remain on the telephone and my objective was to make him press the choke only a tad bit harder. What better game might you at some point ask for?

There was a tad of showering precipitation right off the bat yet the drive was predictable. Well once you move beyond the AMG Merc barreling through our fine state at such corrupt rates. I was on the telephone with Dave for the greater part of the outing and the numbers that he was transferring from their main goal control scarcely checked out. I accelerated a bit to boost the window of my own utility for them yet when they raged by it was totally surreal.

The most unusual part was driving home. I'm never one to avoid caprice of any kind. Unconstrained travels will find no more prominent devotee except for the experience of watching their tail lights vanish with such twist speed and for me to get back to day to day existence was difficult to make sense of. I wouldn't hear from Ed once more until nine o'clock on Sunday when he said basically, "We made it happen. Much obliged to you for all of your help."

What an end of the week that was. I was unable to be any more pleased to have been a piece of the run and to have met Ed through the interaction. Studying him through the ensuing meetings and online entertainment sharing has uncovered that we share significantly more

practically speaking than being on that desolate stretch of the
Pennsylvania Turnpike on a Saturday night in October.

I romantic tales like this on the grounds that the delineate the
vehicle side interest so well. It's not necessary to focus on speeding,
albeit that is plainly a piece of it. This thought is about

taking care of the issues that face energetic street clients consistently.
The test is an embellishment of my crash into work every day, of going
to a supermarket, of going to see grandmother. Ed met and vanquished
that test. I was only glad to be there to witness it.

CHAPTER 17

Roadside Urination & Driver Changes

We were utilizing the Mercedes Trip Computer's reset screen for
every leg of the driving. To save my own mental stability and to
understand what's in store I had reset it once we raised out of
Manhattan and to an acceptable level. It was perusing 104 mph for my
first spell in the driver's seat. Feeling real was excessively new. We
were flying. The vehicle was smooth, murmuring along and hitting
130-150 in every straight. The force of the supercharged AMG V8 was
surreal.

That established the vibe. The sensation was unfathomable, especially
in America.

I invest the vast majority of the energy under as far as possible driving
around in life-sucking traffic in my 631 strength LP640. We forget
rapidly what these vehicles are prepared to do. Ze Germans would
drive this way on the Autobahn each and every day in a CLK320 taxi
since they can and the vehicle can. Dave and Dan were especially
dazzled. I think Dave settled on the choice to claim an AMG vehicle at
some point inside the main hour of the drive. I needed to inspire him to
close down the program on his telephone and get off of Craigslist.

Some vehicles speed up quick from a stop like a Chevrolet
Corvette or a Lamborghini Aventador. Some handle with exceptional
levelheadedness around turns like a Porsche Boxster, V8 Ferrari or
McLaren 650S. Different vehicles voyage easily at high paces
incredibly well like a Rolls Royce, Bentley, or Aston Martin. This
matured AMG monster was jumping from 80 to 130 with as much
balance as I had at any point seen out of a vehicle and eating up each

and every bend. It was totally right at home and neither we, nor the vehicle, were breathing hard. It represented what little edge of vehicle ability we convey on a day to day basis.

The disposition in the vehicle was one of a kind. It stayed dissimilar to any driving that any of us had at any point done. While Dan's wide eyes had gotten back to their typical size there was an inactive conversation around the information entering the vehicle. A framework detailing nothing was more significant than it saying there was something to fear. Clear implied hammer down. For the initial not many hundred miles of the outing that was all there was to it. We saw no police, no traffic, no dynamic development, nothing. Not a really obvious explanation to dial back, so we didn't. It was an encouragement to test the constraints of the vehicle and of my driving. We accepted.

The cockpit discourse was great.

"Nothing on the

V1, Passport

clear as well,

Waze clear,

street ahead twists left concurring the nav

screen, under 30 degrees,

geography goes downhill after the

following curve, nothing on the CB,

scanner hushes up, clear

ahead, right path empty,

move there,

slow Pontiac Sunfire in the left

path, slice the brights to pass,

embrace that shoulder and give her some

additional room, how about we hold them

back from calling 911.

You are doing

extraordinary.

Need any water?

Adjust your seat a little, we needn't bother

with a blood coagulation. Loosen up the grasp

on the controlling wheel.

Car is under control.

You are obvious to utilize the whole street on this

one, remain left. Get that apex.

Next straight seems to be two miles or so.

Waze says there is a vehicle halted out and about however it looks stale.

Clear on Trapster alerts for as may be

obvious. No traffic, no surprises.

Car sounds great, wow the fires up are extremely low

at this speed. Give me five additional miles for each

hour..."

It was liquid. It was motivating. It was working.

We halted without precedent for West Virginia. We headed over to shoulder of the street, peed there, and Dave assumed control over the driving. There was some beginning phase alarm with respect to the next two however my bladder was prepared for excited evacuation.

My first shift was finished. I had traveled 394 miles in 4 hours 17 minutes for a 91.98 normal. This was quicker than the general normal of the Roy/Maher run. I honestly had felt that it could take getting to New Mexico or Arizona to get the typical where it should have been to challenge the record. To have done it within the fourth state felt strange. Further, assuming you require out the fifteen minutes that it took us to endure the initial two miles, the normal was around 98 mph. That was solid for any leg of the outing, especially the curviest leg with the most height change. Presently the time had come to allow the street to fix yet we were entering Ohio, the strictest state in the country for speeding.

Chris Staschiak had organized at the West Virginia/Ohio boundary and left when we were around 100 miles out. I put him on speakerphone for the majority of our communication as a shallow method for building up the fortunate idea of the open door he had surrendered. No matter what the progress of this drive it would enlighten the told-you-so discussions I could get the opportunity to appreciate before long. It was clear as he wandered through his home state he lamented passing up the mission both of us had been plotting for the a long time since his first email to me. We were uniquely in West Virginia for thirteen routine miles, we went through it shortly including the stop. Normal was 86.67 mph for the state, sufficiently quick for not even one of us to lose half of our teeth or steal away with a cousin.

A 100-150 mile cushion among us and a spotter by and large gave us a three hour shutting time. They would go as far as possible and we would be 30-50 miles each hour over it relying upon how empowering their reports were.
Watching the holes contract was exhilarating.

It functioned admirably. There was certainly a risk that a hazard or speed trap could present in the gap between when the spotter would pass through an area and when we would arrive there but our efforts to build our own strategic Waze style group were proving successful. Regardless of whether we tracked down motivation to scrutinize indisputably the utility of their consent to choke up unafraid of hindrance, the association was extremely valuable. Realizing that this was a collaboration and that there were others concentrating profoundly on the venture that day caused the entirety of the drive to feel more significant and exciting.

We were by and large radio quiet to uninvolved gatherings. Megan had attended a Halloween party that evening dressed as a zombie Alice in Wonderland. We traded several instant messages offering minimal more than, "We are ok.
Progress is great. Haven't killed Dave at this point." She had assigned Dan as the "mother of the vehicle" and he should keep her side by side of our advancement and focus on our prosperity over a shameless methodology of succeeding at all costs.

She wound up going through the night for certain companions. Megan find out about the thing we were doing than any other person in the situation since she had been the onlooker to the vast majority of my ten years of exploration and readiness. My advantage in intriguing vehicles and the record most certainly originated before her importance in my life so I guess she had picked in. In any case, I perceive that it was a provoking passionate spot for her to be. Before we were dating, Megan's car skill covered out at the capacity to recognize a vehicle and a truck. Presently she was perched by as her better half sought after one of the most notorious crowns of ill-conceived motorsport. I was certain her folks planned to come around to endorsing me now!

From Chris Staschiak, Ohio Scout

Ed Bolian is one of those individuals that you are pleased to be aware, especially assuming you are an engine oil-for-blood gearhead as am I. Put another way, Ed is out of his f***ing mind. Regularly when you get a lot of vehicle folks together, the tales become quicker than angler at a bar however when Ed says he will get some fantasy vehicle or do some insane drive, you really want to tune in. This crazy person will really do it.

Like Ed, I was generally consumed with getting in a vehicle and driving quick for quite a while. After I saw Ed on MTV in 2004 I needed to reach out to him. The exchange never halted after that.

Initially we discussed plans to get together and do a few conventions. I did the Gumball 3000 in my 1973 Big Block Corvette in 2003 and 2004. In that time I got comfortable with Alex Roy, David Maher, and Richard Rawlings - veterans of similar occasions. Ed and I discussed Bullrun, Players Run, Gumball, future cycles of the AKA Rally he had done, and what vehicles we would chip away at. Ed was currently beginning his rental organization and the sorts of things that he thought up kept on astounding me.

Alhowever our arrangements to drive in an extraordinary vehicle rally never met up, we turned out to be old buddies and talked several times each week. I will always remember the experience of traveling to Palm Beach to co-drive back to Atlanta in the perfect Ferrari 360 Spider that Ed had recently purchased for the rental organization. I had been around supercars my whole life however this was one of those list of must-dos encounters for any vehicle fellow. We impacted up the

Florida Turnpike and onto 75. The most amazing aspect of the excursion, though, was simply getting to know Ed more.

Ed and I experienced childhood in totally different ways, went with various choices, and checked out at life according to alternate points of view. Sorting out the way that Ed Bolian believes is like attempting to tune a carbureted motor. It is rich in its straightforwardness yet muddled to dominate. I love the straightforwardness that he uses to assess and make sense of the world. We each battle in adapting to life. His ventilation techniques are a smidgen more crazy than mine however I surmise speeding the nation over can land you in prison similarly as quick as me punching some windbag in the face.

The conversation of conventions immediately went to breaking the New York to Los Angeles record. Ed has an irresistible energy and he is the best sales rep on earth. He likely missed his calling as some religion chief or road mentalist. Speeding in enormous gatherings is quite simple. In the event that you are not out in any kind of mood of the pack, you are protected. By and large, in my experience, these speeding endeavors are in short explodes. Ed needed to do this without a gathering of vehicles and he needed to go extremely, quick. In spite of certain reservations, he had me hooked.

As Ed began not too far off of arranging his first endeavor in 2008, I was down and out and occupied. I let him keep on trusting that assuming he paid, I would go along. Luckily, life disrupted the general flow for him as well. I went to Atlanta to be a groomsman in his wedding and got to observe the bedlam of the tenant who crashed his Lamborghini and sold the Ferrari. Ed had me out chasing after the Ferrari in the valets of well known Atlanta cafés as we would get reports of sightings however we were unable to track down it. We were generally only one stage behind and Megan was developing increasingly more baffled with anything about a car.

I have never considered anybody to be cool under tension as Ed. It is bizarre. I have talked him through some truly bizarre and insane educational encounters and he is extraordinarily prudent about everything. I guess that is most likely what allows you to accept he can do such crazy things. Watching him attempt them and do them for the beyond a decade has made me a believer.

In 2012 when Ed concluded it was truly time I let him know that I would go however that I was still in no situation to toss in for my half of the bill. That's what seeing Ed acknowledge and push forward showed me he was in another spot with all of this. It was moving toward NYC despite everything me.

As the arranging proceeded, my life got more occupied and it was become doubtful that I would have the option to move away for the time expected to make the endeavor. It seemed like each time I conversed with Ed he had quite recently sold some Aventador or Gallardo. It seemed like he could experience difficulty making the opportunity as well. Fall traveled every which way. Spring 2013 traveled every which way. Then Ed changed. He appeared to understand that it was presently or never. I expect that might have had to do with a ticking clock of one more sort.

I had basically bowed out by then. Ed and Adam Kochanski were arranging in full power and I would do whatever that I might to help from my home in Ohio. I recollect the consider saying that they were going that end of the week in October. I stacked up and prepared for a drawn out night out and about. That sensation of a botched open door began to sneak in. Ed actually assumed that they were probably not going to break it on the principal attempt so I would attempt to move back onto the dynamic program for endeavor two in the spring of 2014. I actually realize that you ought to never forget about this person. I would help as much as I could.

I left the OH/PA line when they were around 150 miles out. Their person in Columbus had this season's virus so my arrangement was to lead them across the entire state. Dave had taken over in West Virginia and it seemed like their normal was solid. Their first scout had served them well and I planned to do likewise. Driving alone in the center of the night in Ohio is exhausting. I can envision their outing was not.

Ed and I remained on the telephone more often than not. There was very little to report. At the point when they got around twenty miles behind me, they continued saying that they were getting little radar blips. I had not seen a solitary cop. Ed at long last requested that I delayed to 30-40 mph and attempt to allow the cop to make up for lost time. They imagined that the continuous blips were an indication that there was a cop between us, driving in a similar heading. At last they appeared to sort out it was some obstruction between the various radar frameworks they were running and they got back on the horse.

I truly can't depict the sensation of watching that vehicle that I ought to have been in go by at 140 mph. I was unable to be more joyful for Ed however I was unable to kick myself any something else for having allowed up the opportunity to back up the driver for that excursion. I'm certain that this won't be the last insane story for Ed. I will be along for the following ride!

Surely We Can't Keep This Up

The full moon was splendid. It was astonishing the amount it further developed perceivability. I had gone this way and that with various lighting arrangements. The notable Cannonball and US Express vehicles seemed to be Group B Rally Cars with helper lights mounted all over the place. Obviously the incandescent lamps that they were enhancing had no place near the capacity of xenon and LED lights of present day cars.

I purchased an immense 30" LED light bar that the ad suggested could sub for the capstone of the Luxor however we were unable to sort out a decent method for mounting it to the front guard so I wound up bringing it back. It had been designed for off road use and was generally to be mounted along the top of the windscreen frame of a Land Rover Defender or Jeep Wrangler so I had also been concerned that it would have made the car more conspicuous than I wanted it to be. We selected to supplant the headlights with a basic HID bulb retrofit pack and they were working extraordinary. We didn't require the high bars however we utilized them a ton of the time in any case.

We were not lamenting our absence of a night vision framework. I realize that a few past clients were extremely glad for them however I had not been persuaded that any of the accessible choices would have allowed driving with the headlights off. Not a single one of them offered perceivability past the headlights so it appeared to be a costly non-advantage. I likewise felt like in the event that I was a clueless Ohio-an and a Mercedes went by me without its headlights on as I was gone to my bingo parlor, hair super durable salon, or Golden Corral family night, then I would be more upset than if the guilty party was utilizing some illumination.

Similarly, I never had an event to deactivate the back lights. The cautiousness of three individuals implied we for the most part distinguished each of the perils before passing them so perceivability of the back lights was a non-issue. The primary worry that we had at the time was not missing a cop but rather having somebody call the police. A vehicle in a compromised state was bound to set off a bizarre 911 recording than a vehicle basically speeding excessively.

The duality of character of the Mercedes AMG vehicles is most likely the tallest credit to themselves. Even after nearly 100k miles of daily driving the cars over the years and scrutinizing the performance statistics in selecting the CL for the trip, I had no idea that it would perform with the unending ferocity the car had that night. We were tearing through the "course" with a psyche blowing measure of speed.

"Without a doubt we can't keep this up the entire time?" Dave expressed from in the driver's seat. "Something must occur sooner or later, right?"

"Indeed, however I think we are developing time quick an adequate number of that we could possibly recuperate from something pretty critical." Dan replied. I could see his brain moving. "Basically, assuming we really want a 90-95 normal, we simply need two minutes at 150 for consistently we are halted. That would wash it out."

I was extremely pleased with their newly discovered and as of now capable Cannonballing abilities. "Precisely, we simply need to bank time where we can and keep on making the most of these chances to go super quick. You are doing incredible Dave and it seems like the course is clear." Foot to the floor.

Whatever score can be found supporting 130-140 mph speeds on a public street, we had it. The steadily ergonomic German seats were kneading endlessly. The scanner and CB hushed up. The as of late adjusted vehicle was cutting a way through the by and large abandoned Ohio streets with zero difficult situation by any means. Even Dan was amazed at how comfortable he was finding the space in the rear seat.

If it were some other kind of drive, the secondary lounge of the CL was unsavory yet on that event he had it organized as his own main goal control. He had an iPad perusing the region on Google maps, checking for the most ideal choices for our next gas quit, shooting a periodic text to Megan or Lisa Black, and offering the kind of encouraging feedback to Dave that he absorbed like a reptile lolling on a warm stone in summer.

Dave said, "Man, this feels fantastic. However, it seems like our karma can't keep going for 30 or more hours. I super expectation it doesn't abandon this leg."

From Dave Black, Co-Outlaw

We trudged our direction down 31st, passed the notorious crossing point of-falsehood, moved down to the entrance to the Lincoln burrow. We impacted through it, up onto I-95, and down to the exit at I-78 (the subsequent bungle spot), converged on and afterward destroyed the fucking street. My strategic bearings (felt like it) were right on the money, and Ed was setting a crazy and to some degree alarming speed through the light traffic. We drew near to guards, cutting in the little holes. I had a concise snapshot of "goodness poop" during this time - the driving was the most forceful I had seen during the excursion. I was trusting this was simply Ed attempting to get comfortable with himself. I returned to calling tactics.

The shower of downpour came as we dealt with the New Jersey rural areas where we had been before. Ed kept a solid speed. Wipers off in light of the fact that the speed beading the water was more effective.

I watched out for the Garmins and on the vehicle's excursion PC to watch the typical increment. The fifteen minutes in Manhattan made it require a long investment to get the normal up. I was hanging tight for the enchanted number "93" - this would be the moving typical that we expected to keep up with to beat Alex Roy's 31:04. Part of me believed that we'd slow down at that point, and even looked forward to slowing down. When we arrived at 93 normal, Ed continued to push with speeds as much as 130 mph. It felt super quick and a piece terrifying. Ed had the difficult assignment of winding through the Alleghenies where we had haze and loads of sharp, blind bends. Anything that concerns I had before were gone at this point. He was kicking ass.

The typical held ascending to 103 preceding we halted, peed, and exchanged positions. It was around 3 hours in and around the West Virginia boundary of Ohio. The driver change and pee break was a comforting experience for the fact that it was so fast, that I knew we could do many of them without even putting a dent in our time. I could never feel constrained to over-drive while fatigued.

As I accelerated, I understood that driving has around a 25 mph lower view of speed than being the co-pilot.

As we moved toward traffic or visually impaired slopes, we'd let off the gas and we'd prompt each other to unwind, and calmly inhale. We'd likewise utilize these minutes to commend each other's driving. Oddly enough, the commendations made a practically actual difference - like I could feel different feel-great synthetic substances siphoning into my veins. It was unusual. Ed gave great compliments but, then again, he is a car salesman.

Driving was simple and tomfoolery. I was in my blissful spot - in the driver's seat, centered, and mindful. The vehicle was a fantasy to drive - strong, planted, smooth, agreeable seats with massagers. I attempted to release my grasp on the wheel, inhale and unwind while apexing bends at 120 mph. My mantra was "smooooooooth." Once I hit the level fields of Ohio, I pounded down.

CHAPTER 18

Continued

We had commonly worked effectively of recognizing dangers and decisively staying away from them. For the most part. After the adequately high normal I had overseen through Pennsylvania, Dave was eager to assume control. Chris was giving us incredible input through Ohio and we were floating by I-70 at an extraordinary speed. I was watching out and Dan was keeping incredible tabs on every one of the information coming into the vehicle. The framework, but as of late devised, was working well.

Dave was passing through Ohio close to the Eastern edges of Columbus.
The setting was beginning to turn out to be more metropolitan. He was in a phenomenal furrow coming to and keeping up with a few exceptionally high paces. I saw a vehicle sitting in the middle. It seemed to be a fair sized American vehicle. I promptly said, "Brakes, brakes, brakes!"

"Goodness definitely, I see the brake illuminates there."

Dave answered. Different drivers ahead were all of a sudden
seeing the cop.

"No, Dave. There is a cop. Hit the brakes." I was sure that we
would have been rescuing him of an Ohio prison several hours later.

He nailed them with all of the beauty of a Floyd Mayweather
homegrown conversation. I think he twisted the rotors, As a matter of
fact. If not, that happened in the near future later. He was voyaging
some place during the 130's the point at which I originally shouted out
and I saw that he passed the cop actually doing 95.

When we went by I could see the cop investigating screen of the
PC mounted in his front seat, missing the scene of our sure-to-be
shining rotors just to his port side. I don't know what he was checking
out for sure other work he was keeping away from however that had
been an incredibly near disaster. That's what we concluded "Cop" was
an adequately reasonable guidance. "Brakes" would be the perceived
reaction to such an order pushing ahead. I expect we owe an obligation
of appreciation to some recently refreshed obscene site for saving us
there.

The stomach response when you barely try not to go to prison is to
slow down.
For this situation you can't do that. In the event that you burn through
five minutes under 90 you want to burn through ten over 100 to
compensate for the offense. Dave shook it off well and got back on the
choke. Dan and I stayed on high alert.

Radar identifiers are genuinely simple gadgets. The best one that I
have at any point utilized is the Valentine 1 framework. It utilizes bolts
to demonstrate which sensor (front or back) is getting the sign. There
are sure blare designs that you learn. Low power K or X band intruder
can be promptly excused as odds and ends shop entryway sensors. A
strengthening signal is moving towards you. Ka is generally no joking
matter and as a rule fixed.

VASCAR or radar mounted to a moving squad car normally
appears as an exceptionally amazing K band signal. Here and there,
however, you will get a cadenced blip of sign up ahead that seems
each 5-10 seconds and rapidly goes away.
That can persevere for a significant distance. It implies you are moving
toward a cop a decent distance ahead, moving in a similar course.
Cruising through Ohio we kept on getting these. The driving protocol

is to go as fast as you can to catch up and identify the threat while never cresting a hill or going around a blind turn without the ability to quickly brake down to within 10-15 miles per hour of the speed limit quickly and smoothly.

Chris had not revealed anything in front of us however I was unable to shake the inclination that we were going to blow past a cop going onto his morning shift and attempting to settle on Dunkin' Donuts or Krispy Kreme for the morning gift. I looked back through the back glass and I saw our second V1 mounted there. The sound had been switched off in light of the fact that it was apparent to the driver and commonly the commotions were repetitive. It was rotating with the windshield mounted one. They were deceiving each other into believing that the danger was there and resonating inside the vehicle. I advised Dan to switch it off and all went calm. Disappointed with the oversight we sped up difficult to compensate for 10-15 mins of relaxing (not surpassing 100-110).

Chris was additionally making some extraordinary time through Ohio. I was anticipating having him hand the rod to David Wiggins close to Columbus yet he actually had a few ground on us and Wiggins was currently at home with seasonal influenza so we proceeded on.

The web is brimming with clasps of hustling drivers doing mind blowing things in vehicles, stunt entertainers practicing vehicle control that makes every one of us need to go to floating school, and different presentations of driving greatness. What Dave did in
the early hours of that morning was something I had never imagined. My idea in retrospect of a co-driver had close to zero insight into what we were really doing that he wasn't stressed over the results. He was going through the most risky state in the Union for speeders so quick I thought my head was going to explode.

The police system changed once we got inside twenty miles of Chris. f he were to run over a decent speed trap he ought to head over to the shoulder and ask the cop for bearings. Like that, he could rest assured that the speed trap didn't move between him passing it and us passing it. He could likewise occupy the cop from seeing us as we floated past with a fast, "Look, a squirrel!" Unfortunately, we never got to test that plan.

It was 227 miles across Ohio on 70. Dave arrived at the midpoint of 108.10 miles per hour.

108! There isn't anything else to say there. It was the single vehicle road course Grand Prix of Ohio. Everything was working. Dave answered extremely well to both a solicitation to rivalry and inspirational statements. I tried to let him know when he made a smooth move and to salute him on his incredible minutes, of which there were many.

It didn't stop. It was 156 miles across Indiana on our course. He arrived at the midpoint of an unbelievable 110.12 miles each hour. This brought our excursion normal up to
99.33 mph. The paces were so incredible thus tenacious that I genuinely recollect very little about the state. The outskirts was a haze as the machine worked perfectly.

Things were working out in a good way. Whenever you take a gander at a guide of the course that we required some investment spent in the Southwestern United States, it is not difficult to figure the paces conveyed in Oklahoma, New Mexico, and Arizona will be the most serious. That isn't true. The midwestern states are generally profoundly watched however are extraordinary chances to construct speed. We did.

It was after seeing those midpoints when I understood that Danny Landoni, a person I had never met face to face and had simply addressed for around ten minutes before that evening, had given me one of the most significant presents I could at any point get. It was the way in to this record. His thorough and empowering reports of what lay in front of us on that game changing night had been an encouragement to drive as quick as I could wherever we went. That driving
tested Dave into driving the manner in which he had and subsequently set the vibe for the whole trip.

CHAPTER 19

Excessive Oil Consumption

It was the ideal opportunity for our first fuel stop. We were in Casey, Illinois - appropriately in the unexceptional center of no place. We got out as high on adrenaline as we had at any point been and honestly it was somewhat of a scramble. I gave Dan one of my Mastercards to go to the far side siphon and make it run while I arranged the close to side and got it into the helper tanks. I think Dave had should eliminate the two covers on the back tanks however the bathroom turned into a higher need. It didn't make any difference to me the least bit. He had procured it.

It was not careful however it was proficient. The Visas worked, the gas streamed, nothing burst into flames, and we were back out and about in nine not-completely rushed minutes. While it stayed hard to judge how quick a three man, three tank, multi charge card, three bladder, woozy early morning refueling break should take; we were content with the work and result.

We made it 815 miles on roughly 64 gallons of gas. That was a normal of 12.73 mpg. Going into the drive I had no clue about how terrible the efficiency planned to get. The greater part of my short spells of high midpoints had been around 15 mpg yet I knew that supporting those paces over these distances would be a lot of more regrettable. A normal of ten or less would have required an additional a fuel stop.

This was a long ways past what we would require. That implied there was not an obvious explanation not to press the gas pedal a piece harder, assuming that were even conceivable. As the chance of breaking the record sneaked in, I pondered regions where somebody might have sped up. With intriguing exemption, we had gone as quick as our quick vehicle would go. We experienced traffic however managed it conveniently. Very little was overlooked. It actually had the sensation of opening a Scrabble game with three seven letter words, significantly increasing each score. Without a doubt, it is going great however that couldn't really be supported all through the game.

I make no statements of regret about being serious. I was not content to be so outmaneuvered by Dave in this situation so it was hammer down when I got in the vehicle for my subsequent driving movement leaving the service station in Illinois. The plan was to have my more youthful sibling, Jeremy, lead us through the Illinois segment. He had moved there several years earlier for a task with a counseling firm in Evanston. As it so happened his better half was away with their fuel controlled vehicle, leaving him with their subsequent vehicle - an allowed to-rent after-tax cut Nissan Leaf. As well as being my sibling, Jeremy is my carbon balanced. His completely energized 89 mile range was not of extraordinary use to us that evening so he offered just passionate support.

Even without a spotter driving us, I was squeezing hard. I was driving extremely quick however it was smooth and agreeable. We had chosen to renounce significant video during the excursion. It had clearly been the focal point of Alex Roy's drive as he was arranging the narrative with Cory Welles however I ruled against it on three grounds.

First - we didn't require it as confirmation. We would have the conventional trifecta of cost receipts, gas receipts, and photographs toward the beginning and finish. We had cell meta information for the majority of those photographs, an evidentiary curio inaccessible only a couple of years earlier. We hosted third get-together observers all through the course and we hosted the effectively processed third gathering following information. It additionally seemed obvious us that assuming were to be attempting to counterfeit the run, it would be simple for the representatives of Waze, AT&T, or Trapster to look at our records and observe we were lying.

Second - the gamble of being pulled over, captured, and having the vehicle appropriated was incredibly high. Having open documentation of how quick we had obliged when and where that had happened would be an encouragement to alternate carrying out prison punishments in every one of the wards we had gone through. The presence of such proof felt terrifying regardless of whether we held the Fifth Amendment honor of not implicating ourselves.

Third, I didn't need anybody attempting to look great, invest investment let a camera know what was happening, and doing something besides committing regard for the street. Whenever Lee and I had spent the 2004 New York to Los Angeles drive recording for MTV, that was the game. That was where our brains were. Have this chance, really take a look at the tape, is the sound functioning admirably, do you think they got that, goodness there's the helicopter - accomplish something insane! It was excessively. It was an interruption we didn't require with this drive's power previously went up to eleven. We have a lot of short telephone recordings we can mince together into somewhat of a feature reel however I felt that was generally that would be necessary.

I was going quick. The initial 85 miles of my leg went by in only 44 minutes. That is a 115.91 normal. It was our quickest leg of the excursion. We were dazzled with one another and satisfied that we were exhibiting ourselves to be the type of drivers to be cutthroat in this blessed space. While we were available however, the vehicle started to struggle.

We were barely nine hours into the excursion. Soon after 6 AM neighborhood Central time, 7 AM Eastern. The vehicle gave me a caution to add oil at the following fuel stop. Obviously the vehicle didn't realize that the following fuel stop was 700 of the hardest miles of its life away. I had driven vehicles with this 5.4 liter supercharged V8 north of 50,000 miles over the past six years. I had never had one consume a drop of oil. This one was at the point of begging for some which must have meant that we were two or three liters low. I had just stuffed two.

We had kept the vehicle going through the principal fuel stop. The goal was to keep the motor and start on until we maneuvered into the parking garage of the Portofino the following day. The reason for this was to keep the Mercedes on-board PC ascertaining as an extra type of confirmation. The GPS beacon was our end-all-be-all of proof however it was extremely difficult to peruse because of the amount of information it would record. It was valuable in assistance as strong confirmation however the more photographable screens made for additional convincing articles. The route framework trip computations and the on board PCs would recount to the story in a speedy and absorbable way.

The oil necessity took steps to thwart that. The oil cap and filler neck go through the driver's side valve cover. I had no clue in the event that I could open the cap with the vehicle running. I expected that it could regurgitate oil all over. I called Charles, our Lambo tech. I called Brian, our administration chief. I called my guide from the Mercedes showroom. Nobody replied. We were 9 hours 4 minutes and 900 miles into an extremely extraordinary drive and I would have rather not taken a chance with the motor exploding in Illinois.

Dan grabbed the paper towels. I pulled over and electronically opened the trunk before shutting off the car. I set about releasing the cap and Dave grabbed a liter of oil. It was orchestral. As I poured the first I decided that it was probably a good idea to put a bit more in because there was no way that the threshold for an alert was just one liter. Dave grabbed the second liter we had packed. I put about a third of it in, tightened down the cap, and then we
hopped back in the car.

The error message went off and all systems were go. Well, they were as much go as they were going to get. The police scanner didn't work at all. It had worked quite well when I was running it around my house but when Forrest and I had programmed it for this trip we had messed up. We went county by county for the entire route through a frequency database web site and put approximately 1,400 frequencies in. It was the most advanced civilian level scanner I could find but it simply could not get through all of them quickly enough to find and grab an active frequency before we moved away from it and the strength became useless. We needed to have separated the country into separate banks of frequencies.

The CB was not working very well either. It had enough knobs and we had enough inexperience to properly booger it up. We played with it and consulted a couple of YouTube tutorials but it did not improve much. The 90 degree flexing of the K40 Antenna was not helping at speed. It appeared based on some gurgled responses that we could broadcast fairly well but such capability did not feel very useful at the time.

We resigned ourselves to a simple idea. Messages from the CB or Scanner could only slow us down. Nothing could motivate us to go any faster. We were driving as fast as we sustainably could every single moment on the road. The occasional blip from the V1 caused a short lift but those were usually dismissed easily. We didn't see any cops set up as speed traps. I recall passing a couple going in the opposite direction where we either braked down to a less conspicuous speed or we used the cover from a tractor trailer to occlude their line of sight.

The logic says if you need an average in the low 90's and you can minimize your stops then you should be able to drive between 95 and 105 most of the time and wind up where you need to be. The idea of going balls out the whole way and only stopping for gas or cops is admittedly sexier but that was not my planned strategy. Alex and I had discussed the driving protocols that led to his time and it was generally apparent that Richard Rawlings and Dennis Collins had done something very similar, albeit with several short pulls up close to 200 mph mixed in for good measure and bragging rights. They cruised along a few miles per hour above their desired average and waited for the average to climb.

David Diem and Doug Turner had claimed to have used a 155-55-0 strategy in their drive, cruising at 155 mph the whole time, slowing to 55 to past cops, and stopping for their five fuel stops and single ticket. In his dissection of their run, Alex Roy concluded that the fuel economy at a cruising speed that high failed to add up and resolved that they must have cruised at 95-110 the entire time. Although his final co-driver David Maher changed the strategy, initially Roy planned to rarely exceed 100 for more than a minute or two at a time. I had gone into the drive anticipating something similar.

The execution of our strategy had taken a turn due to the confidence imparted by some initial success and optimistic reports of what was ahead. We were pushing as hard as we could but it carried with it the looming feeling that it was on borrowed time. I knew that Alex had carried a high 90's average into the first Oklahoma toll plaza when he had a fuel system failure and I had heard that Rawlings was set to break 30 hours until he got caught in some miserable traffic in New Mexico. Would one of the slot machine wheels finally catch up to us and sideline our journey?

Dave had taken over driving once we added the oil and I got in touch with Tom Greulich who was going to lead us through Missouri. We left I-70 and took 255 around St Louis. We gave up the chance to see the iconic arch but we missed a lot of construction based on the instructions from Tom. He was extremely excited to be helping and loved the idea of the record. It seems like just about everyone who has been a car guy in the past forty years has at least contemplated the trip.

It was 172 miles through Illinois. Including the two minute stop for oil, we did it in 1 hour 44 minutes at an average of 99.23 mph. Into Missouri we hopped onto 44 and continued along. Tom was feeding us great info but ultimately there was not much to report.

The Cannonball accounts and the US Express documentation talked a lot about the sensation of seeing the sunrise over St Louis. There were some wonderful aged videos in the Cory Welles documentary that beautifully illustrated the emotions that you feel coming out of the first night of driving. It is difficult to describe the confusingly demoralizing refreshment of not being in jail, the car still running, being on schedule, finally being able to see well, coming across a lot more traffic on the road, and still having about 1,700 miles to go. You want to be able to look at each other as you relish in the victory of getting there with a resounding "You ain't seen nothin' yet!" but in reality you just want to get some sleep and have a shower.

During the time that Tom was serving as our scout car I got an email.
Since Dave was driving I looked down to see what it was. It happened to be a Facebook alert. That seemed like an appropriately mindless distraction from the day's work. It wasn't.

The email said that a friend had just tagged me in a post. Tom Greulich had a new status update - "Up early this morning helping a friend break some records - with Ed Bolian." I texted him immediately asking him to take it down. I knew that the risk was low but the last thing I needed was for one of his friends to know a cop and to put two and two together. If you browse through either of our profiles it becomes pretty easy to glean from a post like that we might be up to no good in a car. He obliged and we continued on our merry way.

Whatever pace the US Express guys were talking about when seeing the sun coming up in St Louis was far behind ours because it was still pitch black. I had never liked night driving. The visibility is worse and hazards are harder to see. In Atlanta there is traffic generally twenty four hours a day. My midnight runs around 285 in college were rarely in as much solitude as I would have liked. Our speeds during the course of the previous night had actually harkened me back to one of the first group drives that I organized at the dealership.

I called ten customers and told them that we were meeting at a restaurant near the start of a less trafficked state highway at 11 PM. We ate quickly and snapped some pictures of the rainbow of assembled Lamborghinis. We had a newly released Aventador, two Twin Turbo Gallardos with over 1,000 hp, and a handful of regular Gallardos there including my blue ex-Kimmi-the- prostitute mobile standing tall in the company of cars with indistinguishably less sordid pasts.

We started a conference call and everyone was using Bluetooth. We sent a guy in a BMW M3 out ahead and all hung back. We spent the next two hours taking turns getting about 2-3 miles worth of clearance and blasting off for as long as we felt like holding the accelerator down. I hit 185 mph with a measly 492 hp. Interestingly the stock horsepower output of a 2004-2005
Lamborghini Gallardo is exactly one less than my CL55 AMG. The guys with more hp were tickling 200 and shooting flames all over the place on each shift and lift. It was an amazing night where no one got hurt, no cars were injured in the making of the

production, and no one who could have gotten upset ever knew about it.

That was the way that Brock Yates and Dan Gurney had described their success in the 1972 Cannonball Baker Sea to Shining Sea Memorial Trophy Dash. Apart from the one ticket Gurney received, they claimed they blasted across the country at speeds up to 172 mph and that no one even knew about it. They said they broke all of these laws that they were protesting against and no one was the wiser, certainly no one had been hurt.

Either they were lying or we were doing things a bit differently. As the sun eventually came up and the roads become more congested, we had to maneuver the car more to maintain pace. Dave and I had some lengthy discussions about the posture of the car and strategies to minimize the risk of having the bystanding motorists call the police. I am sure that despite my best efforts there were a lot of interesting 911 calls as we also set the record for getting flicked off the most times in a 24 hour period. We said that an improvement we would have made was the addition of a scrolling digital message across the rear right section of the bumper with some sincere sounding apologies. Admittedly, reading something on a car at a 50 mph differential is difficult regardless of how upset you are.

Perhaps Yates had been correct and this was just a way the changing landscape of motor vehicle traffic in America was manifesting itself. They simply spent more time with no one around. Of all the interesting statistics that show how different 1970 was from 2013, one that I think it most interesting is the number of households. In 1970 the US Census reported that there were 63.5 million households. In 2010 there were over 114 million.
They were not all in urban high-rises so the geographic distribution of Americans was much more expansive. I think the longest we went without seeing a car was less than five minutes. For the 70's crowd it could have been an hour.

I tried to make sure that there was no steering input as we would pass a car, the same way that you would treat a slalom cone. That meant there would be minimal suspension lean perceivable outside of the car which would

trigger less anxiety from the people we were passing. It seemed to work.

Dave continued to drive through Missouri after picking up in the stop for my stint that had been abbreviated by the oil top off. The system was working. I was constantly giving him feedback that he was doing well, the coast was clear, and it was safe for him to stay on it. The most useful instruction that I recall giving him was that "Dave, I am going to make you drive 10 mph faster everywhere." It was imperative for the passenger to take ownership of how fast the driver could go. When I did that and took the onus of making more frequent instructions and in essence clearing him for acceleration more often, he responded beautifully.

I had left Adam Kochanski with the login information for the GeoForce tracking device. When morning came back in Atlanta I got a text from him. He said, "You guys are really flying. You just need to average 90 and you will break it. It is actually a little bit below that but I am not going to tell you what that is. Keep it up!" There was no bad weather to report and the construction monitoring sites he could check were still clear.

In 2 hours 31 minutes of driving, Dave averaged 105.30 mph on his 265 mile shift. About 11 and a half hours into the drive we stopped to change drivers near Springfield, Missouri. I took over to finish out that tank of gas. I continued out of Missouri and into Oklahoma along the Will Rogers Turnpike and got onto 40. Although the strain of navigation had not been difficult, it was quite a relief to have made it to the road where we would spend the lion's share of the trip mileage. As ridiculous as it sounds, it was like navigating the twisty bits of a race track and finally making your way onto the front straight. However hard you have been pushing, it had to be tempered by not wanting to overrun a turn. Now it was hammer down to an even greater extent.

There was a lot of anxiety at the first toll plaza. Dave pointed out the shoulder where he had seen the blue BMW M5 pulled over in the film. I had ordered toll passes for all areas we would pass through (stupidly in my personal name) so we did not have to stop. We breezed through the toll plazas maintaining a reasonable speed. Many states issue average speed tickets by mail when you pass through toll plazas in less time than you ought to. Fortunately none ever showed up.

Megan had slept in after the Halloween party and did not make it to church that Sunday morning. I got a text message from the guy that taught our newly married Sunday School class with me asking if I was going to be there to help. It occurred to me that I had not told him I was going to be otherwise indisposed that morning. I was driving and we were not responding to most of the text messages, emails, and calls so I let him figure that out on his own.

I was worried about Oklahoma and Texas. The last time I had driven through there in this way was on the 2004 rally and I had gotten five tickets. I eventually got them disposed of but they don't like speeders from other states in Texas. I think they don't like people of any kind that aren't from Texas. I had generally familiarized myself with the speeding and reckless driving laws around the country but had not dwelt on them too heavily. The monster under your bed is a lot less scary if you never think about what he actually looks like.

The five ticket day had been exceptional for me. I don't speed often in routine driving. I was pulled over near my house the other day for going 66 in a 45 that I had always thought was a 55. When the officer approached and revealed my misunderstanding about the speed limit, I asked for some consideration of the fact that I had not had a ticket in about seven years.
When he returned to the car he said, "You know, nines times out of ten, when someone tells me that it is a lie but it has actually been ten years since your last ticket. You have a nice day now." He let me go.

As I actually thought about it, the last ticket I had received was driving to see Megan at the University of Georgia to go out to dinner on the three month anniversary of our first date and it had been a decade since then. The irony abounds.

I do get pulled over a lot but it is frequently just for a police officer to see whatever car I happen to be driving. Getting pulled over in a sports car is fun. There are some easy answers to the normal barrage of cop questions.

"Sir, do you know how fast you were going?"

"Not really officer, I really wasn't trying to speed

though." "I clocked you at 105."

"Well for whatever it is worth, I was not trying to go that fast. If I were, it goes way faster than that. The car is nuts. Would you like to drive it?" Most cops are car guys but they aren't allowed to drive civilian cars while on duty.

"Oh, I can't do that. Besides my belt and gun would hurt those pretty leather seats."

"I am not worried about it, I will be happy to hold your gun." This usually generates quite a good laugh.

"Not today son."

"Well here is my business card, call me sometime and we can go for a ride when you are off duty." An invitation to pick this conversation up at a later and non-prosecutorial date.

I have engaged in that exact exchange many times and always gotten off with a warning. Only one has ever taken me up on the return trip for a ride. I was giving press rides at The Master's Golf Tournament in Augusta, Georgia in a rear wheel drive Grigio Telesto Gallardo LP550 Bicolore. I was sliding around turns on residential streets and generally misbehaving. Before long every cop in Richmond County showed up and I began my routine exchange. After being dismissed and asked to keep it down, one deputy returned a few hours later for his ride. He told me that he knew a road that we could get some speed on and it was just around the corner.

That corner was about twenty five minutes away and I obliged him although my reluctance increased as the trip lengthened. He told me he had been 180 mph in a Corvette ZR1 there. That was interesting. Chevrolet brought the ZR1 badging back in 2009 with a supercharged version of the C6 body cars. They were very quick but I fancied my Italian Bull to be up to besting it. As we drove I asked the cop how the surface of this road was. He told me that it had been awhile since he had been there so he wasn't sure. This was in 2011 so that struck me as being strange. I said, "Really, what year was the ZR1?"

"1991." He said calmly.

"You mean you haven't been to this road in twenty years? How far from here is it?"

"Oh, it was 95 or 6. It is just around this bend." This time he was telling

the truth. As I rounded the next bend in the Southeast Georgia road, I saw it.

"That is a bridge. Bridges are very bad places to speed. They have crosswinds."

"Oh we will be fine, let's see what it can do!"

"That is also a long bridge. We might be able to go fast but that bridge goes into South Carolina and I have a feeling that whatever jurisdiction you enjoy while wearing your work clothes ends halfway along it."

"Oh yeah, but if we need to run I know all of the good places to hide," he offered reassuringly.

"That is not a contingency I was planning on while going top speed hunting with a police officer riding shotgun." I had voiced my concerns and given the little bit of traffic that was on the bridge time to clear. Despite many reasons not to, I took the cop on a ride out onto the bridge. We clipped along to about 160. The air was stable and the surface was fine. I turned the car around and stopped in the street as the single oncoming car made its way into Frank Underwood nation.

I floored the Lamborghini and spun the rear wheels into third gear with the traction control on but limited. I pushed on, redline shifting, and perceiving the childish ear to ear grin of the portly, middle-aged Sheriff's deputy. We ran out of bridge before I could hit 200 but I know we hit the happy side of 190 on the Gallardo's difficult to read speedo. He was thrilled.

I drove him to his house on the outskirts of Augusta where his wife and young daughter were waiting to photograph him getting out of the car. As I climbed out of the cockpit to greet them, his wife said, "Sir, you have made his life. I bet once a week he says something about that black Lamborghini that those purty gals drove in the Cannonball Run movie. Is that what this is?"

"Yes ma'am it

is." Why not

roll with it?

Texas and Oklahoma both have a rolling statute of limitations. That meant that while I would generally be free from being subject to arrest in those states one year from the time of incident, that one year had to be spent
in each state for it to expire. I had no intention of spending that amount of time in either so it was a sobering reality to think that I might be subject to arrest in each state for the rest of my life. Hopefully that was

longer than the rest of this day.

Oklahoma was the only state where we encountered any real construction. There were three areas where the highway bottlenecked down to a single lane and we had to drive 50-60 mph behind a tractor trailer for 3-5 miles at a time. Fortunately the general traffic level was low enough that there was not a buildup of congestion in the merging areas. The times of being forced to go slow were a great chance to grab some water, loosen the grip on the steering wheel, and adjust your seat a bit to avoid cramping. It did seem, though, that I found myself in the driver's seat for every single frustrating leg we faced.

The prospect that many individuals appear to have when they envision what it resembles to drive this quick for such a long time is a possible deadness to it. It is valid when you drive 130-150 mph and dial back to 100 it seems like you could get out and walk quicker. That being said, the insight that we were horribly surpassing as far as possible never left me. The apprehension about capture did. The acknowledgment that the result of getting pulled over going 100 or 150 was possible a similar really filled in as a few comfort in saving your foot in a little longer and pushing a piece harder. At the point when conditions allowed, and they normally did, we were all the while flying. The vibe of persistently flipping a coin and it arriving on heads each and every time never left either.
Surely there was a tails coming.

Hygiene was an issue. I had bought some Neutrogena grapefruit scented facial purging materials. The divine beings have never felt something so astounding. "Pass me a grapefruit" was a famous and energizing solicitation to make. Halitosis was additionally an issue. The accompanying situation happened more than once.

"Dave, would you like a piece of

gum?" "No, I am great." He would

answer casually.

"Dave, I would like you to have a piece of gum."

I traveled 305 miles. It was the longest driving spell that both of us went on for the outing. Because of the traffic and development it was really the most un-testing leg while being the most disappointing. We halted around Yukon,
Oklahoma and Dave dominated. My normal for the leg was 94.82,

decent for how much traffic and the light hour driving. Our midpoints were reliably ten miles each hour more slow during the day than we had seen the past night.

Our side of the road potty break took under ninety seconds. We lauded the choice to make roadside refueling breaks and driver changes instead of remaining similarly situated for the whole tank of gas. I had generally moved toward it however at that point I would begin taking a gander at the math of being halted for 2-3 minutes all at once and would scrutinize the thought. Doing it again I would shut down at regular intervals/200 miles paying little heed to condition.

Dave dominated and got us to our second gas stop.

From Adam Kochanski, GPS Witness

Ed Bolian is somewhat of a puzzler. You never fully know what to think about him or the things he discusses. I met Ed a couple of years prior through a few common companions at the vehicle shows that we both regularly visited. The vehicles that he drove added to the to some degree amazing persona. We could never really tell if he was driving cars he owned or if they were from the dealership but Ed was always building his brand around the outrageousness of Lamborghini and the exotic car driving lifestyle.

Despite the expected hip bounce craftsman, gold chain, white jacket, womanizing, pet croc persona; Ed was unique. He generally left the vehicle shows on Sunday mornings right on time to go to chapel. Our spouses were particularly indistinguishable and managed everything well. Ed made a special effort to welcome me and numerous different folks to his occasions in general. He invited us into the showroom to drive vehicles and appreciate them close by him. Ed was and is put resources into working on the scene of nearby vehicle culture in Atlanta.

One of the primary discussions that Ed and I had about vehicles was about his advantage in Cannonball. I had seen Alex Roy at a neighborhood stop on his book visit and really have a marked duplicate of his book some place. I was aware of the thought and had seen the old films. What vehicle devotee hasn't fallen head over heels for taking an extraordinary vehicle out and opening it up on a long abandoned interstate?

Car fellow discussions are brimming with individuals asserting that they are going to go out and get some insane vehicle, how quick they drove the prior night, for sure their pretentious plans were with their next project. You generally need a genuine grain of salt to persevere through the puff. Ed appeared to be changed. Whenever he first approached our home for supper, he and Megan were driving a blue Gallardo that was a cycle unpleasant around the edges yet was still clearly to the point of making every one of our neighbors ask what was happening the following time our ways crossed. Whenever he discussed the NY to LA drive, it was not the tone of somebody dreaming. It was the tone of somebody planning.

Ed hinted that his co-driver, a person named Chris, was probable going to

back out. He inquired as to whether I was keen on going along. It was a peculiar solicitation, one I was energetic to get, yet an unusual proposition in view of how much time I had known Ed. I let him know that I would converse with my significant other about it.

Ed is excessively trusting. It could emerge out of the need to regard everybody as a purchaser in the vehicle business. It very well may be on the grounds that he is an extremely dependable individual himself. It very well may be from an idealism in humankind that the vast majority individuals have become critical of. I say that Ed is trusting on the grounds that he takes essentially all that I say at face esteem. The distrust that is normally essential in vehicle fellow trades never appeared to be available in him. It is presumably on the grounds that Ed really causes it to seem like anything you need to do, any vehicle you need to purchase, any ludicrous supporting course of action - is conceivable. Typical driving is by all accounts a genuinely howevertless assignment for Ed. He calls me while heading to work basically a couple of times each week and I attempt to reply. Each time we hang up, though, I feel like I am on the cusp of reestablishing my home value credit line and purchasing a Ferrari F430 Scuderia.

Ed had not bought the CL when I met him. He was everyday ing the Gallardo. At the point when he got into no-nonsense arranging mode in 2012, we checked out at each conceivable vehicle choice. I enjoyed a portion of the Audis - the 03 RS6 and 10+ S4s were incredible on fuel,

had arrived at a decent sticker cost, and made great power.
There was a huge load of reseller's exchange choices for themselves and it appeared to be great. Ed held returning to the AMG vehicles however even with Ed balance the bills, I was alarmed at the expense of upkeep. I'm a BMW and Porsche fellow. The Panamera Turbo was excessively and the M5 was out. The M3s I cherished were too little and the fresher ones were an excess of cash to destroy. Ed began to get optimistic and take a gander at Bentleys however at that point the orange Murcielago went along and that was finished. Ed immediately purchased an AMG vehicle and began sending me connects to Amazon shopping carts.

My better half and I had been attempting to get pregnant for some time so I realize that special case lingered. Whenever it worked out, I realize that I must let Ed down without any problem. I truly didn't. He took it quite well. He appeared to be accustomed to having individuals back out of this pursuit. There were no worries and he was as inviting as could be expected for me to remain involved.

As the last group met up, I headed toward Ed's home on the Thursday night before they left. I had met Dave Black at our nearby occasions and
Ed had portrayed his personality to me well. I met Dan Huang interestingly that evening. It was a diverse group without a doubt. It was likewise the most unusual passionate climate I figure I might have at any point found. Nobody appeared to know what to expect.

When they set off, Ed gave me the login certifications for the GeoForce Tracking Site. As they set off I monitored the feed. It took them a couple of moments to step out of the city and into New Jersey yet when they did, it was all business. Ed was in the driver's seat and was arriving at 140-145 in every straight and scarcely dialing back for the turns. In his common introduction exchange that we as a whole love, Ed had said that he didn't anticipate that the driving technique should direct numerous outings past 110. With the objective of a 93-95 mph generally normal to beat Alex Roy's season of 31:04, that seemed like all that sounds vital. Obviously that approach had been tossed at the window some place in the Lincoln Tunnel.

I messaged Ed to tell him that the sign was great and the updates were incessant. It was taking care of information consistently or two. There would be incidental sign holes of 3-4 minutes however with each ping it appeared as though they were accelerating. It was some exceptionally great speed. In the long run I napped off to lay down with my ipad set to the web address for GeoForce on the end table close to me.

When I got up around 8:30 AM on Sunday morning, I revived the webpage. They were at that point in Missouri. The information from the following programming showed that they were cruising along at 136 mph. They had been out and about for ten and a half hours. I connected the directions from the plotted point on the guide. I set that as the objective with the Red Ball beginning stage in Google Maps. They had voyaged 1,055 miles and were in a town that the following programming said was Rolla, Missouri. 1055/10.5 implied that they had a
100.48 mph normal. I did that math a couple of times since it just appeared to be incomprehensible. A 100 mile each hour normal! That appeared to be feasible for a little while, yet for 10 hours?

I switched the computation with the beginning stage where they were and the objective, the Portofino. They had 1,756 miles to go. 31:04 less 10:30 implied they had 20.56 hours to wrap up. That implied that they simply expected to average 85.38 miles each hour to break the record.

I messaged Ed that they were doing extraordinary. I barricaded it a piece and told
them that they simply expected to average 90 to break it. I was stunned, mooched to not be there close by to progress forward to what made certain to be an incredible achievement, yet entirely flabbergasted in any case. I went through the following day regularly checking in and doing a math to find out how the excursion was turning out. They didn't dial back. They didn't overlook anything. I truly can't make sense of the excitement of witnessing it one speck at a time.

I do a ton of track days in my vehicles. Each time, you appear, go through a drivers meeting, and see some new person just out of the display area in his new M3 or 911. They are dressed head to toe in the most recent Alpinestars Stig suit, gloves close by. They go out on the principal lap and twist the vehicle. A greater number of balls than ability. More talk than conveyance. Our own is a universe of cautious online entertainment looks into day to day existence, all around manicured pictures of our redirections and diversions painted for the world, and a presence intended to be innocuous while still self applauding. This wasn't that at all.

This was genuine Coke. Nothing diet, nothing zero calories. It wasn't watered down. It wasn't tempered for the general population. He didn't go out and purchase another Ferrari or BMW F10 M5 demolition hammer for the gig. He did it without anyone else with most of us contemplating whether he was really focused on it. He picked as quite a bit of a dark horse vehicle as could be envisioned for the drive. He concocted no reasons and showed no mercy - only two people who I had seen only a couple of days earlier with positively no thought what they were in for.

What a trip.

CHAPTER 20

Beating The AMEX Algorithm

We halted for gas the subsequent time in Groom, Texas. We had traveled 1,667 miles in 16 hours and 47 minutes. Our general normal was 99.32 miles each hour. That tank of fuel had taken us an absurd 852 miles. We were just 7.83 miles behind a 100 mph generally speaking normal. The moving normal was absolutely dropping as we went on as the day progressed. The delayed 130+ hikes were demonstrating really testing and without scout vehicles after we had left Tom in St Louis. We had left Oklahoma with an in-state normal of 94.78 mph implying that Dave had kept up with practically the specific speed that I had in his latest 260 mile stint.

Before the run I had been worried that there would be a glaring difference between the speed of my driving and Dave's. I was satisfied to be demonstrated so off-base. I don't think either about us figured we might have done any better compared to the next all of a sudden. I will say, and I accept that Dave would concur, that we went quicker on a portion of the legs when he was driving and I was exploring than when the jobs were switched. We would likewise concur that the justification for the slight inconsistency was the surge of guidance coming from the front seat. Whenever Dave had completed his meetings he expected to rest. I'm certain that I expected to rest more than I understood yet he made a superior highlight make it happen. That implied I ended up doing my own cop detecting a smidgen on a more regular basis. Hence I was glad to be taking a portion of the more vigorously dealt and actually troublesome sections.

Our first stop had been nine minutes of almost wonderful execution. This subsequent one was not that. Dave and Dan promptly dispersed to the bathrooms, both showing up genuinely insane. At the point when I opened the storage compartment I could see a couple of deviant drops of fuel aggregated around the line emerging from the siphon for the traveler side tank. At the point when I swiped my Visa it was declined. Darn it.

I ran inside and told them both to get outside to help. Dan snatched the pipe tape from the back tire capacity seat and went to deal with the fuel line. I was swiping each card in my wallet attempting to inspire them to take. A MasterCard

that I only here and there utilized at last got the job done - precious. I advised Dave to swipe his on the contrary side of the siphon. I saw the slight faltering as he considered the expense so I hit him extremely hard upside the head [in my head]. I don't recollect why I strolled behind the structure and peed on a dumpster in the parking area however I did. There was most likely a line or something.

That stop required twelve minutes. It was our most significant length of time fixed by an extensive degree. Whenever we got arranged in the vehicle I had two messages, one relating to every one of the two American Express cards that I convey. Deceitful charges were thought. My cell rang. It was AMEX. The agent reminded me they had dismissed two charges in Groom, Texas on my cards. They had seen the past charge in Illinois only eight hours earlier. There is a genuinely progressed, however not exactly progressed enough, calculation that they use. It told them since neither one of the charges was close to an air terminal and the distance voyaged was done excessively fast to have been finished via vehicle they consequently declined the charges.

I offered no clarification with respect to why these were as a matter of fact authentic charges however I consoled her that my cards wouldn't depart my ownership for the following 24 hours and asked that she endorse all possible charges made to the record. "Assuming I request each and every as-seen-on-television item on the shopping network from a phone in Mongolia simply accept I wanted that rainbow of Snuggies and many, numerous expandable hoses. Allow them to send them on!"

As we went through Texas it was beginning to turn out to be clear exactly how tired we both were. I had napped off for around fifteen minutes during an off shift the principal night and the adrenal high was beginning to diminish. I attempted to rest as Dave drove before however we were stupendously quicker when I was on alarm offering him counsel on where, when, and how to pass. This was a group activity and you never got to quit paddling for very long.

The beg of Texas was routine aside from a game bicycle that attempted to remain with us for a brief period. This additional a component of obviousness and peril I didn't need. The last thing we really wanted was for me to find a bike moving to another lane. It additionally made it appear as though we were hustling, a considerably more unsavory offense than speeding. We happened upon a red minimized vehicle that disliked the bike and made a forceful swing at it. This incensed the cruiser who dashed off. The driver took a similar action at me

as I passed however we continued away without issue.

I had pressed the optics yet they had been especially pointless. The stories of stabilized scopes were intriguing but our line of sight was unlikely to be radically different than that of a static police officer so the visual strain and the distraction from all of the other data sources sounded like quite the tradeoff. They were likewise truly costly and I needed to keep a couple of secret weapons in the event that I basically wasn't anyplace in any kind of mood of the record on this first endeavor and expected to add to the arsenal.

I purchased the returnable optics to have available if necessary yet when I glanced through them it was a lager goggles insight. I had accepted that would be the situation, consequently the perfectly protected Bass Pro Shops unique bundling and receipt back at home on my office work area. I had not expected the visual sharpness of Dan Huang. I for the most part have an intellectual level capacity to recognize vehicles in view of shapes, lights, and other obvious prompts and albeit this was the pre-Lasik Ed, my rectified vision was very good.

He was on a completely unique level. I was surprised at his capacity to see and peruse this stuff. I could scarcely determine what variety a vehicle was when he was perusing us the tag and clearing it as being non military personnel as opposed to police. Exceptional stuff. I was told by an unusual secondary teacher once that there was a task relating to the cultivating of chicken eggs that was just staffed by Asians. It included zeroing in on a spot on each egg to decide ripeness. He said white individuals were unequipped for making it happen. I don't know whether that is valid and I am don't know whether it is bigoted but rather I was beginning to accept it in light of Dan's performance.

Dave's significant other, Lisa had been genuinely radio quiet all through the excursion. Megan had messaged a piece to Dan helping him to take care to remember me. Dave's telephone rang in Oklahoma and it was Lisa. It intruded on one of the applications that we were utilizing and it was in one of the traveler side mounts so I addressed it. She knew to the point of having a "see no detestable/hear no shrewd" mindset about it so she essentially asked how things were going. I told her that they were going well and that we were cautiously optimistic. She said, "Would I like to realize how quick you all are going?"

"That's what I question yet let me say that we are exceptionally pleased with your better half and his velocities are adequate." That felt like the right word.

There was a second in Oklahoma where Dave as driving. I peered down at the Garmin screen which had been assessing our appearance time in view of its projection that we would average as far as possible until the end of the outing. It read 2:04 AM. In my mind we had left at the 10 PM target. That intended that after the time change, assuming we had just arrived at the midpoint of as far as possible until the end of the drive we would match the Roy/Maher season of 31 hours 4 minutes.

It was a stunning sensation, one I had been altogether ill-equipped to encounter. Getting the normal north of 90 mph had felt better. This felt euphoric. We had a shot. Presently we simply expected to not get captured or break the car.

Our rates were proceeding to be around 10 mph more slow during the day. It didn't have anything to do with testicular backbone, anxiety toward imprisonment, or ability; it was traffic. There were only a ton of vehicles and trucks out and about. Every collaboration with one was the point at which we needed to dial back. We had commonly quit caring how quick we passed individuals. In the event that the path was clear we didn't slow down.

I had not been certain the way in which we would return home.

Since I had truly felt that there was an incredible opportunity we would overcome the midwest and take out the white banner I had not made any earlier plans. Assuming we made it the entire way to Redondo Beach, transporting the vehicle home would be costly, as would three latest possible moment trips to Atlanta. That's what we concluded assuming we broke the record, a treat to ourselves is transport the vehicle home and fly. Assuming that we fizzled, we would need to persevere through two additional days of one another's organization in the imprisonment of the CL. Now, as business situated as the drive had been, our understanding was worn genuinely slight.

Dave had enrolled a companion to help us without a second to spare to lead us through New Mexico. Jules Doty drove a ravishing white Porsche 964 and gave us some incredible understanding with regards to what we could anticipate. Dave and Dan were taking care of me extraordinary intel from the on board hardware and we were making amazing time. We had seen not very many police so far yet there was a genuinely extreme window of police movement coming up. The spotter's recommendation was "Disregard the police on the left half of the road...it's a medication bust...they will not see you."

As we drove past he was obviously correct and the nearby police force seemed

keen on seeing what the suspect's vehicle would resemble with the inside totally taken out. While it seemed like we had commonly mixed in through the early piece of the excursion, I accept that our vehicle and Jules' Porsche were the main non-American vehicles in the territory of New Mexico.

As we had moved away from the more populated areas of Texas and New Mexico I had begun to get a couple of opportunities to forcefully let some circulation into the vehicle more. Prior in the drive Dan and I had invested some energy resetting the on board PC information and watching it ascertain the efficiency at 100, 110, 120, 130, 140, and 150. It got down to 11 on the higher finish of that range yet we determined that we were unable to go quick to the point of getting terrible enough mileage for it to matter.

I was speeding up as hard as we had into clearings all through the outing. The vehicle's five speed programmed is very vigorous, as a matter of fact it was the very one that advanced into the significantly more remarkable Mercedes McLaren SLR somewhere in the range of 2005 and 2009. It's control unit deciphered the more grounded choke inputs as a solicitation to downshift all the more promptly, hold the cog wheels longer and execute the movements a touch all the more savagely. It made Dan and Dave a piece anxious. They advised me that regardless of whether it foil our mileage for the excursion attempting to invest that much energy over 140 mph wouldn't benefit us in the event that the vehicle didn't get us there. I consented to slow the speed increase and give the vehicle an opportunity to rest.

I traveled 260 miles which got us into New Mexico. My leg required 2 hours 42 minutes at a normal of 96.30 mph. We were discovering a few less populated region of the southwest and were traveling through at right over the speed expected to try not to get dependent on precious stone meth. I surrendered the reins close to Encino, NM and Dave was prepared to go.

He exhausted rapidly. Nobody could fault him as we had been out and about for around 20 hours. We cut his excursion off at around 210 miles in a totally common choice. The normal for that leg was Dave's slowest at 92.65, still amazing given the situation and higher than the normal of some other crosscountry drive of all time. Even with the sub 100 averages we were seeing in shorter shifts during the day, we were still carrying a moving average that was well over 100. It was a demonstration of how quick the principal night had been.

The greatest side effect of Dave's weakness was not dialing back or dozing

off - it was dissatisfaction. Each time a truck or another driver would pull out before our vehicle Dave would answer with a downpour of exclamations and a plainly jumbling level of outrage. I told him on a few events that we would go quicker for longer if he could unwind. His reaction was generally that he really was loose yet I couldn't help disagreeing. Your mouth and cerebrum can't be simply detached. It was a steady battle however he started to work on over time.
He finished his driving movement, Dan had snoozed off toward the back, and I dominated. Dave was prepared for quite a while to rest.

I detest the utilization of foulness. I feel that Jerry Seinfeld said all that needed to be said when that's what he said "Obscenity is an incredible easy route of parody and the explanation I don't utilize it is that I am worried about the joke quality anguish." I feel the same way about everyday discourse. In the event that I can't come to my meaningful conclusion utilizing adequate and un-questionable

language then I want to attempt once more in my head.
Deliberate and smart discourse likewise causes individuals to appear as though they are more sure about the thing they are doing. That serves me well professionally.

Dave's response to a Buick Lesabre pulling out before him was not hostile to me at all. It essentially uncovered to me that he was less formed at that time in charge of the Mercedes than I would have enjoyed him to be. At that phase of the drive we were both substantially more exhausted than we let ourselves concede. Signals like this were actually quite important in light of the fact that we expected to help each other unwind and remain on track. It was not difficult to see times when that consideration was wavering.

The I-40/Route 66 piece in New Mexico had been under development for very nearly 10 years. Jules had tried saying the development was finished and individuals capable appeared to be really amped up for it also. There were signs each couple of miles saying thanks to the New Mexicans for their understanding. It felt like the rainbow God sent to Noah saying, "I had to do that, sorry, but I won't do it again." Knowing the amount it had held up Alex and Richard I was unceasingly grateful.

The "how can we pull off this?" sensation had not faded. There probably been many police that had been made aware of this and were chasing after us somehow or another. It needs to ultimately find you. We were checking the air for planes or helicopters. It was basically impossible to tell the number of individuals were adversely mindful of what we were doing. We had no genuine decision except for to press on yet things couldn't continue to go that well everlastingly, right?

Rather than an extraordinary and emotional race from ocean to sparkling ocean this was transforming into a genuinely exhausting yet fast drive by three individuals who shared a few exceptionally odd associations preceding the excursion. There were no high velocity police pursues, no furry moves, no brushes with death, and nothing that would have been extremely engaging to watch assuming we had been getting everything on record. The show was all in getting the vehicle, the group, and our attitudes where they should have been in New York. The rest had truly been going down the Hot Wheels track. I had anticipated that the result should be half in view of the wild factors and half on us. The a large portion of that was us, I speculated was 30% in light of readiness and 70% on execution. That was turned around and maybe much more awry. I had done everything that I could to get us to the beginning line with an opportunity. It appeared as though that may be all that we required on this suddenly sublime day.

It had appeared to be insane to reserve a spot at the Portofino before we left so I didn't. There were essentially an excessive number of impediments between New York and Redondo Beach to legitimize a non-refundable lodging. Riding through New Mexico we were under 1000 miles out. The time had come to settle on the decision. I called them and booked two spaces for us. It didn't seem like the lodging was exceptionally dealt that season of year.

I took over in Gallup, NM not knowing what I was available for. Dave was depleted sufficient that he staggered gravely escaping the vehicle. As we entered Arizona the Garmin ETA was 1 AM. That implied a speed limit normal until the end of the outing would have gotten us a 30 hour time. The advancement of the territory was hard to appreciate at speed however frightful when we understood how different the scene was as we went along. One man's holiday spot is another's crosscountry speeding obstacle.

America is an extraordinary country that offers a wide assortment of landscapes.
There were a lot of modest communities spread many miles from anything somewhat intriguing. I recollect the inclination, "What needs to turn out badly in your life to wind up living here? Most likely they can't be generally in witness security, right?" The variety of our nation makes it incredible. Oddly, it was the normal interest among three totally different individuals that was making this group work effectively.

The main region where we saw a ton of police movement, both fixed and moving, was simply into Arizona. The Sanders - Chambers region felt like cop
back street. Bunches of speedy decelerations stand apart on the GPS information in that portion. Luckily there was typically adequate admonition either from the countermeasure gadgets or from Dan's laser Asian vision. The totally open desert left couple of chances for successful concealing spots. It gave the idea that these parkway patrolmen were undeniably more keen on observing travelers crawling into the 90s or medication sprinters than crosscountry ban street racers.

One vehicle truly tossed us. It seems like each vehicle out West is an American truck or SUV. Assuming that you see an extremely spotless, white, late model Tahoe however, you want to dial back. There was one up ahead and it had a few stickers. I was unable to see any lights yet it was by and large sticking to as far as possible, dubious. Dan could see that the tag was legislative yet he was unable to make out any of the other distinguishing characteristics.

A cop it is not difficult to move the other way. A speed trap is for the most part distinguishable. Hypothetically we had seven semi-excess executes to caution us of those - Waze, Trapster, V1, Passport, Scanner, CB, Dan/Binoculars.
The third chance that is inordinately difficult to defeat is a cop before you moving in a similar bearing. The technique is to jump your direction dependent upon him by utilizing the shade of different vehicles and bends to hinder his view until you are right behind him. Then you need to pass the cop at an extremely slight 2-3 mph differential while still under 10 mph over the speed limit.
This happened to us twice.

In everything going on here, I was driving and the vehicle up ahead ended up being a Department of Homeland Security Tahoe. After that was found I passed him rapidly. He attempted to keep up so that a piece might see what was happening yet that was not occurring. I lost him quickly.
The subsequent time was before in the drive. Dave was in Oklahoma and the cop that he stumbled upon was an Indian Reservation cop. Presently as well as smoking Peyote and taking a quarter at a time from bus voyages through senior residents by means of sparkling gaming machines, local Americans get to police their own territory. It is a terrible spot to get pulled over. You would have felt that I was requesting that Dave sing karaoke to a crowd of people of each young lady that he had at any point had eyes only for. He could never have been less open to passing a cop. I thought I must call 911 and report a mishap behind us in the eastward path to get the dispatcher to get this person to bounce the median.

Fortunately, Dave at last made it by him so I didn't need to carry out another wrongdoing that day.

The drive down from Flagstaff was the most exceedingly terrible leg of the excursion. I was crashing straight into the sun. It ought to have been clear that when you drive due West through a whole day you must invest some energy crashing straight into the sunset. It ought to have likewise been predictable that when you drive 100 mph into the sun it really draws out the dusk you get to encounter. I had not mulled over everything. It could never have changed the way that we needed to haggle through the peril yet it would have been great to get ready for it intellectually. While dashing drivers realize that they will be investigating the sun at one point on each lap they put a piece of tape on the part of the windshield that hinders their perspective on the sun. Evidently it does some incredible things. I discovered that afterward from Charles. With our munititions stockpile of each kind of tape we possessed the ability to convey this solution.

The vehicle was disgusting yet that hadn't made a difference up to that point. Each bug and bit of soil on the windshield glared to make perceivability unimaginable. Dave depicted it well. "Maybe we had passed through a prophetically calamitous tempest of beetles whose guts were loaded up with super-stick." When you hit an all around took care of bug going 150 mph it leaves a dash of goo on your windshield in excess of a foot long. Washer liquid was no counterpart for itself and we were passed on to press on.

It was hopeless. The dead spaces in the blinding light were the trucks which couldn't see by the same token. I had on dull energized shades and I was wedging my head against the top of the vehicle to utilize the highest point of the windshield outline as an improvised sun visor. I'm too tall to even think about utilizing ordinary sun visors. They block the whole street from a vantage point currently close to the main event of most vehicles. This was a piece of the outing where in typical conditions a driver would have pulled over, got something to eat, and trusted that the sun will set. We needed to continue to drive and we expected to continue to go fast.

At one point I was moving toward two huge trucks, one behind the other.
The back truck was a FedEx truck who chose to pass the front. I was moving toward quick, around 135 mph. I streaked my lights at the driver and braked hard for a couple of moments prior to lifting to move the vehicle's weight and reestablish the capacity to control. I blared my horn and wound up passing the truck with two of my tires off of the street in the left rough median.

It was clearly and frightening to Dave and Dan yet I had the option to easily recuperate. The transporter probably could not have possibly had the option to find in his mirror because of the differentiation between looking forward and in reverse in those light circumstances. It was as close a call as we had. The main setbacks from the rough terrain outing were a broken lower left haze light that the vehicle actually wears gladly and the dislodging of one of the four laser sticking heads. I genuinely can't completely accept that we never broke the windshield.

The CB usefulness had not gotten to the next level. The Cobra 29 I purchased was gigantically movable and we were excessively unpracticed with it to truly make it happen. I ought to have gone with a straightforward Radio Shack form like I had utilized beforehand. Bonehead resistant was a striking characteristic for our hardware to have.

We wound up just having the option to hear intermittent murmured interjections from the drivers that we passed. The majority of what we heard was their sputtered negative comments about the silver Mercedes four wheeler that was going extremely quick. We utilized the CB to move beyond certain drivers. I would mimic the truck on the left which was obstructing us with a passing move and ask the driver on the option to tap his brakes so I could come past. Then I would pretend to be the trucker on the right inviting the trucker on the left to come on over, telling him the coast was clear.

The wellbeing conversation about the compatibility of this record stays unwinnable. There is, notwithstanding, a superficial concern and afterward a more profound comprehension of the security suggestions that is more fascinating to consider.

We drove the nation over in under a day and a half. Think about all of the drama that you have experienced in a car for the last three thousand miles, which on average in America is four to five months of driving. Consider the quantity of individuals messaging, removing you, converging without looking, painting their toenails, weeping for reasons unknown, eating, drinking, resting, perusing, and doing everything aside from driving. We saw all of that ludicrousness in less than two days.

Driving three thousand miles was more dangerous than the speed. We had one near fiasco with the law and one with a truck however we made it securely on the grounds that each of the three of us were entirely occupied with the undertaking of driving. I keep up with it is probably the most secure inclination time I have spent in the driver's seat. I don't anticipate that that should convey any weight with individuals who will see this as hostile yet I am not shocked at all that this went off without incident.

It was lucky that every one of the three of us stayed committed to proudly policing each other for exhaustion. We were prepared to move forward when any other person required a break. After the nightfall I was in the mountains in Western Arizona. It was appallingly stunning and I got pretty dazed. I was going as quick as possible yet getting extremely drained. I saw a bunch of tail lights in front of me and feeling like getting them was unimaginable. My eyes essentially couldn't adjust from the force of the nightfall prior. I advised Dan to observe us the following service station and to not quit conversing with me until we got there.

This was our slowest segment. I review the on board PC read around 95 mph for the leg. It regularly read somewhat higher than was valid, presumably because of us resetting it in the event that we had a sluggish stretch to support our certainty. The real speed from our following programming was 89.43 mph for 237 miles.

This was our last gas stop. It was in Seligman, AZ. We had traveled 2,390 miles in 24 hours and 24 minutes. That tank had just taken us 723 miles yet with under 500 to go we were more than fine with a deficient refuel. The stop required seven minutes and we were unquestionably not in our best form.

I took a gander at the distance to objective during that last leg and it being 650 miles. We had been driving for almost a whole day and we felt like we were close yet we actually had an outing to Miami from Atlanta to go. It was discouraging however our speed was as yet solid. The general normal by then had really dropped down to 97.95 mph yet it was getting dim and the streets were clearing up of different clients. It was reviving to realize that we each just had another driving spell, we didn't get an opportunity to bungle a refuel, and that it was at last dark.

We crossed the Arizona line in Needles. We had arrived at the midpoint of 93.25 mph across Arizona, all in all an accomplishment given the extended feel of the most recent two hours of our lives. The setting of normal paces on good to go crosscountry drives was restricted. With the quickest time ever in Cannonball contest, Dave Heinz and Dave Yarborough had arrived at the midpoint of 86.9 mph onto a period of 32:51 in '79. David Diem and Doug Turner arrived at the midpoint of 89.4 mph to accomplish 32:07, the quickest season of the US Express rivalries. The Rawlings/Collins Ferrari time in 2007 was 31:59 with a general normal of 87.9. Street enhancements and course contrasts made the below and quicker time conceivable. Alex Roy and Dave Maher had been the main pair to average north of 90. Their 90.5

normal had acquired them at a little more than 31 hours.

The slowest and most unthinkable inclination leg of our excursion was still comparable to each of these. Having their chronicled encounters accessible to expand on could never have been any more significant. Our machine was getting drained however we were soldiering on. We were not free and clear presently though.

During the excursion I dozed two times for 15-20 minutes each time. Dave rested multiple times around thirty minutes each time. I awakened while Dave was driving in Eastern California. We were totally flying by certain trucks. I could barely handle it however I was satisfied that he had kept the speed up. The lights were streaking in a twist speed design. We were South of the Vegas to LA return traffic and the main other street clients were trucks. The visual up ahead was dreamlike. There was an interminable line of trucks only a couple of feet off of every others' guards and a totally vacant path to one side. I had never seen a situation so thickly loaded with no overwhelming occurring. Ordinarily it seems like transporters all need to travel a couple of miles each hour quicker or more slow than the ones close to them so there is a steady passing and maneuvering for position. Here they should have been a pack of trunk-to-tail elephants in a residue storm, never escaping line. It was confidence in that the norm that permitted Dave to barrel past them all. I cleared the slobber off of my cheek and began to set myself up for the last leg.

When the truck route diverted, I remember looking at the stars. There was almost no other light visible apart from our headlights and the moon was casting an eerie glow across the desert. They were so bright and you could see every single one of them. The spectacle was truly beautiful and it offered an unexpected perspective on the undertaking at hand. We were close enough to achieving my decade long dream that I truly felt like I could taste the salty air blowing inland from the Pacific Ocean. In this big experience though, I get a chance to see just how small we are in the eternal vastness of creation.

We all need significance. We all strive for greatness, excellence at a task we are qualified for. Had we found it?

I think it was Dave that alerted me that I sounded like someone enjoying a psychotropic substance while watching Fantasia. I was deliriously tired.

The first question that people ask when you talk about doing something like this is, "What about the cops?" We actually only saw four or five police

parked near the road and only passed ten to fifteen police cars moving in either direction. It was a non-issue. Our detection devices worked well and the visual diligence of having three people in the car was hugely effective. Even as the police loom as the scariest boogeyman seeking to foil such a trip, they had to be treated as a simple variable in a cold and emotionless equation. The further we got into the trip, the more numb and detached that calculation became. The hard science of preparation helped save us in the trying moments. As we fatigued and found ourselves less capable of decision making, we fell back on structured procedure and established regimen to proceed.

I took over in San Bernardino. Dave had driven 214 miles and we had about 209 to go. His average for that leg was 95.82 miles per hour. It was a gargantuan effort. An average like that against the exhaustion we felt made Dave seem like Sampson, hair cut off, eyes gouged out, beaten within an inch of his life but still ready and able to tear the entire house down. He had.

I was glad to have the final leg. It felt right. Dave and Dan were all for it as well.

CHAPTER 21

The Final Push

As we entered the LA Basin we knew that we were probably going to break the record as long as the car didn't break and I didn't get arrested. We voted on whether to take it easy and cruise in with a mid 29s time or to push it with the chance to break into the 28s.

The latter obviously carried a much higher risk of accident, getting lost, or me getting arrested. Dan was pretty content to take it easy but Dave was 100% go. His decisiveness was new. A short day before he was so very along for the ride that he would hardly voice a preference of fast food establishment. 2,500 miles into the craziest game of highway Russian Roulette we had all ever played, he was ready to keep pulling the trigger!

He claimed that this all-out strategy was now the only way he knew how to operate. Sorry Lisa. I was leaning towards slowing down mostly due to the fact that I had not spent any time pondering the implications of decimating the records by more than two hours. Despite that, I agreed to push as long as the other two would stay vigilant. We pushed and I averaged around 100 through the dense Los Angeles metropolis. The traffic in LA had been an unpredictable elephant in every strategy session. There is no time where you can plan with confidence on it being easy, even in the middle of the night.

I said an out loud prayer for continued safety and to get us there without getting arrested. Dan and Dave obliged in a way that was probably beyond what their typical theology would tolerate but I appreciated their camaraderie in the moment. I do doubt God cares that much about this sort of activity but I know Megan was praying fervently that I wouldn't have to do it again. He listens to her.

Dave did say, "You are not going to close your eyes are you?"

The route was generally down the 15, onto the 210, and then the 605 to Redondo Beach. Every navigational instruction got triple repeated and no one was annoyed in the slightest. It sounded more like fingerpainting instructions to four year olds than the last instructions of the greatest outlaw drive of all
time but that was the tone the car needed.

Google, Garmin, and Waze all disagreed on the best route as we snaked into Redondo Beach . A solo driver would have to pick one. A pair of drivers might be able to weigh two against each other. Having a third person in the car meant we could look at them all and objectively decide what was best.
We ended up using parts of the Google and Garmin routes but it was very chaotic. We were tired, it was dark, and we had no experience on the roads. Dan had truly come into his own in the most ridiculous role I am sure he will ever fill in his life, riding from sea to shining sea with no control and the most ambiguous set of expectations anyone could pose.

He compiled all of the data, processed the pros and cons, and seamlessly presented navigational instructions for Dave to confirm and me to execute.
Late in the game, with it all still on the line, we hit a true symphonic crescendo of teamwork.

The only red light we sat at after New York was crossing the street into the parking lot for the Portofino Hotel and Marina. I forgot to use the traffic light changer and we let it cycle. The next morning I checked it when we left the parking area and it worked perfectly. Sorry Forrest.

We entered the parking lot to the Portofino at 11:46 PM PDT on Saturday, October 20th, 2013. We stopped the timers and put the car into park. Each of us grabbed our cameras and began taking pictures of everything
- the Garmin screens, the stopwatches, the other phones, maps, and
  screens.

Our family pet growing up was a 232 pound English Mastiff named Caesar. He is the laziest, goofiest, drooliest, most gentle dog ever and his favorite thing in the world was chasing cats. One day I was out with him and he was running around. After not seeing him for a few minutes I heard a faint panicked meowing. I turned a corner to see Caesar's eyes as big as they could get and a very confused look on his face. He had caught something he had been chasing all of his life and now he had no idea what to do next. I walked over and pried his enormous jaws open, liberating the petrified but completely unharmed kitten.

For a moment we just sat in the car looking at each other in the same way that Caesar had looked at me that day. We had chased it so hard and we actually did it. What was literally the next movement that our bodies needed
to make?

The trip had taken us 28 hours 50 minutes and 26 seconds. We drove 2,813.7 miles at an average of 97.55 mph. Our moving average discounting the 46 minutes of stops was 100.22 mph. Our three fuel stops had taken 9, 12, and 7 minutes respectively. That accounted for 28 minutes of the stopping time. The other 18 minutes had been the side of the road stops for oil, driver changes, and urination.

We traveled through 13 states, 93 counties, passed 5 speed traps and 12 moving police cars using 34 devices and countermeasures installed in a 9 year old car with over 115,000 miles. We were never pulled over and received no tickets during or after the trip. We averaged 13.2 mpg and the top speed reached was 158 mph. It required the work of 29 people in various capacities.

We parked in front of the hotel and asked the Valet to take a picture of us in front of the car. I am sure that three stinky, tired guys and a car covered in bugs having its own stench of fuel was a unique sight to him. He was by no means a wizard of digital SLR functionality but you can tell we are there. We shut the car off.

I called Megan. The emotion was overwhelming. We had the nav computers and multiple stopwatches displaying the time but I still could not believe it. We had beaten the existing record by 2 hours 14 minutes.

How had that been possible? It was just before 3 AM in Atlanta but she answered the phone on the first ring. Tears were streaming down my face and I could barely manage the words, "We did it." She was more relieved than happy or congratulatory. She asked if I was ok and I tried to reassure her even if the composure of my voice didn't. I was too scared that the time was somehow miscalculated to tell her what it was. Dave, Dan, and I had agreed not to tell anyone the exact time until we dealt with a press release. That boundary did not apply to her but I still couldn't form the words.

I managed to tell her that we had beaten it by over two hours. "What?" she yelled. "Are you kidding? How?"

"I know sweetheart. I still can't believe it. We just went really, really fast. Get some sleep and I will call you when I am up in the morning. I love
you."

We went to check into the hotel and dropped the bags in the rooms. I asked the receptionist if she had ever had anyone coming in during the middle of the night talking about Cannonball. She said that she had only worked there for a couple of months and had never heard of it. The valet had not either.

I fired them both but Dave said I did not have the authority to do that. I thought I had just earned the privilege but I guess not. One day I will have to go back there and host a quiz show competition on Cannonball Trivia.

I honestly couldn't believe the time. The lack of fanfare at the finish made it a bit anticlimactic but I was definitely a bit sanguine about the whole thing. We had just beaten a world record that had been pursued for over forty years by a margin of over ten percent. I knew it would be unbelievable to the people I wanted to believe me. I knew that we had proof but the idea of having to prove this kind of a time felt unbelievably daunting.

I texted Adam, my parents, Chris, Ash, Danny, Tom, Jules, Nick, Charles, Forrest, and the rest of the team to let them know that we had done it. I told them that we had agreed not to tell anyone the exact time until we got home, compiled the proof, and arranged the release. We told them all we made it and we were safe. I thanked them all for coming with me on this journey in whatever way they had.

Of course they were all able to figure out that we had shattered the record by the timing of those texts.

We were as hungry as we were tired. Dan looked for nearby restaurants that were open at midnight and found a Denny's. The irony of getting back into a car after that drive was not lost on us. I am not superstitious but it almost seemed morbidly appropriate for us to be involved in some horrific crash on the way to eat an omelet after breaking nearly every traffic law in the United States the day before.

The large Samoan gentleman that was waiting on all two of the occupied tables in the Redondo Beach Denny's was not worried about us being secret shoppers. Dave was not thinking too well which added to the hilarity of each exchange. He put together an order of eggs, bacon, and some hash browns.

The expressionless face of the waiter was difficult to read but there was a clearly condescending, "why is this idiot messing with me" guise as he pointed to the menu and said, "That's a Grand Slam." The most popular item on their menu.

I had an omelet. I think Dan had fried chicken fingers for the eighth time in three days but I could be wrong. We ate and headed back to the hotel.

The Portofino Hotel offers earplugs to help you sleep through the moans of the indigenous sea lions. We didn't need them.

The next morning I woke up around nine and signed onto the hotel wifi. I went to the tracking device web site and logged in. I tried to export the data for the prior two days and the site locked up. I called their support line and asked them to perform the same export. The technician sent me the file and it was missing half of the data including the start and finish of the run.

There was not a good way to tell if the device was reporting during the drive so we never knew how accurate it was. I called them back and they confirmed that they had a server issue but assured me that it was there and that they could get it. He emailed me the full file a few excruciatingly long hours later. It clearly shows when we left, when we arrived, and how far we drove.

As I said, I was truly concerned that even with as much proof as we had, people who had any experience in this event would not believe us. If we did not have a complete set of the GPS data I did not think that we had a prayer. Dave and Dan knew I was nervous about it but the relief of finally getting the end-all-be-all of verification in my hands was unreal.

My favorite image remains one of the nav screens. They tell the entire story. Distance, average speed, moving time, moving average, time stopped, total time driving. The image of the stopwatch is great too. I have never understood how Roy and Rawlings could do this drive and not end up with pictures like that.

Dave and I had breakfast next to the marina. Dan slept. It was surreal to think about what we had just done. The Portofino Inn is now called the Portofino Hotel and Marina and has been recently remodeled. It is a gorgeous place. I had to get back to work and I hated not having a few days to enjoy it.

We drove the car to Lamborghini Newport Beach and dropped it in their service department. I told Pietro, their GM, I would send a truck for it later that week. He was happy to let us leave the car but he never looked at it. A few days later he actually saw the CL in their parking lot and he asked me in his perfect Americanized Italian accent, "What type of crazy race is this mad Batman car built for?" I told him to watch the news in a few days and it would all make sense.

We booked some flights online, UBERed a car to LAX, and flew home. When we had a few minutes before the flight left I decided to

call Alex Roy. He picked up the phone, "Ed Bolian! How does it feel?"
I was caught entirely off guard by the tone and the question.

"It feels good Alex, could you feel it?"

"Well I figured you had done it after the text that you sent
me last week."

"Alex, I didn't text you last week did I?" I checked through our
text log. "Yeah, I haven't texted you in months."

"Sure you did, some time from a random number. 31
something, just a little bit longer than my time."

"I just finished last night

Alex." "Really, well what

was your time?"

"Honestly I can't believe it either but I can prove it. 28:50."

"Are you kidding me? That is unbelievable. I guess you aren't
the only person to do this in the last ten days."

Alex was skeptical but he knew I was telling the truth. He
was and continues to be a great sportsman and competitor.

It turned out that an Ohio man named Greg Ledet had been the
one who had sent Alex the time by text just a few days prior.

His claim was that he had made his fourth attempt at a New York
to Los Angeles drive on Columbus Day weekend, just a week before.
He claimed to have done it in 31 hours 17 minutes in a BMW 335xi
sedan, leaving from the Trump Hotel and finishing at the Santa
Monica pier which would make it the

third fastest transcontinental driving time ever. I have gotten to know
Greg very well since our drive and he has never been able to show
even a circumstantial piece of evidence that he actually made the drive.
As I said before, I find it emotionally useless to spend time believing
that people lie about this sort of thing so I have given him the benefit of
the doubt.

Right before we got on the plane I made a social media post.
"For those who know what I am talking about - we did it. Thank you
for all of the thoughts and prayers. More to come soon." I checked in
to tag it as being at Los Angeles International Airport to offer a small

clue.

Before they closed the cabin door and told us to shut our phones off I was seeing all of the congratulatory replies scroll in. People who I had not seen or talked to in years knew exactly what it was and had understood back then what it meant to me. Those who had no idea found it to be the most intriguing thing ever and begged for an explanation. A few days later they got it.

CHAPTER 22

Catharsis

Dave, Dan, and I settled into our three adjoining exit row seats on that plane bound for Atlanta. The catharsis of the record was still washing over me. There had been so many times in my life that I finished a task only to immediately feel the need to go onto the next one. This was clearly different. It seemed to be setting in for the other two as well. The emotional overload of falling into something significant at the last minute and then investing so much of themselves into it over the course of the prior two days was hitting the guys hard.

I loved how it meant something so different to each of them. They can speak for themselves but I will try to explain it from my perspective. Dan had enjoyed it as the adventure of a lifetime. He had risen to the challenge and added something to his resume that he had never been looking for. It appealed to the car guy in him but the idea of being called upon seemed to be the reward in itself. I think he took pride in being the kind of guy that you ask to do something like this. He should.

It has been three years now as I put the final touches on this book and I am still not sure that either Dave or I completely know what the experience meant to him. It was a new pearl in a string of personal reinvention. Leaving Apple, a new job, another new job, two Lamborghinis, a new circle of friends, and now the Cannonball had made him a person that I doubt the two year younger version of himself would have recognized. He should be proud of that. I am proud of him.

He had impressed himself in some ways he was clearly not anticipating. As someone who keeps a very fluid life direction, I could see Dave trying to see how much he wanted this drive to be his personal brand. As we flew home he was uncontainably curious about what the next week would look like.

The five hour flight was an interesting opportunity to debrief. Dave was desperately trying to think of any strategies that would have improved the time. I could not tell if this was purely academic or if the next weekend he

wanted to be back in New York at the starting line. The part of the conversation I think I enjoyed the most was the explanation of what the odds were that anyone ever got that same chance to get the right combination of positive outcomes to each of the variables that could have foiled the trip.
Could the Cannonball Slot Machine ever throw all 7's again? That served as a supplementary rationale to explain why I was so happy.

It also probably helped explain why I looked like I could not have been more relaxed if I had just spent a week getting twice daily massages in Bora Bora. If my blood pressure and pulse were any lower on that flight home I would not have been able to open my eyes. It was the level of relaxation where you can actually hear your occasional heartbeat and feel your skin start to warm up rhythmically because the blood isn't moving very quickly through your veins. It feels awesome.

Since it was a complete toss up as to whether or not the public reaction would be positive or negative, we agreed that I would be the initial face of the story. Dave and Dan still wanted to be able to pass the Google-your-name portion of a job interview and so they were very pleased not to be in the proverbial driver's seat for the next steps in the process.

I messaged Richard Rawlings and talked with he and Dennis Collins about our time a couple of days after we got back. They were both invigorated at the possibility of such a period yet exceptionally distrustful. They were exceptionally satisfied that we had stuck to the most customary Cannonball start and end focuses. Richard appeared to be unequipped for really making sense of the possibility of our experience with us just accomplishing a 158 mph maximum velocity. He had generally rushed to say that they had arrived at 207 mph (nine miles each hour quicker than the maker expressed maximum velocity of a 1999 Ferrari 550 Maranello) on a few events during their drive.

At the time they were gone to Jupiter, FL to film with Burt

Reynolds for Fast and Loud. He later let me know that they had talked about my time and that Burt had passed along expressions of congrats. It is hard to get a lot cooler than that.

I called Brock Yates Jr. who currently puts together the Cannonball One Lap of America occasion that his dad began in the 1980's. I let him know the amount I thought about his dad and how affectionately I recollected the discussion I had

with him almost 10 years earlier. I let him know that we had broken the record and our objective in all of this was to honor the tradition of Cannonball and the part of American car history it addressed. Brock had Alzheimer's and did not remember anything about Cannonball but I told his son I wanted to find a chance to visit his father and stepmother (Pam) at some point soon to pay tribute to the man who had motivated me for the last ten years to accomplish this ridiculous dream.

I reached out with Doug Demuro, who was beginning to do most of his editorial composition for Jalopnik - an internet based vehicle blog that had broken the narrative of Alex Roy breaking the record in 2007. Doug composed and delivered the story on the Wednesday before Halloween. They talked with an anonymous worker of the following organization (truth be told, the CEO) to affirm the precision of the following information. The Jalopnik publication staff reached Waze also to validate our cases. They wouldn't deliver their records however unobtrusively re-inforced the information. The article became a web sensation rapidly. I was informed it was the most perused article ever on their site.

The story was on each significant organization, it was the most tapped on article on CNN.com for a 24-hour time span on Friday, November first. There were in excess of 500 TV specifies, more than 1,000 articles, incalculable blog and gathering conversations, radio meetings, magazine comments, and so forth. This drive I thought could scarcely make a difference to the American vehicle lover local area turned into a shot heard round the world.

My compatibility of this remained as a conspicuous difference to that of Yates and the first Cannonballers of the 1970s. On one hand, the likenesses are amazing, yet actually the soul could never have been considerably more unique. They were distraught that individuals were saying that they couldn't do something.
They were putting forth a defense for a more elevated level driving

permit for qualified drivers and testing another foundation. It was a dissent of a thought and it was intended to show that speed limits were pointless and that interstate watch organizations were inadequate.

Our objective was not that by any means. I don't completely accept that that speed cutoff points ought to be abrogated. I feel that the measurements of progress are off yet I imagine that they work really hard. Our drivers instruction programs, authorizing prerequisites, and general driving conventions are no place near where they would should be to have higher or no speed limits.

If you have any desire to raise speed restricts this is the manner by which you get it done. You start by putting the punishments on exercises that are genuinely hazardous. Foundation $5,000 required and uninsurable fines for the accompanying - to blame mishaps, DUI, messaging, utilizing the telephone, and running red lights. Fines go to support a full scale execution driving schooling system that can be privatized. Street and composed tests should be directed at regular intervals. A permit is quickly suspended at every offense until paid. Get three fines in a single year and permit is suspended for the following a year. Raise speed limits on controlled admittance roadways 5 mph each year. There is no expense of execution and no misfortune in income for government. Cops would never legitimize investing energy composing $250 speeding tickets in the event that they could be pursuing $5,000 messaging fish. It wouldn't make it man's down to drive a rich. It would make it basic for individuals in no situation to bear the cost of a five thousand fine to be cautious and follow the rules.

It would eliminate street clients and provoke a colossal interest for quality public vehicle. Government could step in to make up for that shortcoming. This additionally has the additional political advantage of being unobjectionable. Nobody can say that it is a poorly conceived notion to punish individuals for causing mishaps and drinking or messaging while at the same time driving. Maybe on the off chance that I were not totally unelectable by the Google measures as a government official now I could run for Senate and make that my platform.

Can I actually be captured for this? The rules of restriction have lapsed all over the place however Texas and Oklahoma which keep on rolling at whatever point I am in each state. In that first year window it would have been troublesome yet not feasible for a cop to foster reasonable justification to get a warrant to capture me or Dave and to open an examination. They would have to show verification of which of us was driving in their ward and rather unequivocally where we sped. This could be just about as simple as referring to traffic camera film or however we have not had any issues. Most police are vehicle folks and as long as you don't attempt to shame them with your speeding takes advantage of, they will quite often be genuinely great games after a safe outcome.

A wrongdoing plugs association conveyed a ton of messages to neighborhood Georgia police areas beseeching them to figure out how to capture me. The shoot incorporated an extremely un-hateable image of me with Megan from my Facebook profile.
There were some web petitions circling empowering different states that we passed through to find and capture us. None got numerous marks. The story was shared on Facebook in excess of multiple times from the CNN article

as well as a comparative number on the Jalopnik site. The CNN article had more than 5,000 remarks posted. CNN Television named my outing the "Best Commute of 2013."

Interestingly, I have not been reached by anybody saying that they are genuinely chipping away at an arrangement to break my record. I truly do get asked frequently on the off chance that I have any interest in breaking my own record. Absolutely not until somebody breaks it but rather in all honesty, in the event that I had ten endeavors and $250k to toss at it, I question I would have each of the wild factors adjust to try and make it conceivable to break the record. When you begin including the hypothetical probabilities of the gambling machine factors - of having no awful climate, no development projects, no mishaps that cause gridlocks, light times of heavy traffic where unavoidable, a full-ish moon for perceivability, no issues with the vehicle, not hitting any creatures going across the street, having the option to facilitate with a group, and by and large being mentally prepared to do as such; it begins to get asymptotically near difficult to recreate.

A couple of months following the record, I was conversing with Richard Doherty.
He coordinated the 1980-1983 US Express occasions subsequent to taking an interest in Cannonball and being frustrated in the exposure bazaar of 1979 and the stopping of the occasion. The tales from these

folks never get old to me. I don't think his head took off of his cushion soon after their last 1983 running where he didn't trust somebody would call welcoming him on another crosscountry race. I let him know how in each discussion I had with somebody who had done this kind of drive, they generally advertised "indeed, on the off chance that this hadn't happened..." situations where they would have sped up. I felt like the main individual to have felt like I was unable to go any quicker. All that went right definitely couldn't all go so well again.

Many analysts and companions have offered different arrangements on the best way to work on the time. As I mull over the potential enhancements that I might have made to bring down my time, this is the thing I have come up with:

• Pay for fuel in cash (eliminates credit card issues). Race car dump cans, fuel trucks on the side of the road or alongside the car while moving on the highway, etc. are overkill. The advantage is not worth the risks. Fuel volume on our trip was perfect. No need for more. We did need a fuel additive to cope with poor quality gas in the Western US. I had planned to take some but forgot.

• Have companions at each gas stop to help siphon, clean the windshield, and oversee logistics.

• We utilized Waze on an iPhone. It is smarter to utilize it on a 3G/4G tablet.

• A quicker vehicle - a Bentley Continental GT Supersports 2+2 ($100-130k current worth) would be the most ideal choice. This would make periodic 180 mph spells conceivable without losing taking care of ability.

• Lead vehicles out of Manhattan to obstruct convergences (Rawlings/Collins did this)

• Working CB and Scanner

• Slightly stuff the vehicle with oil to start the drive.

• At this point you can likely piece the extra tire and jack. An opportunity to supplant it would most likely make it almost difficult to break the record and the additional room will make the drive more agreeable. At any rate, move it to an all the way far removed location.

• Stabilize or mount the optics so that individuals other than Dan can utilize them.

• Find a smart method for saying 'sorry' to individuals who you pass. This could be a looking over LCD sign along the rear of the car.

• A cleaner run would diminish stress.

• Deploy more scout vehicles all through the country.

Each of these thoughts would save 1-5 mins in general. Joined they are not to the point of defeating issues with any of the factors that we had great results with. A tempest, gridlock, mishap, vehicle issue, or ticket would probably end any possibility enhancing our time.

During a meeting that I did on CNN, the hosts asked what I would do straightaway. The hosts at the Today Show in New York were comparatively intrigued by what befalls somebody after they go through a day and a half violating pretty much every transit regulation in the country. I responded to that as indicated by my better half, my next experience to anticipate was having kids. The ticking clock that was not mounted with twofold stick tape to the dashboard of the Mercedes had not eased back its rhythm. We got pregnant the following month and found out on
January 1, 2014. Graham Edward Bolian was brought into the world at 3:12 on August 20,
2014. He was 7 lbs 4 ounces, 20.5 inches long.

In the fallout of the record declaration, I came to figure out that our oddball time preliminary style drives were not by any means the only current translation of the Cannonball inheritance. Quickly following the declaration of the Roy/Maher/Welles record, a man from San Francisco named John Ficarra had a thought. He was sickened by the cash no-object approach at the record pursuit and was enchanted by the as of late sent off 24 hours of Lemons hustling series (perseverance track dashing in $500 vehicles). He concluded it would be fascinating to mix the two and The 2904 was formed.

This is a more drawn out story for one more day yet after our drive, Ficarra reached me. He said that they had run the occasion multiple times and assuming they planned to rehash it, they needed to zest it up a little. The reason was that each group could spend something like $2,904 which was illustrative of the mileage of their unique New York to San Francisco course. They had additionally done the occasion from New York to Los Angeles. Like Lemons rules, wellbeing related things were not included in the spending plan. That's what he said assuming I were keen on joining their cheerful occasion, it could do just that.

I let him know that I couldn't want anything more than to do it and experience the drive in a bit of an alternate way. It likewise offered me the opportunity to keep investigating various answers for this issue I had been kicking around for my whole grown-up life. I bought a 12 proprietor, 2 mishap, rescue title, airbags recently sent, outline harmed and fixed, 8 shades of white and yellow 2002 Mercedes S55 AMG on Craigslist Las Vegas for $1,500. The lady selling it had loaned it to her little girl to head to Hollywood to turn into a well known celebrity. The vehicle had stalled and she had never become renowned. The driver's window was stuck down, the suspension was imploded, the measures didn't work, and the mileage was unknown.

I purchased the vehicle and had it sent home. Dave "Klink," Chris Staschiak, and I drove the vehicle among a field of eleven vehicles to win the 2015 running of the occasion with a period of 32 hours 5 minutes, making it the quickest time ever in a cutthroat New York to Los Angeles style occasion. This was not by any means the only Cannonball related report of 2015, however.

2015 denoted an unforeseen renaissance in the idea of cutthroat crosscountry driving. It appeared to have been filled by the prevalence of the
report about our run yet it was a blast of innovative translation around a similar thought. During the year, there were twelve new "Cannonball" related records asserted. They were:

- Solo Atlantic to Pacific Record - David Simpson - 27 hours 49 mins

- Atlantic to Pacific Record - Vic Echeverria, Bill Farmer - 26 hours 19 mins

- Shortest EV Charge Time NY to LA (Guinness directed) - Carl Reese, Deena Mastracci, Rodney Hawk - 12 hours, 48 mins

- EV NY to LA Record - Carl Reese, Alex Roy, Deena Mastracci - 57 hours, 48 mins

- Autonomous Car NY to LA - Carl Reese, Alex Roy, Deena Mastracci
– 57 hours, 48 mins

- Motorcycle NY to LA Record - Carl Reese - 38 hours 49 mins

- 3 Wheeled LA to NY Record - Alex Roy and Zach Bowman - 41 hours 49 mins

- EV Coast to Coast to Coast Record - Carl Reese, Deena Mastracci - 6 Days 6 hours 22 minutes

- Coast to Coast to Coast Record - Pierce Plam, John Ficarra, Alex Richter - 5 days 10 hours 49 mins

- Solo NY to LA Record - David Simpson - 34 hours 33 mins

- Competitive Event NY to LA Record - Ed Bolian, Chris Staschiak, Dave Klink - 32 hours 5 mins

- John Ficarra set a standard of having taken an interest in 7 cutthroat Cannonball-style events

It was an astonishing year to be related with this specialty. Additionally, there was a side project of a side project made. Honoring The 2904, which itself honored the Cannonball Baker; a few New Zealanders made an occasion called the C2C Express. As well as restricting the buy financial plan at a round $3,000, all partaking vehicles must be worked preceding 1980. I was approached to partake in the second running of this in September 2016 alongside individual 2904 contender Arne Toman and Forrest Sibley. We dressed as the Blues Brothers and drove a 1974 Dodge Monaco Bluesmobile to a triumphant season of 34 hours 17 minutes.

2016 was likewise an incredibly miserable time for the Cannonball people group. From the get-go in the year, Richard Doherty died. In October, we lost Brock Yates. I had the pleasure of writing an eulogy for my late legend for Jalopnik and it brought back all of the feeling that this section of my life had involved. The amazing flood of affection and reverence from the motorsport local area was ample and well deserved.

I continue to receive calls of congratulations and camaraderie from various past Cannonballers, US Express guys, and even heard of other small events of this kind that have happened over the past few decades. It is a fascinating organization of maniacs to presently be responsible for yet it has been an extremely fun ride.

The action item from this experience is basically the way that magnificent God can permit our experience on this planet to be. It is an account of a motivation, personality, and an exceptionally remarkable test. Crosscountry record breaking won't ever be a standard objective or action and it shouldn't be. I believe this story should act as an outline that there is likely an out of the container thought out there that can turn into your Cannonball record.

I am the most fortunate person on the planet. Not so much for winning, not for getting by, and not for staying away from prison. At an exceptionally youthful age I saw that as "thing." I observed a test that could distract my awareness, both interest and legitimize a perpetual series of penances and steady responsibilities, become a fixation, and be an extreme wellspring of pride in accomplishment. Through the bend of my commitment with the test it went from an interest, to a thought, to an objective, to a test, to a way of life, to a fixation, to something that I would do nearly anything to accomplish. The groundbreaking circular segment uncovered more about myself than it did about driving.

It was at the preliminary second when I realized nothing was off the discussion table when I realized I had tracked down it. It existed in the crossing point between my inclinations, capacities, and mental self view. There was nothing that could mark additional resounding boxes for me.

The drive spoke to my interests, illuminated the picture of myself I believed the world should see, showed the traits about me I am generally partial to, and assisted me with grasping the defects inside me. The Cannonball Record could scarcely have been a more dark dream yet I genuinely accept there was nothing else on Earth that I might have achieved that would have made me this content.

There is anything but a remedy to propose for how to see as your "thing" and this isn't intended to be a self improvement guide. Composing this has been an individual festival for me to think back on how my point of view advanced regarding this journey. The development was the award. I have heard a ton of motivational speakers teach thoughts of working at what you love, picturing achievement, and remaining devoted to your dreams.

That is just fine yet that isn't what got me here. I do those things however they couldn't have ever driven me to this as an objective. This happened in light of the fact that I let myself be presented to it from the beginning and I never gave any confidence to the large number of reasons it couldn't or ought not be finished. Because of my overall absence of regard for rules and limits, that acknowledgment came decently effectively for me however it could be a test to some. Push through it.

The obstructions in this pursuit effectively shown how all that makes me broken as an individual really made me qualified for this. The unwavering inconspicuous gravity pulling me toward it never given up for a whole ten years. Things could hold up traffic and pull me this way and that for a brief time frame however the flowing development was toward the truth of this event some day.

My preference for improvisation over structure, my indignance to authority and my unique moral interpretation of the world, my love of cars, my faith in the unknowable, and even the psychopathy that desensitizes me; it all came together to make me a person who could contend.

The two individuals remaining close by in the Portofino parking garage are a demonstration of the uniqueness of this kind of pursuit. En route, I tracked down a perpetual line of individuals who thought that it is intriguing or fun. They proposed to help, to talk about, and even to dream close by me. Whenever it came time to act however, there was something wrong with it. It was not their thing. Where technique moved from fun and energetic to not allowing anything to hold up traffic, the wheat and the waste separated.

I wound up with one person who needed to go on an excursion and one that simply wasn't doing anything that end of the week. The experience was totally unique for themselves and I totally love them both for it. It really could not have possibly occurred without them. Assuming Dave knew every one of the motivations to dial back as I did he could never have kept up with and refined the speed. Assuming Dan had assembled the vehicle with me he would have involved everything in the hypothesis in which we expected it as opposed to adjusting it to our nearby necessities as he saw them.

At the poInt when everything in a real sense became real I observed the arranging was the last thing I needed to relinquish to go after triumph in a last push. Assuming I had waited for a completely working vehicle and the group that I was expecting, I

would in any case be dreaming while at the same time tarrying. Whether you accept that it is God, the universe, or simply irregular occurrence pulling you toward your creation it will immediately turn out to be evident that it's anything but an objective that we get to head to voluntarily. For my purposes, this is a God thing.

Even however there were long periods of a gravitational draw toward compatibility, achievement was neither ensured nor likely. The wheels of the gambling machine were completely unchangeable as far as I might be concerned. Wearing clerical attire, an intoxicated Dean Martin kidded to Sammy Davis Jr. that God was their co-pilot in Cannonball Run. The cosmically far-fetched open door we needed to finish our drive in such a stunning time supported to me God was with us in a considerably more genuine sense. Assuming I had hesitated any more in the rental business, wedded some unacceptable young lady, sought after other narrow minded desires, surrendered to the enticement of separation, or wouldn't praise Him through my gradual victories - I could not have possibly gotten it done. My God is faithful.

"For I know the plans I have for you," announces the Lord, "plans to thrive you and not to hurt you, plans to give you trust and a future."

Jeremiah 29:11 (NIV)

My story is one of shifting back and forth between times of pushing as hard as possible with dismissal for the dangers and the times of tolerating exhortation and respecting the course where I expected to go.

Basketball gave approach to business

Ivy League gave way to modest nearby school and

expendable assets Journalism wound down and Supercar

Rentals was born

I gave my own childishness the rearward sitting arrangement and let myself love Megan

She showed me when the time had come to release Supercar
Rentals and to go to

the dealership

Those penances in the end made the determination to pursue a
    fantasy that had generally been there in a more grounded yet
    more dependable way

A healthy lifestyle at last gave way to the lenient trigger to take
           the necessary steps to make the last push

And, after its all said and done, my group and my thoughts
        needed to respect individuals that God put in my
        way at the perfect time.

It is my decision to see it in like that. I could take possession and
say that I implied for everything to happen similarly as yet that would
be completely false. The rhythmic movement of inclination versus
"being curious to see what happens" made this so valuable for self-
awareness. Now and again I paddled upstream, on occasion
downstream. The breeze was at my back and furthermore blowing in
my face. Now and again the ground disintegrated, different times it was
the main thing holding me up.
Somehow, however, I got constantly closer.

Winning was without a doubt the good to beat all prepared cake.
It was one of the existence minutes where the result was actually all
around as great as you envisioned it very well may be. The genuine
award, however, was the street that took me there. It was a support
when I expected to limp through the harder times in my day to day
existence. It was the expectation for something extraordinary when all
the other things attempted to pull me down. It remained there as a
signal up ahead reminding me it was there while I was occupied with
the remainder of life. Critically, when I seriously required a success, it
was still in that general area. At the point when the magnificence of
life gets through the difficulties that we face, our responsibility is to
just ensure that we are centered around the game and that we wind up
doing what we want to. The principal flush after at last finding time to
fix that interminably running latrine could never be as satisfying in the
event that it hadn't invested such a lot of energy torturing you in the
background.

Perspective is basic. What we really want to do is make a solid
attempt as we can and afterward let the tension off briefly. Let the

world around settle as it will. Enjoy some time off, appreciate how far we have come. Then we can get ready to push again.

I acclaim my God for each progression of the way that drove me to Cannonball and for grasping me to bring me through it. My two sincerest petitions to God are that my infant child come to be aware and love that equivalent God the way that I do and that one day he will view as a "thing" of his own that he can endeavor to prevail. Assuming one day he will cry similar bittersweet tears bliss I did as I remained on that moor sitting above the Pacific Ocean in the night on October 20, 2013 then he will realize he tracked down it. On that fine day, there will be two most joyful individuals in the world.

Now go get yours!